TEENAGERS
AND TEENPICS

TEENAGERS AND TEENPICS

THE JUVENILIZATION

OF AMERICAN

MOVIES IN THE 1950S

Revised and Expanded Edition

Thomas Doherty

 Temple University Press
PHILADELPHIA

Temple University Press, Philadelphia 19122
Copyright © 2002 by Temple University
Published 2002
Printed in the United States of America

⊗ The paper used in this publication meets the requirements of the American National
Standard for Information Sciences—Permanence of Paper for Printed Library Materials,
ANSI Z39.48-1984

Library of Congress Cataloging-in-Publication Data

Doherty, Thomas Patrick.
    Teenagers and teenpics : the juvenilization of American movies in the 1950s /
    Thomas Doherty.
        p.   cm.
    Revised and expanded edition.
    Filmography: p.
    Includes bibliographical references and indexes.
    ISBN 1-56639-945-9 (cl. : alk. paper) — ISBN 1-56639-946-7 (pbk. : alk. paper)
        1. Motion pictures—United States—History. 2. Motion pictures and youth—
    United States. 3. Teenagers in motion pictures—United States. I. Title.

PN1993.5.U6 D53 2002
302.23'43'0973—dc21   20011052514

To Sandra

Contents

Acknowledgments

In his *Autobiography*, Benjamin Franklin smugly attests that he would be happy to live the same life over again, "only asking the advantage authors have in a second edition to correct some faults of the first." In this spirit, I have exploited what Franklin might call the present felicity to polish and expand the first edition of *Teenagers and Teenpics*, published in 1988 by the now-defunct Unwin and Hyman, by correcting typos, purging mistakes, repairing syntax, and blue-penciling a few boneheaded comments. In addition, the last chapter, which as before tracks the permutations of the teenpic since the 1950s, has been updated with ruminations on some recent trends, notably the grim legacy of the AIDS epidemic on the teenpic genre. Otherwise, for better or worse, the original text remains intact.

The first edition owed a great deal to a good many people, in whose debt I remain. John Raeburn was unfailingly generous with his time and incisive with his criticism. William Paul shared his enthusiasm and considerable expertise. At the University of Iowa, back during the age between punk rock and the hairspray bands, an exceptionally sharp and humane group of teachers and friends offered encouragement: Rick Altman, James Carey, Wayne Franklin, Rich Horwitz, Brooks Landon, Cindy Larson, Richard Dyer MacCann, Albert Stone, Sherman Paul, Paul Soucek, Bruce Sternfield, Michael Wall, Robin Wood, and everyone clustered around the Bijou Theater and University Film Board, whose repertory programming served as the informal film studies curriculum on campus. Bruce A. Austin, Ernest Callenbach, and the late Fred C. Clarke lent emotional and editorial support. Roger Corman was kind enough to interrupt an editing session and answer questions from a flustered scholar-fan. The National Endowment for the

Humanities financed my attendance at a provocative seminar with James Gilbert at the University of Maryland. A platoon of librarians and archivists provided helpful guidance through their research collections, in particular George Barringer of Special Collections at Georgetown University Library, Patrick Sheehan at the Motion Picture Research Division of the Library of Congress, and Mary Corliss and Terry Geesken at the Museum of Modern Arts Film Still Archives. My sincere thanks also go to David Thorburn and Lisa Freeman, who worked on the book during its first life, to Micah Kleit at Temple University Press for midwifing the rebirth, and to Naren Gupte of P. M. Gordon Associates for guiding the project through production. In reading the manuscript for gaffs, Michael Anderegg, Andrew Hudgins, and Sandra Doherty each displayed an annoying thoroughness in detecting authorial lapses. Finally, and not least, the new edition has benefited mightily from the keen eye and kind suggestions of Jeffrey Miller.

TEENAGERS
AND TEENPICS

1

American Movies as a Less-than-Mass Medium

Like all great arts the motion picture has grown up by appeal to the interests of childhood and youth.

Terry Ramsaye, 1926

Films have to be made for the majority and the majority in the United States are teenagers. It's different in France and Italy where the majority are adults.

Joan Collins, 1957

Strictly speaking, American motion pictures today are not a mass medium. As any multiplex marquee attests, theatrical movies cater primarily to one segment of the entertainment audience: teenagers. Without the support of the teenage audience, few theatrical movies break even, fewer still become hits, and none become blockbusters. In America, movies reflect teenage, not mass—and definitely not adult—tastes.

This was not always so. Prior to the mid-1950s, movies were the mass medium of choice for a vast, multigenerational audience that motion picture industry officials invariably envisaged as "the public." Movies may have "sprung from minds essentially juvenile and adolescent," as Terry Ramsaye wrote in his landmark motion picture history, *A Million and One Nights* (1926), but their images captivated all kinds. Will H. Hays, president of the Motion Picture

1

Producers and Distributors of America (MPPDA) from 1922 to 1945, always insisted that movies were "art for the millions . . . speaking the language of all men of all ages." Unlike high opera or classical music, they sought no "specialty audience" but aspired to be a truly popular art, a "universal entertainment" for the entire family. "The commercial success of the screen," declared Hays, "is based on its appeal to the general public—men, women, and children." In the 1930s and 1940s, that all-embracing ideal mirrored Hollywood's pluralistic audience. By and large moviegoing *was* a familial, almost ritualistic activity, with children, adolescents, young couples, housewives, breadwinners, and the elderly partaking together of the liveliest of the arts.

The rise of television and the collapse of the old studio system destroyed that kind of universality. Since the 1950s, moviemakers have been forced to narrow their focus and attract the one group with the requisite income, leisure, and gregariousness to sustain a theatrical business. The courtship of the teenage audience began in earnest in 1955; by 1960, the romance was in full bloom. That shift in marketing strategy and production initiated a progressive "juvenilization" of film content and the film audience that is today the operative reality of the American motion picture business. The process whereby "movies for the millions" became a less-than-mass medium is best revealed in the genesis and development of what has become the industry's flagship enterprise, the teenpic.

The Exploitation Film

The teenpic is a version of the exploitation film, a loose though not wide-open category for motion pictures. Lingua franca in the regions of the motion picture industry and academic film studies alike, "exploitation" has three distinct and sometimes overlapping meanings. In its two broadest senses, "exploitation" refers both to the advertising and promotion that entice an audience into a theater and to the way the movie then endears itself to that audience. As the object of exploitation, the movie is passive, a product to be advertised and marketed; as the subject doing the exploitation, the movie is active, an agent that caters to its target audience by serving up appetizing or exotic subject matter. In its third, categorical sense, "exploitation" signifies a particular *kind* of movie.

In early industry parlance, "exploitation" meant only the process of advertising and publicity that accompanied a movie's theatrical release.

Hollywood's platonic ideal: three generations of American moviegoers exit a theater in Dixon, Illinois, 1947. (National Archives)

Motion pictures reached maturity during the "ballyhoo years" of the 1920s, and studio executives well recognized their medium's dependence on effective advertising. "The better the picture, the greater must be the exploitation campaign," declared Columbia Pictures vice president Jack Cohn in 1933. "Good pictures do not sell themselves. We will never have phenomenal box office successes without the combination of a great picture and adequate exploitation."

To help exhibitors attract an audience, the major studios maintained permanent full-scale "exploitation departments" or used the services of special agencies skilled in public relations. "Exploitation men" were responsible for devising eye-catching advertisements and concocting newsworthy stunts linked to the movie in question. During the 1930s, the *Film Daily* included an "Exploitation Digest" in its yearbook that listed "a comprehensive summary of stunts for exploiting any type of picture" and encouraged studios to submit their favorite exploitation scheme of the past year. Hal Horne, director of advertising and public relations for United Artists, described a publicity stunt for *White Zombie* (1932) that defines this most basic meaning of "exploitation":

> When *White Zombie* was ushered into the Rivoli Theater in New York, all Broadway was startled by the sudden appearance of nine Zombies on a boardwalk erected above the marquee of the theater. Thousands packed the sidewalks and gasped with amazement as the nine figures, faithfully garbed and made up to simulate actual members of the *White Zombie* cast, went through a series of thrilling dramatic sequences. . . . The doll-like figures of the girls were dressed in white flowing robes and the men looked just as if they had been dug up from the ground with wooden splints on their legs and battered facial expressions. . . . Crowds gathered all day lured there not only by the drama enacted above the theater front but by the *White Zombie* sound effects records which included the screeching of vultures, the grinding of the sugar mill and the beating of the tom toms, and other nerve wracking sounds.

For his studio's best exploitation effort that year, Arthur L. Mayer, director of advertising, publicity, and exploitation at Paramount, chose a promotional perennial, the contest. Some sixty thousand entrants were given screen tests in "a nationwide search for a non-professional actress to play the Panther Woman in *Island of Lost Souls* [1933]." (One Kathleen Burke got the role.)

The industry's most outrageous exploitation ploys are a cherished part of Hollywood lore. Paramount's Adolph Zukor recalled the promotional campaign for a movie called *The Green Parrot* wherein a number of trained green parrots were to be set free in selected newspaper offices to squawk the movie's title. The birds performed well, but the plan was canceled when the title was changed. Universal's Carl Laemmle told of the press agent who publicized his client's latest jungle opera by checking into a first-class hotel under the name of T. R. Zan, sneaking a lion into his suite, and then ordering ten pounds of steak from room service. Laemmle approved of the "original manner" of such exploitation but counseled the less inventive to herald upcoming attractions the traditional way, through contests, "newspapers, lobbies, theater fronts, window displays, printed matter, and the like."

Since the wild days of vintage ballyhoo, promotional techniques have more than kept pace with the industry's technical improvements.

The publicity campaign for the modern theatrical movie is a precision media assault based on communications theory, depth psychology, and dead-on demographics. Today, exploitation, hype, or what is still sometimes called ballyhoo is a sophisticated national advertising campaign, the cost of which often surpasses that of the multimillion-dollar feature in the spotlight. As in Jack Cohn's time, an adequate exploitation strategy remains crucial to a movie's box office fortunes, with trailers on cable television and Web sites serving as the digital-age equivalents of the posters and playbills of yesteryear. Since the MTV-fueled success of *Flashdance* (1983) and *Footloose* (1984), rock video tie-ins have been instrumental publicity shills, while the prerelease buzz created online for *The Blair Witch Project* (1999) quickly established the Web site home page as an essential cyberspace lobby card.

Communications rather than marketing defines the second meaning of exploitation. It refers to the dialogue a movie establishes with its viewers. A movie is said to "exploit" an audience when it reflects on screen the audience's expectations and values. The implicit corollary is that it does so in a particularly egregious and manipulative way through subject matter that is particularly accessible or disreputable.

When movies shifted their emphasis from spectacles such as Thomas Edison's *The Electrocution of an Elephant* (1903) to dramas such as Edwin S. Porter's *The Great Train Robbery* (1903), moviemakers found that their narratives had to conform to traditional expectations or risk confusing, offending, or otherwise alienating audiences. Taking their cues from the carefully ordered middle-class world of popular nineteenth-century novels and plays, motion picture pioneers like Porter and D. W. Griffith shaped their narratives for audience approval at the same time that they created a unique filmic grammar. After *The Birth of a Nation* (1915), feature-length dramas achieved ascendancy over the picturesque slapstick of one- and two-reel comedies. The great silent clowns of the next decade—Charles Chaplin, Buster Keaton, and Harold Lloyd—made sure that their gags and bits of business were played out within a well-wrought narrative framework. "After we stopped making wild two-reelers and got into feature-length pictures, our scenario boys had to be story-conscious," recalled Buster Keaton. "We couldn't tell any far-fetched stories. . . . It would have been poison to us. An audience wanted to believe every story we told them." In short, moviemakers learned early on that theirs was fundamentally a storytelling medium and that stories affirming an audience's beliefs were the most successful at the box office. The wise moviemaker "exploited" what was known about an audience by catering to its desires and meeting its expectations.

By 1930, a coherent Production Code could credibly posit a set of standardized audience values to guide moviemakers in the construction of their narratives and hence in the exploitation of their audience. For all its rigidity, the moral universe established in the Code expressed a rough cultural consensus: that crime should not pay; that virtue should be rewarded; that the good, handsome boy should get the good, pretty girl. As such, the Hays Office merely codified a set of narrative and thematic requirements that most commercial moviemakers observed anyway. In exploiting a culturally heterogeneous mass audience (and in creating a culturally homogeneous one), Hollywood would have had to adhere to conventions, Code or no Code. Exploitation, then, whether defined as a promotional or a communications strategy, has always been part of the American motion picture industry.

The modern sense of the term as a pejorative description for a special *kind* of motion picture ("the exploitation film") is more recent. In 1946, the show business bible *Variety* spoke of "exploitation pictures" as "films with some timely or currently controversial subject which can be exploited, capitalized on, in publicity and advertising." That *Variety* felt compelled to put "exploitation picture" within quotation marks and to define the phrase for a savvy trade audience indicates both its recent coinage as industry vernacular and its relative unfamiliarity as a production strategy. At this early date, "exploitation picture" seems to have had no negative connotations but was used simply to refer to a timely picture with a clear promotional tie-in. As examples of exploitation pictures, *Variety* cited mostly mainstream, major studio products such as RKO's *Back to Bataan* (1945), which was "released almost simultaneously" with the return of American forces to the Philippines, and Warner Bros.' *Hotel Berlin* (1945), whose release was "a race against Russia's entry into Berlin and the end of the European war." By these standards, a mainstream, big-budget prestige project such as producer Sam Goldwyn's *The Pride of the Yankees* (1942) qualifies as an exploitation picture: based on the life of Lou Gehrig and featuring many of his former teammates, it hit screens a brief thirteen months after the first baseman's death in June 1941.

By the mid-1950s the name had picked up the bad reputation it still retains. To qualify easily for motion picture exploitation, subject matter now had to be timely *and* sensational, not simply timely after the fashion of a war movie or celebrity biopic. Like their immediate predecessors, 1950s exploitation pictures drew on the public curiosity and free publicity surrounding a popular current event. These films were "exploitation naturals" because the real occurrences that inspired them had already aroused widespread interest and charted a clear promotional path for "ad-pub" (advertising-publicity) departments. For example, the juicy libel suits involving *Confidential* and *Whisper* magazines wrought MGM's *Slander* (1956), which concerned an unscrupulous editor of a *Confidential*–like scandal sheet and whose promotion was cued to the timely real-life tie-in: "MGM brings America the FIRST insider account of how the scandal magazines operate!" promised the ad copy. But to a degree unthinkable a decade earlier, the 1950s exploitation picture favored the bizarre, the licentious, and the sensational—and, following the Hollywood mainstream, depicted same with escalating daring and explicitness. In delving unashamedly into often-disreputable content and promoting it in an always-disreputable manner, the exploitation label acquired a pejorative distinction its exemplars usually lived up to.

As a production strategy, the 1950s exploitation formula typically had three elements: (1) controversial, bizarre, or timely subject matter amenable to wild promotion ("exploitation" potential in its original sense); (2) a substandard budget; and (3) a teenage audience. Movies of this ilk are *triply* exploitative, simultaneously exploiting sensational happenings (for story value), their notoriety (for publicity value), and their teenage participants (for box office value). Around 1955–56, "exploitation film" in this sense had become fairly common usage within the motion picture industry.

The 1950s exploitation picture responded to history with a distinctive speed and selectivity. Typically, the lapse between an event's appearance in the newspapers and the movie that exploited it was remarkably brief. For example, on October 4, 1957, the successful launch of the Russian satellite *Sputnik* stunned the nation. The soon-to-be-legendary Roger Corman, already one of the era's cagiest producers of exploitation pictures, felt sure that he could "cash in on the satellite craze" if he acted quickly enough. He immediately contacted his distributor, Allied Artists, "and told them I could have a *Sputnik* picture in movie theaters across the country in two months time. They said, 'Sure, do it.' It was one of the fastest movies ever made. The script was written in less than two weeks. Six weeks after that the film *[War of the Satellites]* was being shown Coast to Coast." Throughout the 1950s, any sensational happening amenable to filmic rendering was likely to cause a rush to the Title Registration Bureau of the Motion Picture Association of America, an office whose files chart the era as well as the *New York Times Index*. In August 1958, the under-ice voyage of the submarine *Nautilus* had producers racing for the title *Atomic Submarine*. The first response of one enterprising moviemaker to the shooting down of U-2 pilot Francis Gary Powers in May 1960 was to file for the title *The True Story of Francis Gary Powers, American*. After Fidel Castro drove Fulgencia Batista y Zaldívar from Cuba on January 1, 1959, and before his communist agenda was widely known, producer Jerry Wald secured the revolutionary's cooperation for a film project based on the Cuban revolution. Under an agreement signed in Houston in April 1959, Wald acquired the rights to film Castro's life, the dictator agreeing to "turn over to Wald complete facilities in Cuba, including the army." Castro wanted Marlon Brando to play Fidel and Frank Sinatra to play his brother Raoul. Ernest Hemingway was his first choice to write the screenplay. Sam Katzman, a founding father of the exploitation movie, may have known something neither Wald nor the State Department knew: within weeks of Castro's victory, he registered the title *The Rise and Fall of Fulgencio Batista*.

Overtaken by history, some movies became inadvertent exploitation pictures. The FBI's capture of the Brinks robbers in January 1956 inspired the rerelease of Universal's fortuitous *Six Bridges to Cross* (1955), a heist movie filmed in Boston. Within an hour after the FBI cracked the case, exhibitors in Boston, Providence, and Lowell, Massachusetts, had rebooked the revamped "exploitation picture." Likewise, when Grace Kelly's role as a princess in *The Swan* (1956) became a real-life fairy tale, a standard costume drama was transformed into a Monaco exploitation movie. For sheer cynical opportunism, nothing matches Columbia's rerelease of *Cell 2455, Death Row* (1955) on the eve of Caryl Chessman's execution in May 1960. "Columbia Blasts It!" shouted the ad copy; "Timely as Today and Sizzling as the Hot Seat!" (Actually, Chessman went to the gas chamber.) Like Corman with *War of the Satellites* (1958), the resourceful exploitation moviemaker aims to get the movie into theaters in time to benefit from (transitory) public curiosity. The classic tag line for exploitation movies remains "as timely as today's headlines!"

Not every headline, however, warrants an exploitation movie. During the 1950s, commercial moviemakers shied away from quickie low-budget features about the Salk vaccine, Dwight D. Eisenhower's heart attack, or the decline of the inner-city tax base. Exploitation material, then as now, was outlandish, mildly controversial, and a little licentious—and if the movie wasn't, the advertising was. A survey of the era's history bears out the exploitation movie's twin impulses to the timely and the sensational. If the event is trendy or controversial enough, chances are an exploitation movie, somewhere, has documented it. The more enduring furors of the 1950s, like rock 'n' roll and juvenile delinquency, spawned whole exploitation cycles, historically bound clusters of films sprung from a common source.

In 1956, ten years after its initial comments on the "exploitation picture," *Variety* submitted an authoritative definition, revised and updated, for the "so-called exploitation picture": "These are low-budget films based on controversial and timely subjects that made newspaper headlines. In the main these pictures appeal to 'uncontrolled' juveniles and 'undesirables.'" Together, these three elements—controversial content, bare-bones budgets, and demographic targeting—remain characteristic of any exploitation movie, whether the scandalous material is aimed at "adults" ("sexploitation"), African Americans ("blaxploitation"), or gorehounds ("axploitation"). But because the demographic target under the most intense and incessant fire remained "juveniles"—teenagers—the exploitation film became associated mainly with its most familiar version: the teenpic.

The Teenpic as Genre

Like many movie labels, the term *teenpic* may be more reliable as a bibliographical entry than as a critical category, but it conjures a commonsense impression of a group of kindred motion pictures. In this, the designation "teenpic" is similar to the customary classifications—musical, comedy, western—that have long lent order to an otherwise unmanageable inventory of Hollywood product. The usual handle for these clusters of seemingly similar films, a word left as yet intentionally unspoken, is "genre."

As much a linguistic convenience as a serviceable organizing principle, the concept of genre is one of the most fruitful yet contentious approaches in film scholarship. In the decades since Robert Warshow's trailblazing essays "The Gangster as Tragic Hero" (1948) and "Movie Chronicle: The Westerner" (1954), genre-based film studies have multiplied steadily, nearly matching auteurism as the critical vantage of preference for popular, if not academic, film books—though even in an academy smitten with semiotics, deconstruction, cultural studies, and other esoteric methodologies, scholarship grounded in genre is voluminous. The approach has obvious advantages. Genre brings an Aristotelian coherence to disparate subject matter, permits easy movement from particular close description to general qualitative prescription, and, not least, acknowledges the common sense, in audience and artist alike, of a movie's membership in a wider filmic community.

The etymology of the word *genre*—by way of the French from the common Greek and Latin root *genus*, meaning "kind," "stock," or "birth"—is itself suggestive. The source word generates a ready association with the classical mind, particularly the rigorous nomenclature and ideal forms of Greek philosophy. Genre criticism aptly begins with Aristotle's *Poetics*, which first applied the orderly frame of Greek thought to the arts. In positing categories for mimetic form, the *Poetics* set a procedural precedent that has challenged the interpretive dexterity and frustrated the organizational mentality of commentators on the arts ever since. Although for scientific inquiry the Aristotelian model proved congenial—two hundred years ago, Linnaeus devised a system of binomial classification for the animal world that remains basic to the natural sciences—for aesthetic inquiry Linnaean classification never led to linear progress. The modern literary critic is not discernibly closer to a definitive notion of tragedy than his baffled medieval forebear, Averroës.

Taking their miscues from the literary tradition, early genre studies in film tended to appropriate the zoological model. Typically they sought to create a Linnaean taxonomy for motion pictures by discerning "essential" formal and thematic qualities and cataloging required visual markings ("icons") for easy identification. As a method proper, genre criticism is variously inductive, deductive, and a combination of both. The inductive critic dilutes the characteristics of likely members into common group properties; the deductive critic, by contrast, posits a Platonic "supertext" (either real—"*Stagecoach* is the definitive western"—or ideal—"all westerns showcase frontier landscapes") and works a textual suspect into the prefabricated framework. The older the generic applicant, the better the approach seems to work. In a classical studio era populated by *The Plainsman* (1936), *Stagecoach* (1939), and *Jesse James* (1939), genre criticism offers the tidy satisfactions of orderly arrangement and assured placement.

At the same time, the definition of genre has had to be flexible enough to accommodate marginal applicants that fail to meet the agreed-upon standards but nonetheless seem qualified to fill the slot. In 1981, Thomas Schatz's *Hollywood Genres* submitted a definition instructive in its looseness: a genre film is "one which involves familiar, essentially one-dimensional characters acting out a predictable story pattern within a familiar setting." Like pornography in Justice Potter Stewart's famous remark, it seems genre is a matter more of unspoken recognition than of dictionary definition: we know a western when we see one.

Or at least we used to. Since *Destry Rides Again* (1939), to take an oft-cited milestone, even ostensible westerns have resisted attempts to fence them in, no matter how wide the generic boundaries. Classical westerns, deconstructionist westerns, parodic westerns, urban westerns, revisionist westerns, postrevisionist "straight" westerns—by the time a *Rancho Notorious* (1952) or *Johnny Guitar* (1954) is corralled into its appointed place, the film is bent totally out of shape. Similarly, because story patterns mingle more readily than animal groups, even seemingly incompatible types such as the western and film noir crossbreed with disturbing promiscuity. Films such as *Meet Me in St. Louis* (1944), *It's a Wonderful Life* (1946), and *Colorado Territory* (1949)—to say nothing of the self-reflexive genre efforts of the poststudio era, such as *Little Big Man* (1968), *Cabaret* (1972), or *The Long Goodbye* (1973)—defy simple classification.

By the traditional measures of genre affiliation, teenpics are as elusive as any postmodernist motion picture amalgam. Paramount's *King Creole* (1958), for example, is at once a star vehicle for Elvis Presley, a musical, an urban crime drama, a familial melodrama, and (stretching things only slightly) a signature film noir of director Michael Curtiz. Both within and outside generic borders, exceptions, originals, and hybrids disrupt the system. And, as with scientific frameworks, when anomalies proliferate out of control, a paradigm shift beckons.

An alternative approach probes the development, not the definition, of genres. It begins with a recognition that anomalies and double entries are endemic to the very concept and proceeds to address the problem by sidestepping it. The standard genre questions of classification, of ideal form, even of meaning are subordinated to the primary question of inception: where do genres—or, for the present purpose, where do teenpics—come from?

From a methodological standpoint, the critical departure is not without its own problems: it assumes but does not define the shared—and, for most viewers, unquestioned—sense of what a genre is; it appropriates the referential convenience of genrelike categorizing without observing its standards and practices; and it makes ready use of the vocabulary of genre. Perhaps the best compliment to the efficacy of "old" genre theory is that it is virtually impossible to talk about Hollywood movies without drawing on it—without accepting some of the major distinctions, without speaking the troublesome file names, and without succumbing to the temptation to add to the catalog by submitting, for instance, "rock 'n' roll," "weirdie," and "clean" teenpic chapter headings.

But whatever the downside in critical consistency, an approach that places the interrogative "Why?" before "What?" has one overriding advantage: it can actually be answered with a degree of certainty. Explaining the inception of the teenpic seems a more enlightening enterprise than debating its essence. A phenomenon whose peculiarity was first noted in the mid-1950s, the teenpic can be marked with some precision along Hollywood's historical time line. The date of a phenomenon's occurrence is a good index of the reasons for its appearance. The teenpic, then, begins around 1955, a product of the decline of classical Hollywood cinema and the rise of the privileged American teenager.

2

A Commercial History

n America, moviemaking has always been dependent on commercial validation. With few exceptions—propaganda films mandated by the exigencies of wartime, vanity productions underwritten by wealthy eccentrics, and an always marginal avant-garde cinema—motion picture production responds to the immutable laws of consumer demand. Virtually all movies begin as commodities made for a marketplace—not just commodities, to be sure, but at least commodities.

In this light, the history of American motion pictures may be viewed as a commercial history, the story of businessmen and entertainers trying to gauge the barometer of public taste for financial profit. Movie patrons voice their preferences by casting an economic vote at the box office window; moviemakers tally the tickets and respond accordingly. If one year the public indicates an infatuation with gangster films, as the lucrative returns from *Little Caesar* and *The Public Enemy* signaled in 1931, it follows logically that the next year will see many more.

In practice, of course, the creation of motion pictures is not so static and deterministic. A purely economic equation fails to explain the experience of a viewer "spellbound in darkness" before a screen. Likewise, the motives of the capitalists themselves, the studio executives and producers whose prime task is to turn a dollar, don't always match up with a bottom-line analysis. Even Jack Warner and Harry Cohn, two of Hollywood's sternest and stingiest money-men, had instincts other than the acquisitive. If anything, Hollywood cinema under the moguls demonstrated a level of craft, art, and social responsibility that more than justified its profit margins. The economic means influence, not determine, the cultural meaning.

Still, a movie is an expensive and high-risk product in an intensely competitive entertainment marketplace. It has to be bankable figuratively to be bankable literally: that is, likely to turn a profit if it is to obtain initial financing. To justify its commercial existence, it must return its negative costs (the price of a negative of a completed film) plus distribution, exhibition, and promotional expenses. The product's consumer, the moviegoing public, has to be vigorously courted and satisfied if a moviemaker wants to stay in business. Since the mid-1950s the most dependable suitors have been exploitation films; the most seducible clients have been teenagers.

Exploitation films derive from a commercial strategy first practiced in earnest during the 1950s and attributable mainly to the economic disorders then afflicting Hollywood. For the motion picture industry, the 1950s were a frightening decade for reasons that had nothing to do with atomic warfare or the House Un-American Activities Committee. What was truly dreadful was an apparently irreversible decline in movie attendance and the radical disruption of the industry's integrated and efficient institutional structure. These two ailments created the financial desperation that led to the emergence of the exploitation teenpic.

From "Gilded Hussy" to "Erstwhile Big Eight"

For most of the 1930s and 1940s, the motion picture industry was dominated by a handful of companies, the so-called Big Eight. Five "majors" (MGM, Warner Bros., Paramount, Twentieth Century-Fox, and RKO) and three "minors" (Universal, Columbia, and United Artists) accounted for well over 80 percent of the movies exhibited across America. Most of the balance was taken up by less solvent "Poverty Row" companies—Monogram and Republic Pictures being the best known and most enduring—which specialized in inexpensive B pictures. In a large metropolitan area, a dedicated moviegoer might also come across a foreign import or a "specialty market" feature, such as Yiddish-language films for Jewish Americans or "race movies" for African Americans. But for the average patron, especially in smaller communities, "the movies" meant the Big Eight and their B-picture appendages.

This period of oligarchic control, known as "classical Hollywood cinema" to most film scholars, dates from the early 1920s, when the major studios consolidated their power, until the decline of the system in the 1950s. With few exceptions, classical Hollywood moviemaking was a rationalized, assembly-line business supplying a more or less standardized product to an enthusiastic and reliable audience. Studios and individual movies competed, but moviegoing itself was guaranteed, just as automobile manufacturers offered different models to consumers who need not be sold on the advantages of driving. The Hollywood machinery ran so smoothly that individual production units developed easily identifiable stylistic qualities and narrative tropes. The glossy escapism of an MGM musical, the gritty working-class realism of a Warner Bros. melodrama, and the European flair and sophistication of a Paramount comedy all testify to a time when Hollywood's market was certain and its means of production uniform. Little wonder that envious businessmen in other fields spoke of Hollywood as "that gilded hussy, the motion picture industry."

Only during the early years of the Great Depression was Hollywood forced to reckon with declining profits and retrenchment. Before the crash of 1929, the rush to convert to sound technology and the intense competition for exhibition venues seriously overextended the financial resources of the major studios. As the magnitude of the nation's disaster became apparent, weekly attendance plummeted from the estimated 110 million in 1930 to 60 million in 1932. The close of 1932 found the fortunes of the business "at their lowest ebb." Several theater chains went bankrupt, Paramount and RKO went into receivership, and Warner Bros. and Fox teetered on the edge of ruin.

The industry weathered the crisis by tightening budgets, lowering ticket prices, and, beginning in 1934, enforcing the culturally soothing Production Code. By mid-decade, despite the continuing nationwide depression (or perhaps because of it), Hollywood was back in the money. In 1934, weekly attendance rebounded to 70 million, and from 1935 to 1939 it stayed in the range of 80 to 90 million. The renewed patronage is often attributed to Depression America's twin need for emotional sustenance and shelter from the elements. Whatever the reasons, the industry was once again on course, a unique reversal of fortunes in a stagnant economy. Several of the major studios actually capitalized on the crisis by using their superior resources to crush independent competition and otherwise consolidate their economic hegemony. Although film historian Garth Jowett is correct to point out that the motion picture industry did not, as is sometimes supposed, come through the "terrible thirties" untouched, it fared pretty well on balance, especially in comparison with the rest of American business.

The resilience Hollywood demonstrated during the Great Depression anticipated a lucrative war record. Homefront consumers, glutted with discretionary income and limited in their spending options, flocked to the movies. By 1945, weekly attendance was at a steady 95 million; domestic gross receipts for the industry as a whole had risen from $1,002,560,000 in 1941 to $1,500,000,000 in 1945, with comparable gains in net profits for most of the major studios. This flood of black ink put Hollywood in the "soundest financial condition in its history" as it entered the postwar period.

Unlike many industries that had ridden the war boom to unprecedented profits, Hollywood had little reason to fear conversion to a peacetime economy. Any misgivings about labor problems and increased production costs were offset by the anticipated reopening of the movie-starved European market. Besides, the Great Depression had shown that movies were a cultural necessity virtually immune to economic downturns. Reflecting a widespread optimism about the future, Terry Ramsaye, then editor of the *1945–46 International Motion Picture Almanac*, wrote rhapsodically of an "ever-beckoning anticipation and promise for tomorrow."

The events of 1946, the first full year of peace, were heartening. In one stroke Congress increased industry profits 64 percent by repealing the federal excess-profits tax. A boost in foreign business delighted distributors, and a surge in weekly attendance to a postdepression high had exhibitors ecstatic. Financially secure, and with every reason to expect continued prosperity, the motion picture businessman of 1946 could look forward confidently to the best years of his life.

What followed was one of the most precipitous collapses in the annals of American business. In quick succession, and with devastating effect, Hollywood was beset by a series of plagues almost biblical in their variety and cruel persistence. The visitations were of three kinds—economic, political, and cultural—and their cumulative effect left the lately vigorous industry prostrate.

First, and with dizzying suddenness, the economic situation deteriorated. The most crippling development was the Supreme Court decision to apply the Sherman Anti-Trust Act to the motion picture business. The Paramount Decree of 1948 ended a decade-long on-and-off dispute between the Department of Justice and the major studios by ordering the vertical disintegration of the motion picture industry. The Court ruled the triple-threat monopoly of production, distribution, and exhibition, which several of the majors had enjoyed since the silent era, in restraint of trade and required studios to divest their theater chains. This structural dismantling terminated the old studio system. With the studios unable to guarantee each of their films a venue, the assembly-line production system that had defined the classical Hollywood cinema was no longer sustainable. The decree also disrupted the industry's circular system of financing, wherein profits from exhibition were reinvested in production of new features. Throughout the 1950s, Hollywood's agile accountants circumvented the spirit of the divorcement decree, but the security and predictability of vertical integration were things of the past.

The Paramount Decree was the most serious blow to the hegemony of the studios, but other developments contributed to the desperation of what were rapidly becoming known as "the erstwhile Big Eight." In August 1947, the British government imposed a 75 percent tax on all American film company earnings, and overseas markets elsewhere initiated similar protective measures. To encourage their local film industries, foreign governments often required that a percentage of Hollywood's overseas profits be "frozen" within the host country. To gain access to these frozen assets, a Hollywood moviemaker had to produce abroad, thereby underwriting foreign film industries. The lure of cheap on-site labor and the proven box office appeal of exotic locales lessened the sting of the arrangement. By the early 1950s, it made more economic sense to shoot in a picturesque foreign location than to recreate it on a Hollywood back lot. "Join the picture business and see the world" was the joshing motto as the popularity of picturesque dramas such as *The African Queen* (Kenya, 1951), *Roman Holiday* (Rome, 1953), *Three Coins in a Fountain* (Rome, 1954), *Summertime* (Venice, 1955), *Soldier of Fortune* (Hong Kong, 1955), *House of Bamboo* (Tokyo, 1955) and *The Bridge on the River Kwai* (Ceylon, 1957) served notice that Hollywood-the-place was dispensable to postwar moviemaking.

The domestic economic climate became equally unfavorable to the old studio system. Once Hollywood lawyers and agents realized that capital gains were taxed at a lower rate than salaries, they urged their high-priced clients to back private production companies and reap the benefits of corporate profit sharing rather than take a studio salary. Attracted by freedom as well as finance, big-name producers, directors, and stars rushed to form independent production companies, "indies" in trade jargon. In 1958, United Artists vice president Max E. Youngstein hailed an "independent revolution" that had supplanted "the one-man studio czar system." By his reckoning, independents accounted for only 1 percent of Hollywood output in 1951; in 1958, their share had risen to at least 50 percent, including three straight winners of the Best Picture Oscar: *Marty* (1955), *Around the World in Eighty Days* (1956), and *The Bridge on the River Kwai* (1957).

In one sense Youngstein's much-vaunted "era of the independent" was something of a misnomer. The indies routinely leased big-studio facilities and employed their distribution networks. More significantly, the best of the independent producers and directors (Elia Kazan, George Stevens, John Huston, William Wyler, Stanley Kramer, and Hal Wallis) and all of the big-name stars who formed independent companies (John Wayne, Jimmy Stewart, Burt Lancaster, and Kirk Douglas) had been nurtured within the old Hollywood system and emulated its professional standards. But occasionally, as in *On the Waterfront* (1954) and *Sweet Smell of Success* (1957), the artistic sensibility was truly as "non-Hollywood" as the financing.

Concurrent with the economic maladies was a political assault undertaken by the House Un-American Activities Committee (HUAC) and several powerful private organizations, most notably the American Legion. Beginning in May 1947 and continuing with varying degrees of drama and intensity until the mid-1950s, HUAC and its ideological allies subjected the motion picture industry to intense scrutiny, questioning its loyalties and challenging its very right to exist as an independent business. The criticisms culminated in a series of highly publicized congressional hearings. Held in October 1947 and presided over by J. Parnell Thomas (R–New Jersey), the most notorious investigation was a boisterous spectacle starring a recalcitrant band of filmmakers dubbed the Hollywood Ten. Under the more temperate chairmanships of John Woods (D–Georgia) and Harold Velde (R–Illinois), HUAC continued to subpoena and harass Hollywood artists throughout the early 1950s.

Moviemakers were no strangers to tangles with hostile officials. Since the days of the nickelodeon, ambitious city council members and zealous ministers had made points with their constituencies by delivering jeremiads against the civic and moral lapses of screen entertainment. Not infrequently, ad-pub departments welcomed a healthy dose of controversy as a way to inject new life into a failing feature. The attention from HUAC was different in degree and kind: this was not a dispute with the Chicago Board of Censors over cleavage but a sustained assault on the industry's lifeblood, the people who made the movies. The HUAC hearings were less concerned with condemning movie content than in claiming live victims, professionals whose political leanings called their patriotism into question. To chronicle here the investigations and the Hollywood blacklists is unnecessary; these are some of the most exhaustively documented chapters in motion picture history. What does bear mention is the constraint the political pressure put on the initiative and creativity of American moviemaking at the very moment it was most in need of those qualities. During the height of anticommunist fervor in 1948–54, what Robert Warshow described as "the present atmosphere" redirected creative energies and limited options for the popular arts. Commercial moviemaking always operates within fairly rigid boundaries, but under the watchful eyes of Congress and the American Legion the permissible range of alternatives was, for a time, constricted even further—though the atmosphere was never so stifling as to bring about "the end of intellectual content in Hollywood for more than a decade," as film historian Charles Higham claims.

More fearful than Hollywood's blacklist, however, was its red ink. The immediate postwar surge in attendance had been remarkably short-lived; by 1949, Americans were deserting the movies in droves. The great exodus to the suburbs permanently altered the leisure habits of Hollywood's once-faithful audience, as millions of couples settled down to raise families and purchase expensive new consumer goods. For such couples, the cost in time, money, and trouble of an excursion to a downtown theater was a dubious investment, particularly with a convenient alternative available in the living room.

"The Electronic Monster"

Of all the plagues to descend on Hollywood in the 1950s, television was the most debilitating. The new medium forever ended the cultural hegemony of the movies. In 1947, the total revenue of the TV networks and their affiliated stations was $1.9 million; by 1957, it had skyrocketed to $943.2 million. In 1960, eight of ten American homes had at least one television set turned on an average of five hours and five minutes each day. Scorned in the beginning as a derivative, subordinate form of entertainment, television achieved ascendancy over the movies with such dazzling speed that it had already upended the cultural hierarchy by the time Hollywood began to respond in earnest to its challenge.

From its defensive official slogan ("Movies Are Better Than Ever") to the overweening nostalgia and desperate boosterism of the trade journals, Hollywood's public relations counterattack bespoke nothing so much as imminent doom. Eric Johnston, president of the Motion Picture Association of America (MPAA), spent the decade dutifully putting up a good front. In 1957, he quoted *New York Times* TV and radio critic Jack Gould to the effect that television had reached a crisis, that it had "ulcerous problems," that "after 10 years of bedazzling audiences with the new joy of staying home [television] is now scraping its barrel to keep its audience at home." The next year, *Television Age* coolly submitted the humiliating news that "if box office figures haven't proved it, and television ratings haven't proved it," a specially commissioned research study had: "More people watch movies on the home screen than on the big screen."

Because the television audience grew as the movie audience shrank, Hollywood made the obvious connection. Although changing patterns of suburban life and multiplication of leisure options also contributed to the drop in attendance, these developments were esoteric and difficult to calibrate. Industry old-timers, remembering what movies had done to vaudeville, were especially wary of the new medium and longed for the days before "the electronic monster halitosised up our lives." In attempting to reverse its decline, Hollywood reacted mainly to the manifest threat from television. The nature of television—its physical shape, episodic format, and family-oriented content—largely determined the nature of American motion pictures in the 1950s.

There were two ways movies could outflank television: (1) do what television could not do in the way of spectacle (form) or (2) do what television could not do in the way of controversial images or narrative (content). In short, "make 'em big or make 'em provocative." During a decade painted as conservative and conformist, the motion picture industry, with a vigor born of desperation, became more technically innovative, economically adventuresome, and aesthetically daring than at any time in its history.

Many of the striking optical effects and "gimmick" processes of the 1950s had been around for years, but neither producers nor exhibitors

"The electronic monster": suburban Americans mesmerized by Hollywood's nemesis, 1955. (Quigley Photographic Archive, Georgetown University Library)

had wanted to absorb the retooling expenses for the new projection techniques. Television forced the issue. To enchant consumers out of their living rooms, the studios, led by Twentieth Century-Fox and MGM, ballyhooed a fascinating array of new cinematic devices designed to heighten the theatrical experience and diminish the twenty-two-inch, low-definition TV screen.

Fred Waller's Cinerama was the first of the new processes to gain prominence with the phenomenal success of *This Is Cinerama* (1952), a nonnarrative spectacle created solely to showcase the new process. Inventor Waller intended Cinerama, which encompassed an arc of about 140 degrees, to approximate the viewer's peripheral vision, an arc of approximately 160 degrees. Cinerama utilized a three-lens camera in filming and required three projectors in exhibition, each projecting a third of the total image on a screen roughly three times larger than normal. Multiphonic sound recorded on six tracks added to the sensory bombardment.

Initially, audience reaction to Cinerama was enthusiastic. As more than a gimmick, though, the process had insurmountable problems. First, exhibition was prohibitively expensive. Seating renovations and installations of special screens and projection equipment came to

$250,000 at one New York theater. (The retooling costs for Todd-AO, a 65mm widescreen process developed by producer Michael Todd and the American Optical Company for *Around the World in Eighty Days*, were even heftier: $400,000 at one venue.) Second, Cinerama was a nightmare for projectionists: the margin lines between the three projected images were clearly visible. Finally, for all its technical complexity, Cinerama was dramatically retrograde. The half-dozen or so Cinerama films released during the 1950s were basically travelogues with peripheral vision, pure spectacle in a narrative medium. Only *How the West Was Won* (1962), the last big Cinerama entry and by then a case of "too much too late," managed an integration of widescreen frontier landscapes with western narrative conventions.

The cinematic technique most commonly associated with the 1950s is the three-dimensional process promoted by Milton Gunzberg. Polaroid glasses were necessary to complete the 3-D illusion of a specially photographed 2-D motion picture. Audiences shrieked delightedly as natives appeared to throw spears at them in *Bwana Devil* (1952), the first of the 3-D films, or as tongues of fire leapt from the screen in *House of Wax* (1953). "This is the year," exulted Eric Johnston, "that will go down in motion picture history as 1953-D." It too, however, was a short-lived craze. Exhibitors never knew how many pairs of Polaroid glasses to stockpile. Viewers complained of headaches, and the movies screened in 3-D, such as *Man in the Dark* (1953), *It Came from Outer Space* (1953), and *Gog* (1954), may have been as responsible as the glasses.

In the end, only CinemaScope, Twentieth Century-Fox's widescreen anamorphic process, gained wide acceptance. Employing a special lens that compressed an image in filming and spread it out again for projection, CinemaScope increased the aspect ratio of the projected image from the standard "Academy ratio" (width to height) of 1.33:1 to 2.55:1 (later, 2.35:1). Cinematographers had more trouble adapting to the new process than did exhibitors, and this relative ease of conversion won the widescreen sweepstakes for CinemaScope. Encouraged by the huge success of *The Robe* (1953), the first CinemaScope movie and number-one box office attraction of the year, Fox estimated in 1956 that 36,197 theaters in forty-one countries had made CinemaScope installations, with domestic theaters accounting for 17,408. Just in case anyone missed the point, 'Scope movies self-consciously called attention to their scale. In *The Girl Can't Help It* (1956), Tom Ewell appeared in a precredit sequence and pushed out both sides of an

Widescreen retaliation: a CinemaScope point-of-view shot from Twentieth Century-Fox's *The Fly* (1958). (Courtesy of Twentieth Century-Fox)

Academy-ratio screen into the CinemaScope format. In the aptly titled *Bigger Than Life* (1956), director Nicholas Ray was marginally more subtle, framing a pitifully tiny TV screen in the center of a cavernous expanse of 'Scope screen space. Ultimately Fox's success with Cinema-Scope forced Paramount to deploy its own widescreen, though non-anamorphic, system, VistaVision (1.85:1). By the end of the decade, most movies, even rereleases originally filmed in Academy ratio, were projected in aspect ratios of 1.66:1 or 1.85:1.

If nothing else, all the frenzied technical activity kept the copyright lawyers happy, and the nomenclature was at least as inventive as the photography: HyptoVision, Psychorama, glamorama, naturama, thrillerama, technirama, hypnovista, percepto, emergo, cinemiracle, and regiscope, the last a process using electronically animated puppets. The gimmickry reached its apogee in the "scent sweepstakes" between Walter Reade Jr. and Michael Todd Jr. Reade's "AromaRama" disseminated seventy-two different smells during *Behind the Great Wall* (1959). Todd's *Scent of Mystery* (1960) employed an "olfactory process to end all processes" called smell-o-vision, which spewed out some thirty different aromas, including roses, banana, onions, tobacco, gasoline, and the specially concocted title perfume. The quality of most such films produced solely to exploit a gimmick process was unwittingly summed up in *Scent of Mystery*'s ad campaign:

> First, they moved—1893
> Then, they talked—1927
> Now, they smell—1959

Blockbusters, Bs, Bardot, and *Baby Doll*

The technical changes in motion picture form encouraged a shift in the kind of motion pictures the big studios financed. To a greater degree than ever before, the industry channeled vast sums of money into fewer and fewer projects. The divorcement decree alone had mandated some of this: without captive venues, marginal films of limited appeal were more difficult to book than the high-powered blockbusters, whose grand scale and big stars could be counted on to generate business. Moreover, the growing internationalization of the motion picture business provided compelling economic reasons for a change in production strategy. In 1953, box office returns from foreign markets surpassed domestic business for the first time, accounting for some 60 percent of total receipts. The action-packed, simply plotted blockbuster was the form that most easily and profitably crossed national borders.

The 1950s blockbusters were high-profile spectacles, "twice as big and half as good," featuring casts of thousands, exotic locales, and eye-popping set designs. Rome was burned, the Red Sea parted, and the heavens stormed, all in widescreen "movie color." Although the blockbuster mentality also infected musicals and war stories, it reached its most egregious form in the so-called antiquity kick. Studios scoured the Judeo-Christian tradition for passionate stories suitable for picturesque rendering. *Samson and Delilah* (1949), *Quo Vadis* (1951), *David and Bathsheba* (1951), and *The Robe* (1953) set an early pattern for a DeMillian series of overblown biblical epics that captivated the foreign audience and lured a goodly number of lapsed Americans back into the ritual of moviegoing. *The Ten Commandments* (1956), *Ben-Hur* (1959), the 1959 reissue of *Samson and Delilah*, *Spartacus* (1960), *King of Kings* (1961), *Cleopatra* (1963), and even *Exodus* (1960) are legacies of this "sword and sandal" or "lust in the dust" cycle.

The blockbuster mentality forced a continuing reduction in the number of films produced each year. The first casualty was the venerable B picture. The standard B picture was an evanescent genre effort, usually a western or crime melodrama, whose main economic function was less to round out an evening's entertainment than to lower overhead by keeping soundstages busy between productions of prestigious A features. In an exhibition practice that first became widespread during the depression, the B played the lower half of a double feature, providing a sidebar treat to the featured medium- or big-budget attraction. When moviemaking was an assembly-line operation with guaranteed outlets, the Bs, plus newsreels, cartoons, and serials, were a cheap way to keep the production machinery well oiled. At the same time, they offered exhibitors a steady supply of rotating features. By the early 1950s, however, with *The Lone Ranger* and *The Roy Rogers Show* readily available on television, the cheap genre fare that defined the old B pictures lacked theatrical appeal. With production costs rising and revenues dropping, the traditional B became too expensive to justify its commercial existence. In 1952, Warner Bros. and Twentieth Century-Fox dropped B pictures from production; Jack L. Warner even labeled them "a menace to the industry." As the trade press punned, the Bs were buzzing off.

In first-class metropolitan palaces, the dearth of Bs went generally unlamented. Such theaters adapted their exhibition strategy to blockbusters, supplementing the featured attraction with one- or two-reel shorts on current topics or with brief travelogues. But for small neighborhood theaters—"nabes" in trade jargon—the departure of the Bs and a concurrent reduction in the number of medium-budget films presented a major problem. Unlike a large downtown venue, the nabe drew from a limited audience and, in order to attract the same moviegoers week in and week out, required a steady supply of changing features. In small communities, even a popular blockbuster "played out" in a matter of weeks. The nabes depended on Bs and medium-budget films to fill the gap between releases of A features. Despite the loss of B pictures, as late as 1954, 70 percent of the nation's theaters still operated double features. With the wait between A features growing and the supply of alternative fare declining, many exhibitors faced a serious shortage of product.

The production end of the business, meanwhile, opened a second front in its campaign against the small screen. This strategy attempted to outflank television with "mature" or "adult" content. But where the change in cinematic form required only an advance in technology, the change in motion picture content, in the moral universe Hollywood had posited for so long, required a cultural revolution.

Since 1930, the motion picture industry had operated under a strict and, after 1934, rigorously enforced Production Code. The Production Code Administration (PCA), theoretically a creation of the Motion Picture Producers and Distributors of America (which became the Motion Picture Association of America in 1945), was in fact the fiefdom of Joseph I. Breen, a no-nonsense censor who from 1934 to 1954 made sure every movie passing through his office met the Code's exacting standards in matters of morality. From the studios' point of view, this was an expedient accommodation. The Breen Office standards were, in general, consistent and comprehensible; they were certainly preferable to the vagaries of local censorship boards. Equally important was the fact that an imprimatur from Breen, an upstanding Irish Catholic, kept at bay the powerful Legion of Decency, the pressure group that monitored movie morality for the Roman Catholic Church. During the 1930s, a Legion-sponsored boycott of a motion picture could spell box office disaster. In Philadelphia, attendance dropped 40 percent when church authorities ordered parishioners to boycott local features. The Code may have annoyed a few Hollywood artists and outraged the National Council on Freedom from Censorship, but for moviemaker and audience alike it was a convenient arrangement. Not until the mid-1950s did the economic desperation of the industry coincide with a revolution in public morality to produce significant changes in the world the movies depicted and upheld.

Several factors contributed to the industry's realization that the Code had outlived its usefulness. In big cities and university towns, owners of small theaters found an appreciative market for the right kind of foreign film. One of the few success stories for the exhibition end of the business, the "art house" played (in theory) to a sophisticated, upscale audience, though Brigitte Bardot's epochal unveiling in *And God Created Woman* (1956) proved the market for foreign art was not limited to eggheads. Despite cries that "the so-called Art Theatre" had become "the dumping ground for the European celluloid garbage bucket," Arthur L. Mayer, a prominent importer and exhibitor of foreign film fare, estimated that there were eight hundred art houses in the United States by 1958 (up from fewer than fifty in the prewar era), and the number of foreign films imported had risen from 93 in 1948 to 532 in 1957. When the Supreme Court, in a case involving an Italian import, *The Miracle* (1951), appeared to grant motion pictures the same First Amendment rights as print media, the conditions seemed right for an all-out challenge to the Production Code's authority. In confluence with wider changes in American culture and motivated by a keen sense of self-preservation, the motion picture industry moved gingerly into zones it had traditionally left untouched.

Lending dignity to the venture was a generation of serious artists who stood ready to create intellectually respectable movies about forbidden themes. Otto Preminger's *The Moon Is Blue* (1953) is the obvious landmark: the director's refusal to delete the word *virgin* from the film, and United Artists' decision to release the movie without Code approval, made it the first meaningful challenge to the status quo since Howard Hughes's obstinacy about the advertising for *The Outlaw* (1943). Ironically, television supported the growing consensus that the Code needed revision. Live TV dramas regularly broached subjects forbidden to Hollywood. For example, the movies were not permitted to depict narcotic addictions or kidnapping, but the network censors imposed no such limitations on television. "TV's *Dragnet* gets away with narcotics 'exposees' pictures can't, and because of a Production Code set up over twenty years ago," complained the *Hollywood Reporter* in 1952. "No wonder competition's tough."

By the mid-1950s, more and more pictures were treading on territory that had previously been taboo and, in spirit, moving away from Code subservience. *Variety*'s Abel Green scanned the unclean, un-Breen output of 1956 and paired old sins to the new cinema: drug addiction (*The Man With the Golden Arm*, 1955), homosexuality (*Tea and Sympathy*, 1956), "poor white trash" (*God's Little Acre*, 1957), "happy pills" (*Bigger Than Life*, 1956), abortion (*Bachelor Party*, 1956), and unconsummated marriage (*Baby Doll*, 1956). "A motion picture so daring you'll ask: How Did They Dare Make It?" went a typical tag line.

So "daring" was the new spirit that Hollywood began challenging the HUAC intimidation. By mid-1955, *Storm Center* (1956) was in preproduction, a film about a librarian (Bette Davis) vilified by right-wingers for refusing to remove procommunist books from her shelves. "The companies are now producing material they wouldn't touch a couple of years ago," said its screenwriter. A revision of the Code in 1956 was an act of self-preservation that, while maintaining the PCA's authority, forfeited the certainty of the old standards. Motion Picture Association of America president Eric Johnston revealed the prevalent confusion in a clumsy defense of the revisions that called the new Code "neither tighter nor looser than the old one" but more modern. Whatever the case, the very uncertainty over what was permissible created great artistic and entrepreneurial opportunities.

Inevitably, toward the middle of the decade, Hollywood capitulated to television. Most of the studios' troops had long since gone over to the enemy anyway. When RKO and Warner Bros. sold their motion picture libraries to television, the rest of the industry paused only long enough to scream, "Traitor!" before following suit. The ready cash was too desperately needed to resist. In 1956, Fox's Spyros P. Skouras admitted that without the $30 million from library sales to television, his studio would have ended the year in the red. Another accommodation proved even more profitable: led by Columbia and Warner Bros., the major studios threw in for a piece of the video action, with subsidiaries specializing in production of network shows. Fox's Darryl F. Zanuck expressed the new pragmatism: "Television has been a big blow to us. Let's take it and turn it to our advantage."

T(V)KO'd Exhibition

The cozy symbiosis between television and the studios may have been a boon for the production end of the business, but for exhibition the alliance was a devastating betrayal. Together with the decline in attendance and the product shortage, Hollywood's aid to the enemy made for a near-constant state of animosity between producers and exhibitors. Said one angry theater owner, "It'll be a whole new era for TV, and the theaters will be left out in the cold. I can't see how the companies, who have grown fat off the theaters, can think they'll be able to serve two such deadly competitors as theaters and TV without condemning one to death, especially since one medium gives away its entertainment free." A colleague agreed. "How can the theaters play both sides against the middle? Someone is going to lose out and you know it's going to be the exhibitor."

Feeling jilted by the studios, exhibitors turned for comfort to an eager group of independent moviemakers who stood ready to elbow in and fill the marquee void. Traditionally, exhibitors had been reluctant to book indies for fear of jeopardizing relations with the Big Eight. With the Big Eight erstwhile and product scarce, the nation's theater owners, particularly the nabes, were compelled to cultivate alternative sources of supply. By the mid-1950s, they were "wide open and hungry" for indie product that was cheap, regular, and exploitable.

The experience of Steve Broidy, president of Allied Artists (formerly Monogram), was typical. In common with other moviemakers outside the majors' circle, Broidy had struggled for years against the majors' stranglehold on choice exhibition venues. Exhibitor desperation for inexpensive marquee filler finally allowed him to make some headway. "The major producers' label alone no longer sells a picture," a prominent exhibitor told Broidy. "It's only what's on the screen that counts.

There's a ready market for good pictures. You produce them and we'll show them." Indeed, to ensure a source of supply, some exhibitors invested in motion picture production themselves. American Releasing Corporation, the early version of American International Pictures (AIP), received 20 percent of its early financing from theater interests. Company president James H. Nicholson, himself schooled in exhibition practices, knew there was an appreciable market "in the smaller houses" for "the formula pic, if properly planned as to title, type, and story."

Exhibitors would not give the indies the same favorable rental agreements they gave to the majors, but this too could work to mutual advantage. "We don't get the same terms as the majors," admitted Nicholson in 1956, "but we consider our returns satisfactory since we have a streamlined operation with low overhead." Low-budget moviemaker Herschell Gordon Lewis described the arrangement more colorfully:

> How could I convince [theater owners] to set aside a week's playing time for my picture? Well, I could give them better terms: a sliding scale from twenty-five to fifty percent, instead of demanding a ninety-ten split in my favor on the first couple of weeks. So they figured to themselves, in their warped weasely little minds, "If I play this fellow's films to a half-filled house, and I keep sixty percent of the gross, I am far better off than playing to a filled house where I keep only ten percent of the gross." So economics worked in favor of the low budget producer.

In short, by the mid-1950s, exhibitors were willing to deal with any moviemaker carrying a 35mm print.

The "formula pic" peddled by the low-budget producers and played mainly in the smaller houses was a scion of the B picture and, in appearance, all but indistinguishable from its parent. Like the old studio B, it rounded out programs and filled up marquees during fallow periods between major releases. (To increase potential play dates, American International Pictures developed a policy of releasing its features during "slow" periods when major product was unavailable.) Also like the B, the formula pic was cheap—in relative terms probably cheaper than its predecessor. In the domestic market of the mid-1950s, a low-budget indie feature would yield perhaps $450,000 to $500,000 in distribution revenues, down from $600,000 just a few years previous. Their total cost, then, could not exceed $225,000 per feature, industry rule of thumb then being that a picture's gross should be double its negative cost. More often the price tag of a low-budget indie was closer to $100,000. A 1956 deal between indie producer Robert L. Lippert and Twentieth Century-Fox, for example, called for the production of six low-budget black-and-white CinemaScope pictures at $100,000 apiece. AIP also figured its early budgets in the $100,000–$200,000 range, though many of its 1950s projects surely never saw six figures. Moviemakers kept costs in line by limiting shooting schedules to perhaps two weeks, sometimes a matter of days, and, in AIP's case, making sure the feature was in release within ninety days after shooting.

Means of production aside, the new secondary fare was different from the B in two respects: subject matter and audience. Unlike the Bs, these movies, whether solo or in twin combinations, had to stand on their own, not as sidebars to a top-drawer A attraction. Though made on B-level budgets, they had to have A-caliber drawing power. Without the luxury of a guaranteed audience or an A attraction host on which to attach itself, the secondary fare of the 1950s required a special "hook" to entice audiences, a gimmick or "exploitation angle." Although the trade continued to refer to any low-budget formulaic movie as a "B," by the mid-1950s the nomenclature no longer fit. In 1955, *Variety* spoke to the difference in an article on Sam Katzman's production unit at Columbia:

> While Columbia has dropped what may be referred to as the "formula picture," it has substituted the "gimmick" picture. These are low-budgeters with an exploitation angle. They usually feature lower case names, actors who receive between $20,000 and $30,000 per picture. The Sam Katzman unit at Columbia is especially active in grinding out films of this type. Some of them may never play Broadway, but they still chalk up respectable grosses in the hinterlands. . . . A once-over of the Katzman titles gives a good indication of the type of fare exhibitors can expect from Columbia. . . . They include *Creature With the Atom Brain, It Came from Beneath the Sea, Chicago Syndicate, Gun That Won the West, Teenage Crime Wave,* and *Devil Goddess.*

At this date, Katzman's selection of subject matter still retained an echo of the B tradition, with "an occasional western" continuing to appeal to patrons in what were called "the smaller stations." By the next year, however, Katzman and his rivals at AIP had discarded the B mentality altogether. Independently of each other, they developed a distinct strategy for the new secondary fare, the essential component being audience, not subject matter.

In late 1956, *Variety* described the new product wrought by the changing relationship between exhibitors and indie producers:

> In recent months exhibitors have clamored for film fare that would appeal to teenage customers whom they regard as their best audience. . . . According to a circuit booker, the product shortage has brought about a new theory of assembling a show, a practice that has been adopted by several indie producers and distributors . . . the distribs, according to the booker, launch these pictures with a hefty advertising campaign. "They line up a big group of theaters," he explained, "and grab their money and run. It's not legitimate film fare as such. It attracts an audience that many of us in this industry consider undesirable." . . . The theaterman, who books and buys from a large New York circuit, said that if the theaters could possibly afford it, they would bypass these pictures. He pointed out that playing these films in the New York metropolitan area is only a recent policy and has been brought about by (1) product shortage and (2) the absence of acceptable secondary films. The lack of business, he noted, has forced the circuits to play "the type of pictures that attract peculiar audiences."

Only in the motion picture business would so tantalizing a consumer group as teenagers be considered "peculiar" or "undesirable." Few in the industry were as farsighted as AIP's James H. Nicholson. Fresh from his company's first big success, a double bill of *Girls in Prison/Hot Rod Girl* (both 1956), Nicholson proclaimed the demographic reality: "From an exhibitor's standpoint, the teenage audience hasn't been satisfied. . . . These kids are today's customers."

3

The Teenage Marketplace

The trouble with teenagers began when some smart salesman made a group of them in order to sell bobby sox.

PTA Magazine, 1956

These days, merchants eye teenagers the way stockmen eye cattle.

Dwight Macdonald, 1958

In 1904, the pioneering psychologist G. Stanley Hall announced a momentous discovery: the American adolescent. Like America itself, adolescents had always been around, but before Hall no one had taken particular notice of them. In lectures to progressive civic groups and in articles for national magazines, he and a band of energetic followers first popularized the concept of a developmental phase that began with puberty and ended with mature adulthood. Through their efforts, what had previously been "childhood," "youth," or "young adulthood" became a distinct experimental realm called "adolescence."

For the concept's originators, adolescence encompassed a much longer phase than it does today. In *The Boy-Girl Adolescent Period* (1911), a widely read compilation of articles written for the popular middle-class journal *American Motherhood*, Emma Virginia Fish told parents that adolescence was "the period bounded, loosely speaking, by the years twelve and twenty-five." For obvious biological and psychological reasons, however, early experts on adolescence concentrated on the formative and stressful "teen years." For less obvious economic and social reasons, conscientious parents turned increasingly to authorities like Hall and Fish for help in rearing their children amid the temptations and confusions of industrial urban America.

Sanctified by psychologists and recognized by every parent, a young person's "teen years" soon came to describe social status as well as chronological age. By the 1920s the novel quality of adolescent life in America was the topic of art and anthropology alike. F. Scott Fitzgerald's *This Side of Paradise* (1920) caused a sensation by exposing the gulf between Victorian parents and their jazz babies. Its eighteen-year-old protagonist, Amory Blaine, lives in a world of "vast juvenile intrigue," "petting parties," and girls "deep in an atmosphere of jungle music and the questioning of moral codes." Beset by multitudes of youthful offenders, the legal system reached the same conclusion as the literary salons. Juvenile court judge Ben B. Lindsey's book-length polemic, *The Revolt of Modern Youth* (1925), warned of "the strenuous, strict, and self-denying conventions of the strange Flipper-Flapper world," where a young girl petted at fifteen and drank at eighteen; "a world whose ways, customs, purposes, vision, and modes of thought were as unknown to her parents . . . and teachers as the social customs of Mars." Although Fitzgerald's classmates were hardly profligates, there was, as cultural historian Frederick Lewis Allen commented, "enough fire behind the revelations to make the Problem of the Younger Generation a topic of anxious discussion from coast to coast."

In their landmark survey *Middletown* (1929), Robert and Helen Lynd noticed another difference between adolescents and their elders: the community's young males, unlike their fathers, actually *enjoyed* going to school. Offering one of the first sociological descriptions of the self-contained teenage universe, they wrote, "The high school, with its athletics, clubs, sororities and fraternities, dances and parties, and other 'extra curricular activities' is a fairly complete social cosmos in itself, and about this city within a city the social life of the intermediate generation centers. . . . In this bustle of activity young Middletown swims along in a world as real and perhaps even more zestful than that in which its parents move."

Not that all professional observers put American youth in the same fish tank. Based on research conducted in 1941–42, A. B. Hollingshead's *Elmtown's Youth* (1949) concluded that class, not age, determined the social behavior of what were still being called "high school adolescents": "We believe that one of the important things this study highlights is the diversity of behavior exhibited by adolescents in the different *classes* in their day-to-day activities. We might have assumed that in a community the size of Elmtown with a stable, white native-born population, there would be more uniformity in the behavior of this group than we found" (emphasis added).

Although class consciousness was apparently still acute in Elmtown (and in the social sciences), age consciousness was taking hold elsewhere, the unprecedented and unaccountable generational differences being more strikingly noteworthy than the usual and understandable economic disparities. By the end of World War II, according to the *Dictionary of American Slang*, the term *teen-ager* had entered standard usage: "The U.S. is the only country having a word for members of this age group, and is the only country considering this age group as a separate entity whose influence, fads, and fashions are worthy of discussion apart from the adult world. Before circa 1935 U.S. teen-agers considered themselves as, and were considered, young adults and not a special group." In postwar America and in Americanized foreign countries, the teen years became a unique transitional phase between childhood and adulthood, in some senses an autonomous and in most cases a privileged period in an individual's life.

1950s Teenagers as Subculture

In 1958, the critic Dwight Macdonald took notice of "a new American caste" with "a style of life that was *sui generis*." The seemingly sudden appearance of the recently spawned life-form inspired levels of nervous trepidation, hopeful expectation, and outright xenophobia reminiscent of the opening reels of *The Day the Earth Stood Still* (1951). Truth to tell, 1950s teenagers *were* strange creatures, set apart from previous generations of American young people in numbers, affluence, and self-consciousness. There were more of them; they had more money; and they were more aware of themselves as teenagers.

In density alone, the massive teenage presence was something of a statistical anomaly. After a deep "population trough" in the worst years of the Great Depression, birthrates in America gradually accelerated during the late 1930s and throughout the war years showed a marked increase. As a 1982 study for the Brookings Institution noted, "Even *before* the baby boom officially began in 1946, there were substantial gains [in the birthrate]. The number of 5-through-9-year olds grew 24 percent between 1940 and 1950; children in this age group were born during World War II" (emphasis added). Reaching adolescence in the latter half of the next decade, this generation of wartime babies, not their celebrated younger siblings of the great baby boom of 1946–57, became the original teenagers.

The first teenagers came of age in surroundings that, by the standards of their parents and the rest of the world, were luxurious. Although the popular memory of the 1950s as an edenic era of near-universal economic prosperity has improved with time, the image of postwar affluence is by no means all misty nostalgia. Emphasizing John Kenneth Galbraith's "affluent society" at the expense of Michael Harrington's "other America" slights the condition of millions of poor and low-income people, but from a cold historical vantage the impressive fact is not that so many continued to have it bad but that so many more started having it good. To an unprecedented degree, the wealth spread from Wall Street to Main Street, a "movement toward [income] equalization" and a vast "diffusion of well-being" that improved the material lot of virtually all segments of society. Contemplating an especially pertinent graph charting a rising line of progress, economist Harold G. Vatter noted with wonder "the steady rise in aggregate real personal consumption expenditures, *a rise which rarely faltered, and on an annual basis never declined, from 1946 through 1961—a remarkable historical phenomenon.*" By almost any economic criterion, the decade warrants its superlatives; in any survey of the national largess, teenagers must be counted among the prime beneficiaries.

Dollars and demographics are two necessary measures of the first teenagers' originality, but the decisive element is generational cohesion: an acute sense of themselves as a special, like-minded community bound together by age and rank. Of course, all contemporaries who share the same experience of war, economic dislocation, or cultural revolution acquire a generational comradeship that comes with common berth on a mutual voyage through life. What lent 1950s teenagers a sense of group identity both peculiarly intense and historically new was that their generational status, their social position *as teenagers*, was carefully nurtured and vigorously reinforced by the adult institutions around them.

In the marketplace and the media, at home and at school, the teenager was counted a special creature requiring special handling. Sheer numbers and group proximity born of the population shift from rural to urban and suburban areas encouraged a collective and standardized response; the very nature of a complex bureaucratic society assured it. For the first time, the essentially private psychological and physical development of the American adolescent was accorded a dramatically public recognition. At once socially special and specially socialized, 1950s teenagers experienced the same things together—through their assigned place in the burgeoning consumer economy, in the increasing uniformity of public school education throughout the states, and in national media that doted on their idiosyncracies. Even in the family, helpful guidebooks such as Dr. Dorothy W. Baruch's *How to Live with Your Teenager* (1953) and Paul H. Landis's *Understanding Teenagers* (1955) discouraged innovative, individualized treatment. In short, the collective and standardized implementation of the traditional tools of socialization—child rearing, schooling, commerce, and culture—cemented intragenerational identification as surely as it cultivated intergenerational integration.

Grouped together, teenagers became a group. "In a real sense, the teenage group is self-sufficient now as in no previous generation," Landis observed in *Understanding Teenagers*, reminding parents that the "teenage problem" was a "new problem" and attributing it, interestingly enough, to collective treatment: "For the first time in history, young people have to live in large groups." When discussing the teenage problem, editorialists tended to employ the taxonomy of animal husbandry ("herds," "packs," "droves"), but academics turned naturally to the language of ethnography: teenagers were a "caste," a "tribe," indeed, a sort of "subculture."

In sociology and anthropology, the disciplines that jointly stake the best claims to possession, "subculture" is a designation with several varied but distinct meanings. In its crudest vernacular usage, it describes any discernible subgroup within a broader, presumably dominant and arguably monolithic society. By this light, in American terms, groups as diverse as Southerners, nudists, Mennonites, and the Hell's Angels are all national subcultures. In the more precise language of the social sciences, subcultures are commonly defined by racial, ethnic, regional, and class boundaries; described by language, values, and folkways; and authenticated by historical permanence and cultural continuity: Boston Brahmins, Jewish Americans, and inner-city African Americans taking their place under the big umbrella of "American culture" (itself a tenuous and troublesome concept). As the prefix indicates, subcultures are not autonomous; they exist in relation to a precedent or dominant culture. All considerations of subculture take cognizance of the relationship, and most emphasize it. In this sense, groups with a nominally separatist stance toward American culture, such as the Amish of the Midwest or the Hasidim of New York, are autonomous "cultures" in their own right: they are not really "in" America in any meaningful way.

The relationship of the subculture to the dominant culture may take many forms: easy accommodation and peaceful coexistence, imitation and assimilation, antagonism and opposition. Not infrequently, as in the experience of Jewish Americans, the subcultural group reacts in different ways at different times while its individual members negotiate their own personal responses. The familiar immigrant groups and their customary strategies of adaptation and resistance, however, make up only one part of the national experience of subculture. If the open spaces of nineteenth-century America attracted the traditional (and ready-made) "subcultures of birth," the urban confinements of twentieth-century America nurtured modern (and made-in-America) "subcultures of behavior." These were rejectionist, "alienated" groups such as delinquent gangs, bohemians, social cliques, and sects religious and political; groups whose membership joined by choice, not birth, and whose folkways, if less enduring, were often no less rich and formalized. With varying degrees of force and self-consciousness, their stance toward the surrounding culture was oppositional, a subcultural posture warranting the separate designation of "contraculture" or "counterculture."

The term *counterculture* was suggested in 1960 by sociologist J. Milton Yinger, to apply when, among other conditions, "the normative system of a group contains, as a primary element, a theme of conflict with the values of the total society." Reflecting the consensus outlook of sociological research in the 1950s, Younger had in mind "deviant" subgroups in clearly defined locales, such as "street corner societies," delinquent gangs, and imprisoned criminals. As a coinage of the 1960s, "counterculture" is, characteristically, a more amorphous concept. It usually refers to the demographic bulge of legend, the Woodstock-weaned "youth culture" ostensibly united by age, style, and sensibility. Although both subcultures are by definition oppositional, members of the 1960s version were presumed to have a participatory awareness their 1950s forerunners lacked, a heightened sense of themselves as an alternative to the dominant (Establishment) culture that made for a more self-conscious and calculated assumption of antagonistic values.

In defining the cultural status of 1950s teenagers, the conceptual movement from "contraculture" to "counterculture" is pertinent in three ways. First, the myriad contracultures of the 1950s were small local gangs limited and defined by neighborhood and peculiarities of place; the singular counterculture of the 1960s was a broad national group, lent a kind of community by the more intangible shared experiences of growing up mass-mediated in America. Second, where contracultural groups were typically defined in class and economic terms, the counterculture was described in generational terms (thus the tandem designation "youth culture"). Finally, a different value adheres to each label. To outside observers, contracultures were delinquent and deviant, a true social disease demanding curative action for the well-being of the body politic. By contrast, the oppositional stance of the counterculture, certainly among its righteous participants and often among chroniclers, was seen as a positive and pure response to the greater illness of the dominant culture. Additionally, if contracultures were treatable outgrowths in a basically healthy organism, the counterculture was a potentially terminal affliction.

Although neither "contraculture" nor "counterculture" is an especially current term in recent studies of subculture, the residue of their opposing perspectives is readily detectable. Especially when applied to so-called youth cultures—whether gangs, student groups, or broad generational coalitions—cultural conflict tends to take on connotations of moral worth. Contracultural "deviants" and countercultural youth movements are aggrandized or condemned in proportion to the degree of moral legitimacy accorded or denied the dominant culture. Generally, this means youth is free, pure, creative; the opposition is uptight, corrupt, stifling.

Sounding a theme that echoed incessantly throughout the next decade, psychologist Edgar Z. Friedenberg voiced the standard academic allegiance in *The Vanishing Adolescent* (1959), proclaiming that "it is the fully human adolescent—the adolescent who faces life with love and defiance—who has become aberrant." Similarly, a standard Marxist variation on the Freudian perspective celebrates youth subcultures as subversive and potentially revolutionary, a social phenomenon signaling and "signing" the human costs of class oppression and capitalist dehumanization.

Given the breadth of the demographics and the looseness of the cultural bond, 1950s teenagers might seem fit candidates for any of the available ethnographic categories: like a subculture, they can best be understood in response to a dominant culture; like a contraculture, they thrive on conflict; and like a counterculture, the community is national and generational, not local and class determined. But none of the terms imparts the historical novelty and social peculiarities of 1950s teenagers, and each conjures misleading associations: the permanence and tradition of a time-tested ethnic subculture, the criminal deviance of a contraculture, and the avowed confrontation of a cou Indeed, to think of 1950s teenagers as possessing their ow whether a sub-, contra-, or counterculture—is at best only cally accurate. By the light of anthropologist Clifford Ge nently reasonable definition of culture ("an historically t pattern of meanings embodied in symbols, a system of inhe ceptions expressed in symbolic forms by means of which mei nicate, perpetuate, and develop their knowledge about and att ward life"), 1950s teenagers created only something *like* Teenagers might be granted special "knowledge about and toward life," but they lack the requisite historical perpetuity. tional culture disappears with age, the "patterns of meaning" t ted by the "symbolic forms" of each generation remaining dis locked in time: the attitude of the 1950s rockabilly fan, say, be years away from his 1990s successor, who adopts the same "s forms" of dress and language for quite different "patterns of me

Rather than concoct another prefixed neologism, however, t *subculture* can be a serviceable shorthand designation for the dis experience and values of 1950s teenagers—with some allowanc the term describe the collective and national experience of oi first generation of American teenagers (1955–60), and only thos ileged enough to partake fully of the leisure and consumption af by the "parent culture," an evocative designation for the dor American culture of the same period. That rough historical boundary also avoids confusion with the succeeding, storied "youth culture/counterculture" of the 1960s and the attendant demographic and historical forces distinct to that generation. Limiting membership to the "privileged," actually a populous and broad spectrum of American society, is a necessary recognition of the membership exclusions made by any subculture, not an invidious distinction.

Naturally, just as teenage subculture is not wholly autonomous, parent culture is not wholly hegemonic. In culture as in the home, the relationship is dynamic and symbiotic, marked more by accommodation and negotiation than by isolationism and open warfare. The cultural borders between the two are largely unmarked and freely traveled, with a good deal of territory shared in trust. Despite the alarms and skirmishes, the incursions by both sides are not alien invasions but family feuds waged on common ground. After all, these are blood ties.

The Blue-Jeaned Storm Troopers

The tribal rites and manners of the teenage subculture were the topic of anxious inquiries from concerned clergy, baffled parents, tireless social scientists, and an alarmed Congress. Generally, the reports back to civilization were not encouraging. A soaring teenage crime rate put the "problem of juvenile delinquency" high on the national agenda. Senator Estes Kefauver chaired a well-publicized subcommittee that spent years investigating delinquency's causes; J. Edgar Hoover ranked "the juvenile jungle" right up there with communism as a threat to American freedom; and New York police commissioner Stephen P. Kennedy spoke darkly of "teenage criminals carving out almost exclusive domains in the realms of robberies, burglaries, and auto thefts." Despite disclaimers that delinquents were but a small minority of the total teen population, the media fixed on the image of the urban juvenile as a switchblade-brandishing menace. The decade's representative juvenile delinquent may well have been the notorious Joseph Schwartz of Chicago, a seventeen-year-old who beat a black youth to death with a ball-peen hammer to prove he was tough enough to wear the jacket of a local street gang. Harrison Salisbury called the troubled youth of the 1950s "the shook-up generation"—though adults seemed to be doing most of the shaking.

Throughout the decade, cultural guardians likened American teenagers to barbaric hordes descending on a city under siege. *Cosmopolitan*'s special issue in November 1957 was typical: "Are Teenagers Taking Over?" queried the cover, while the inside copy only half-jokingly conjured the image of "a vast, determined band of blue-jeaned storm troopers, forcing us to do exactly as they dictate." But even as editorial writers, law enforcement officials, and parents were shoring up the barricades against teenagers, the business community was welcoming their arrival at the gates, and with good reason: there was a fortune to be made selling trinkets to the invaders.

Whatever the consequences for American civilization, the "invention" of the adolescent was an immediate boon to the nation's emerging consumer-based economy. In the nineteenth century, young people had fueled the Industrial Revolution with their labor; in the twentieth century, they would fulfill a more enviable economic function as consumers whose leisure vicariously validated their parents' affluence. G. Stanley Hall himself had condemned the nineteenth-century economic environment as "one where our young people leap rather than grow into maturity," arguing that "youth needs repose, leisure, art, legends, romance, and, in a word, humanity, if it is to enter the world of man well equipped for man's highest work in the world." At midcentury the business of satisfying youth's need for leisure and art would reshape American culture.

Newsweek labeled it "the dreamy teenage market," and *Sales Management* christened the thirteen-to-nineteen age bracket "the seven golden years." In 1959, *Life* reported what by then was old news: "The American teenagers have emerged as a big-time consumer in the U.S. economy. . . . Counting only what is spent to satisfy their special teenage demands, the youngsters and their parents will shell out about $10 billion this year, a billion more than the total sales of GM." Moreover, as the Bureau of Business Research noted, those billions were all "largely discretionary," which in entrepreneurial terms meant that teenage pocket money was up for grabs.

Since 1950s businessmen were as confused as everyone else about what teenagers wanted, they relied on a relatively new method to help them lead the kids to market: the opinion survey. "Appeals to teenagers are increasingly based on findings and theories of researchers into the mores and motivations of the high school set," commented the *Wall Street Journal* in 1956. "Some of the researchers are independent consultants, others work for advertising agencies or magazines. But they share at least one thing—claims to almost decimal point measurement in the teen marketplace." Prominent among these market research organizations were Eugene Gilbert and Company, Teen-age Survey Incorporated, and the Student Marketing Institute. They provided the raw statistical data used by clients to attract teenage consumers and, ideally, to instill a "brand loyalty" maintained into adulthood.

On one point of marketing strategy the consulting firms all agreed: peer opinion was much more decisive than adult opinion. Eugene Gilbert, the so-called George Gallup of the teenage demographic, advised that the surest way of finding a market among teenagers was "to sell a product to the leaders in school; what they approve counts for far more than what Mom and Dad approve at home." In a typical teen-targeted ploy, Hires Root Beer used part of the $3 million allocated for a teenage promotion campaign to pay popular high school girls to ask for Hires soft drinks on dates. More insidious were R. J. Reynolds, whose Camel cigarettes were featured up front on Alan Freed's CBS radio show *The (Camel) Rock 'n' Roll Dance Party*, and the American Tobacco Company, which "conducted a careful study of teen musical tastes" to guide the Lucky Strike–sponsored TV show *Your Hit Parade* and which marketed a cigarette brand (Hit Parade) named for the show. The cosmetics, grooming, and fashion industries reaped ever-increasing fortunes from sales of special teen-targeted products. Manufacturers of expensive consumer items (typewriters, radios, phonographs, and televisions) also scrambled to produce and promote items in order to cash in on the seemingly bottomless new market. In 1955, Chevrolet paid what may have been the greatest tribute to the American teenager's purchasing power when it marketed a V-8 "to create the image of a 'hot car' to attract the young market." Of course, all this special treatment from Big Business was crucial in establishing and reinforcing the subcultural identity of 1950s teenagers.

Chevrolet's tactics acknowledged the important consumer role teenagers played as "secret persuaders" in a family's big purchases. Besides the estimated $10 billion at their personal disposal, they exerted a strong, if difficult to measure, influence over their parents' preferences. Adults, in fact, seemed eager to appropriate certain teen tastes. Fitzgerald had noticed something similar during the Jazz Age, which became "less and less an affair of youth" and more and more "like a children's party taken over by the elders." In the 1950s, market research firms began to document a peculiar trend in consumerism, one that in the 1960s would become a commonplace of American life: teenagers were often the opinion leaders for the rest of the culture.

Of the $10 billion in discretionary income at the disposal of teenagers, *Life* estimated that 16 percent (about $1.5 billion) went to the entertainment industry, with the rest divided among fashion, grooming, automobiles, sporting equipment, and miscellaneous consumer goods. Although creators of entertainment had always paid some attention to the youth market, the demographic realities of the 1950s encouraged them to consider it as never before. Henceforth teenagers would have a major, sometimes dominant, voice in determining the nation's cultural diet. The first item they called for was rock 'n' roll music.

On the Beat

Until the mid-1950s, the music industry, like the rest of American society, used race as a selection criterion. *Billboard*, the industry's journal of record, divided its popular song charts along racial lines: best-selling songs mostly by white artists on one chart, rhythm-and-blues (R&B) songs by black artists for the growing black audience in the urban North on another. The difference between (white) pop and (black) R&B records was more than skin deep, however, for each had a characteristic style and means of production. The pop charts were dominated by smooth orchestral kitsch pitched mainly to adults by powerful national record companies. (Patti Page's 1953 hit "The Doggie in the Window" on Mercury is the usual example.) R&B songs were generally recorded and marketed by small independent companies and featured a rollicking four-four beat, raw vocalizing, and vaguely licentious lyrics, or "leer-ics" as the trade papers quickly dubbed them. (Ruth Brown's 1953 hit "[Mama] He Treats Your Daughter Mean" on Atlantic is exemplary on all counts.) Because musical tastes and radio airwaves were not as easily segregated as public facilities, R&B made steady inroads with the white audience. Teenagers, enthralled by the music's beat, volume, and unadorned passion, were especially enthusiastic.

In 1954, "Sh-Boom," an Atomic Age rhythm-and-blues tune by a black vocal group called the Chords, attracted a substantial following among white teenagers. *Billboard* acknowledged the song's success and biracial appeal by listing it on the "white" pop charts. Although black acts such as the Mills Brothers had previously placed on the pop charts, "Sh-Boom" was the first rhythm-and-blues tune with an undeniable "black" flavor to cross over successfully. The popularity of the Chords' original rendition of "Sh-Boom," and the even greater success of a white "cover version" by the well-named Crew Cuts, broke the color line in popular music, much as the Supreme Court decision that year broke the color line in public education. Integration, in fact, progressed more smoothly on the charts than in the schools. In 1957, the year President Eisenhower ordered federal troops into Central High

School in Little Rock, Arkansas, *Billboard* reporter Gary Kramer switched the name of his column from the racially restrictive "Rhythm and Blues" to the pluralistic "On the Beat." "No abstract categories prevent the teenager today from buying records by Fats Domino, Elvis Presley, Bill Haley, Carl Perkins, or Little Richard at one and the same time," Kramer explained. "The trade therefore must revise, and perhaps abandon, some of its old boundary lines."

The crossover success of "Sh-Boom" heralded teenage ascendancy within the music industry. In 1955, Bill Haley and the Comets launched rock 'n' roll's classic era with 2 million sales of "Rock around the Clock." By 1956, the year Elvis Presley purchased his first pink Cadillac, it was clear to anyone with a radio that teenagers determined and defined American popular music. Some station managers held out against the teen onslaught, calling rock 'n' roll "the worst influence ever to hit the music industry—a disgrace" and refusing to program it "for the good of the youngsters." But as *Billboard* noted, "the typical management attitude today [November 1956] is that a judicious amount of rock 'n' roll, timed for peak teenage listening hours is obligatory."

Radio programmers, record company executives, jukebox operators, and phonograph manufacturers had two options: they could either challenge rock 'n' roll or exploit it. (The third option—ignoring it— Elvis Presley rendered impossible. "The ostrich act and wishful thinking," *Billboard* gently cautioned, "would seem definitely uncalled for.") Within the music industry, challenges to rock 'n' roll came mainly from people who had made their mark in the pre–rock 'n' roll era. They were understandably fearful of the new music and undertook an impassioned assault on it. In an oft-cited 1958 speech to a disc jockey convention, Columbia Records A&R head Mitch Miller lectured his listeners: "You went and abdicated your programming to the 8–14-year-olds, to the pre-shave crowd that makes up 12% of the country's population and zero per cent of its buying power—once you eliminate pony tail ribbons, popsicles, and peanut brittle. Youth must be served—but how about some music for the rest of us?" Miller, the man responsible for "I Saw Mommy Kissing Santa Claus," "Mule Train," and other adult fare, had his figures wrong, but his sentiments were echoed by many old pros. In *Rock 'n' Roll Is Here to Pay*, a brash bottom-line account of the popular music industry, the rock historians Steve Chapple and Reebee Garofalo cite an extreme response from entertainer Sammy Davis Jr.: "If rock 'n' roll is here to stay, I might commit suicide."

Hostile record company executives and performers denigrated the new music in aesthetic terms, but their main complaint was economic. They had invested heavily in traditional pop in the early 1950s and were appalled when semiliterate hillbillies and black ex-dishwashers on upstart record labels usurped their places in the music industry. Their desperate efforts to defuse rock 'n' roll and divert the dollars of the teen market were sometimes hilariously off-key. At one point, segments of the industry tried "to wean the teenagers away from rock 'n' roll" with a campaign "to establish the polka and 'commercial corn' dance music as the next national craze."

Unaccountably, Steve Wolowic's Polka Band failed to knock Gene Vincent and the Bluecaps off the pop charts. Later that year, in a small but significant move, Milwaukee jukebox operators confirmed the supremacy of rock 'n' roll by removing polka music from their playlists. "Most of our volume comes from younger people," explained an operator, "and they look at polka music as strictly square. The older people, who like to hear polkas, are not as a rule jukebox patrons."

The polka business aside, for the music industry as a whole, rock 'n' roll was a financial shot in the arm unlike any since the invention of the gramophone. In 1956, "more money was spent on records than at any time in history," and the "single most important trend" was the "big jump in the number of rhythm and blues disks" on the charts. Many in the business recognized the wisdom in a *Billboard* editorial that year:

> Should an artist, record manufacturer, or disk jockey be so foolhardy as to buck trends in repertoire and performance, he will run second best to those who are quick to capitalize on popular tastes. . . . The consumer—the kid with the 89 cents in his pocket—is ready and willing to lay his cash on the line for what he likes. Those who won't give him what he wants may be well-intentioned, but they will lose out to someone who will.

Thus, despite aesthetic misgivings and vested interests in the old music, industry professionals moved quickly to capture their share of that kid's pocket money.

For the major record companies (RCA Victor, Columbia, Capitol, and Decca), the standard procedure was to produce a "cover version" of an R&B tune originally recorded by a black artist on a small independent label. Capitalizing on hefty advertising budgets, systems of national distribution, and consumer racism, the majors were often able to outsell the R&B original with a note-for-note "cover," as was the case with "Sh-Boom." Decca and RCA displayed special foresight by moving beyond cover versions to cultivate their own in-house rock 'n' roll performers. Bill Haley and the Comets' "Rock Around the Clock" wasn't the first authentic rock 'n' roll tune, but because Haley recorded on Decca, whose resources backed the song's boost from the film *Blackboard Jungle* (1955), it made the first significant impact. RCA landed an even bigger catch when, in November 1955, it bought Elvis Presley's contract from Sun Records for $35,000, a sum thought excessive at the time.

Sizable segments of the industry were likewise more eager to cash in than to condemn. Phonograph manufacturers, "recognizing the growing importance of the teen-age buyers in the record and phonograph field," developed special one-speed record players for the stacks of 45 rpm singles favored by teens. (RCA, in a promotion presumably aimed at Dad, offered a Glenn Miller album with the purchase of their model.) Teenagers accounted for some $75 million in pop record sales yearly, with millions more from product tie-ins exploiting the passion for rock 'n' roll. Presley alone was a minor growth industry, with over fifty items bearing his imprint, including lipstick in Hound Dog Orange, Heartbreak Hotel Pink, and Tutti Frutti Red. For countless record producers, performers, songwriters, disc jockeys, television announcers, agents, managers, and concert promoters, rock 'n' roll was the fresh new sound of a cash register ringing up unheard-of profits.

Other forms of mass entertainment were quick to note the lucrative impact teenage consumers had on the music industry. The musical revolution that was rock 'n' roll carried with it attendant stylistic changes in grooming, fashion, and attitude that were met by an array of teen-targeted accoutrements. Advertisements for these products helped support new entertainment ventures aimed at teens, such as the teen magazine and the teen-oriented television program.

The first "teen-type" magazines, *Dig* and *Teen*, appeared in 1955, and a dozen more were on the market by 1960. Circulation averaged a few hundred thousand each, but actual readership might well have tripled that. Teen-type magazines were easy to spot: they had names such as *Teen World, Modern Teen, Teenville, Teen Time, Teen Screen, Teen Parade, Sixteen, Hollywood Teenagers, Confidential Teen Romances, Flip, Dig, Hepcats,* and *Teen Today*. Though "young people's magazines" after the fashion of *Youth's Companion* and *St. Nicholas* had been publishing successes since the turn of the century, and *Seventeen* had been around since 1944, the teen magazines that flourished in the mid-1950s were no instructional manuals designed under the approving eyes of parents and teachers. "There have always been magazines for young people," commented a professor of journalism, "but these new ones are unlike anything that ever existed before." Where the old, established youth periodicals spoke in an adult voice and offered guidance into maturity, the new teen magazine addressed the teenager as a peer and advised him—or more often her—on how to become a more attractive and popular teenager. They were not concerned with passage into adulthood but with making the "teen time" more enjoyable. The conventional teen-targeted magazines such as *Ingenue, Seventeen, Junior,* and *Senior Scholastic* eventually followed suit, though not quite as egregiously.

Teenage advice books adopted a similar tack, as the titles of two early trendsetters attest: Edith Heal's *The Teen-Age Manual: A Guide to Popularity and Success* (1948) and William C. Menninger's *How to Be a Successful Teenager* (1954). Addressing a largely female readership, Heal suggested "ways of becoming the popular and successful Teen-Ager you want to be" and urged young girls, in language that had more to do with present popularity than future vocation, "to make a career out of the teens." In a brief prefatory note, the author subordinated her standard professional credentials to a more important endorsement of the book's expertise: "Because Teen-Agers are the only real authority on the Teen Age, this book has been submitted to the alert and critical eye of a Teen-Age Board. The board not only read the manuscript but contributed to it. The author acknowledges with gratitude—and admiration—the candid 'No's' that called for many revisions in the book." A homey blend of clinical psychology and Dale Carnegie, Menninger's advice book was even more forthright in its generational alliances. In a helpful chapter titled "How to Live with Your Parents," the attitude was brazenly conspiratorial:

> What can you do to reconcile your parents to the fact that sometimes what your friends think and do about certain things is more important to you than what Mom and Dad have to say about it? Well, it's not always easy. It's only natural that your parents don't have as high an opinion of your friends' ideas as they do of their own. But with patience and reason, the trick can often be turned.

With publishing enterprises flourishing, the potential teenage audience for television loomed even larger. As the nation's emerging consensus medium, television generally cast a wide demographic net, but portions of the networks' scheduling had long been aimed at narrower, more or less distinct audiences: daytime soap operas for housewives, morning cartoons and *The Howdy Doody Show* for children, sporting events for Dad. When the rock 'n' roll explosion of 1955–56 hit, television was surprisingly open to the raucous new talent. Even after Elvis Presley's scandalous gyrating performance of "Blue Suede Shoes" on the Dorsey Brothers' *Stage Show* on January 28, 1956, variety programs such as *The Steve Allen Show*, Chrysler's *Shower of Stars*, and *The Ed Sullivan Show* regularly sandwiched top rock 'n' roll acts in between jugglers and stand-up comics. Although networks kept a "particularly cautious censorship ear open for material that might lead youngsters astray," they generally did so without regard to race or tempo. For example, NBC banned "I Can't Say No" from a television production of *Oklahoma* but let pass Little Richard's licentious "Long Tall Sally." "How can I restrict it when I can't even understand it?" explained the network's censor.

The preferred teen-targeted TV format for affiliate stations was a locally produced music show featuring teenagers as performers or audience. A partial listing includes *Time Out for Teens* (KGLO-TV, Mason City, Iowa), *High Time* (KPTV, Portland, Oregon), *Teenage Dance Party* (KTVR, Denver), *Teen Hop* (KODF-TV, Joplin, Missouri), *Top 10 Dance Party* (WHBQ, Memphis, and WTVD, Durham, North Carolina), *Spotlight on Youth* (KHJ-TV, Los Angeles), and *Teenage Party* (WRVA, Richmond, Virginia). The most famous of the low-overhead late-afternoon teenage dance shows was Dick Clark's Philadelphia-based *American Bandstand*. In August 1957, ABC put Clark on network television, where he drew one of the largest audiences in daytime television with a format built on "furrow-browed teenagers" doing a "sagging zombie-eyed shuffle."

The branch of the entertainment industry that stood to gain most from exploiting the teen audience was the one longest in coming around: motion pictures. Despite radical changes in the form and content of American movies, and the enormous outlays in money and creative energy each entailed, the motion picture industry had been unable to lure the popular audience away from television. Only gradually did it come to realize what the rest of American business already knew: teenagers were a bonanza waiting to be mined.

Who Goes to the Movies?

The curious thing about Hollywood's courtship of the American teenager was how long it took the industry to make the first move. Despite the "mysterious aura of adoration" surrounding James Dean and the "wild cultist attraction" for Elvis Presley, moviemakers remained generally blind to teenage advances. "Hollywood . . . is regarded as lax in catering to this all-important segment of the population," *Variety* reported in August 1956. "No determined effort has been made to extract the full capacity of the 13 to 19 group by making pictures especially geared for the youngsters or building performers with 'built-in' teen appeal."

Part of the trouble was that until the 1950s, Hollywood had only the dimmest idea of who its audience was: the only statistical information the industry really heeded was the daily box office report. In 1957, Martin Quigley Jr., the influential editor of *Motion Picture Herald*, put it this way: "In the 'good old days' of dimming memory no one in the industry—be he producer, distributor, or exhibitor—took interest in the question Who Goes to the Movies. The answer was plain—Everyone who was not too young, too old, too sick, or living in the remotest backwoods." As a result, moviemakers tended to be in the dark when it came to gauging what kind of features "everyone" wanted. In his 1933 study of the motion picture industry, Howard T. Lewis of the Harvard Business School found: "No wholly satisfactory method of determining the possibility of [box office] success has ever been devised by any [film] company. The method followed is still one of guessing; the producers don't know just what the public wants and it's doubtful they ever will know."

By and large, the forceful personalities who ran the old studio system depended on little more than instinct to anticipate audience tastes. Columbia's Harry Cohn claimed he could tell an unprofitable picture if his behind squirmed during the screening. The prospect of "the whole world wired to Harry Cohn's ass" (as screenwriter Herman J. Mankiewicz wisecracked) may have been daunting, but his methodology made a certain sense. Moguls like Cohn, Jack Warner, and Louis B. Mayer had a sympathetic connection with their audience that their urbane successors lacked; by the mid-1950s, both the audience and the studio executive type had changed. As the moguls and producers who came to power during the go-getting 1920s were replaced by 1950s-style organizational men, the distance between the middle-aged financiers who made the movies and the juveniles who patronized them rendered Cohn's seat-of-the-pants method hopelessly antiquated. At the same time, the scale of the industry—the logistical complexities and the money at stake—had made moviemaking a bigger gamble than ever. Yet, compared with their fellows in the automobile or fashion industry, motion picture executives still made production decisions in a stunningly haphazard way.

In January 1946, the Motion Picture Association of America officially acknowledged modern business procedures by creating a special department of research. The next year, in a special issue of the American Academy of Political and Social Science *Annals*, department head Robert W. Chambers lamented that so many Hollywood executives made decisions in a statistical vacuum. Reiterating the viewpoint of MPAA president Eric Johnston, Chambers wrote that "from the standpoint of statistical knowledge . . . the motion picture industry probably knows less about its audience than any other major industry in the United States." He appealed to Hollywood to devote more of its resources to the emerging science of demographics.

Elsewhere in the same issue, communications theorist Paul F. Lazarsfeld presented a quantitative analysis of movie audiences. Lazarsfeld reported that "scrutiny of available data" showed "age [as] the most important personal factor by which the movie audience is characterized," and "the decline of movie attendance with increasing age is very sharp." Perhaps his most significant finding concerned "opinion leaders": "In an overwhelming number of cases they are young people, many of them below twenty five years of age. This is a very remarkable result. Our general notion is that the young learn from the old. In the movie field, advice and acceptance definitely flows in the opposite direction." In other words, Lazarsfeld was telling the industry—in 1947, at the height of its prestige as a business and its maturity as an art form—that it appealed mostly to youngsters.

This was not the conventional wisdom. Despite pleas from exhibitors, the MPAA refused to abandon its concept of moviegoing as a familial outing for Mom, Dad, and the kids. In 1950, Leo Handel's landmark study *Hollywood Looks at Its Audience* documented an ongoing juvenilization of the movie audience, but moviemakers stoutly ignored the warning. "You can show them [any data] you want," said one frustrated exhibitor, "that's still a long way from getting them to comply." Understandably reluctant to surrender cultural dominance, they ignored survey after survey telling them that the "typical moviegoer U.S.A." was a teenager. "Hollywood officials hire you to help them," complained public opinion pollster and business analyst Albert E. Sindlinger, "but when you don't tell them what they want to hear, sometimes they don't trust your accuracy." Walter Brooks, a respected adviser on exhibition practices, voiced a common industry attitude toward the bearers of bad tidings: "You can prove almost anything by the statisticians. . . . The statisticians assemble all sorts of figures to prove what has happened, and to predict what will happen in the future. Personally, we think the statisticians themselves should be laid end to end—to prove that what they find depends on who pays their fees." Although the great audience for movies no longer existed, the industry did its best to maintain the cherished fiction of service to a grand, broad-based "public."

There were two main reasons for Hollywood's astigmatism. First, the "industry" wasn't really run like other industries in the way it went about selling its products. Moviemakers came out of a show-business carnival tradition of "ballyhoo"; few had any faith or expertise in the modern marketing techniques other industries had been using for decades, much less in newfangled forms of consumer seduction such as motivational research and depth psychology. As late as 1956, a *Variety* reporter who visited the offices of Albert E. Sindlinger and Company, the market research firm specializing in movie data, expressed wide-eyed wonder at the "mass of coded index cards teeming with data, charts, graphs, and tape-recorded interviews. The inquisitive caller is avalanched with information about ticket sales and why they're good, bad, or indifferent." Not until mid-1957 did the Opinion Research Corporation, at the behest of the MPAA, conduct "the first nation-wide study of the American motion picture audience ever undertaken by the motion picture industry itself."

The second reason for the resistance was that many industry professionals—producers, directors, and screenwriters—had "adult" artistic sensibilities. Whether nurtured in the classical Hollywood studio system or recently graduated from New York stages, they were unwilling to allow juveniles to dictate the exercise of their talents. "Making a picture purely for the teenage market is a big mistake," said Douglas Sirk, whose own films were marketed mainly to women. Despite box office reports and statistical data, many in the industry continued to work against their own economic interests by making movies for an audience that really didn't go to the movies that much: married adults with children.

Although the concept of the movie theater as "the center of family entertainment" was encouraged at the industry's highest levels, a growing chorus of voices from the exhibition end of the business and in the

Statistical schooling: researcher Albert E. Sindlinger bears the bad tidings to the MPAA, 1956. The ascending line on the graph traces population; the bottom line charts motion picture attendance. (Quigley Photographic Archive, Georgetown University Library)

trade press called for a recognition of the new demographic realities. A survey for the *Motion Picture Herald* Institute of Industry Opinion reported in 1956, "The need for pictures appealing to the 15 to 25 age group was listed as most important by all classes of exhibitors and producers as well, but distributors placed it fifth. The heavy percentage of opinion for this one factor . . . is one outstanding factor of the survey." Martin Quigley Jr. repeatedly used his editorial forum to point out that "the most important single area for the present and future well-being of the motion picture industry is the youth of the country. In particular, this means those in the teens up through the mid-twenties." "The juvenile market is growing steadily and the 'teen-age' audience looms as more of a b.o. [box office] factor than ever," agreed *Variety*, regularly noting that "the demand for teenage pictures is coming from all quarters—from small theaters as well as large circuits."

Despite the accumulating research evidence and urgent demands from certain quarters of the industry, many moviemakers remained recalcitrant. In 1958, producer Sam Goldwyn expressed the anachronistic sentiments of the holdouts when he affirmed, "I believe in making pictures a man can take his whole family to see"—though by that late date most men were doing no such thing. Quigley warned that "it would be futile to adopt an ostrich-head-in-the-sand attitude and pay no heed to the fact that in relation to their numbers those in the 15 to 25 age group are the motion pictures' best customers," but even for those who acknowledged the importance of the teenage audience, the time-honored mandate of "entertainment for the entire family" died hard. One exhibitor with a better grasp of statistics than of adolescent psychology suggested that "what we need today at the theater is a gimmick to create an incentive to teenagers to come in to their neighborhood theaters, enjoy themselves, and bring their families with them."

Such naive comments highlight the industry's double difficulty: moviemakers had first to recognize that the teen audience was crucial to their economic future and then to court it successfully. Having identified the problem, they still needed a solution. "We know . . . that the juvenile audience is off even though there are more kids around than ever," lamented one producer. "What we need is a study to indicate to us which way we could get those patrons back again." Appropriately, statistical studies by market research firms were less instructive than the example of producer Sam Katzman, one of Hollywood's legendary fast-buck boys. The success of Katzman's teenpics led the industry into the earnest exploitation of the teenage moviegoer.

4

Rock 'n' Roll Teenpics

Catering to the teenagers' taste has leveled our song standards to the point of vulgarity, banality, infantilism. . . . Can
this happen to the movies under the prospect of their getting
hungry enough to start indulging the banal, untrained, irre-
sponsible tastes of the average teenager?

James Fenlon Finley in *Catholic World*, 1957

For those producers, distributors and exhibitors who *know
their markets*, produce pictures *with their markets in mind*,
and *merchandise them to those markets*, the rewards will
be fabulous in years to come.

Albert E. Sindlinger, 1958

lthough the old studio system had always produced its share
of features with a frankly adolescent appeal—notably Monogram's juvenile melodramas, Republic's westerns, and Universal's science fiction—the Dead End Kids, the sagebrush
sagas, and the space patrols were ancillary operations, after-
thoughts in a vigorous enterprise whose "money business"
lay elsewhere. The postwar period thus found the motion
picture industry, if not quite oblivious, then at least unwisely
inattentive to teenagers, snubbing the movies' most devoted
patrons as it tried to reentice the popular audience that sustained Hollywood's classical era. Prior to 1956, there was no
industry-wide consensus on the vital importance of the
teenage market, much less an earnest assault on it. The

54

success that year of a Sam Katzman production, *Rock Around the Clock*, and the popularity in its wake of an imitative cycle cast from the same mold, first testified unmistakably to the present power and future ascendancy of the teenage moviegoer. After *Rock Around the Clock*, the industry campaign to attract teenagers would be concerted and conscious. Katzman's makeshift "quickie" signaled new production strategies and gave rise to a new kind of motion picture: the teenpic.

"Jungle Sam" Katzman

As recounted in his official studio biography for Columbia Pictures, Sam Katzman's backstory faithfully follows the approved course for Hollywood minimoguls: born in 1901 in New York City, of Jewish heritage, an ambitious boy departs from the career path chosen by his father, a professional musician, and enters the motion picture business while still in his teens. Serving an apprenticeship with the old Fox Film Corporation, he advances from prop boy to assistant director and by the early 1930s has moved into independent production, debuting with *His Private Secretary* (1933), starring John Wayne, and made in six days for $13,000. Some twenty years later, by Columbia's reckoning, Katzman had more than 350 action films to his credit. At the peak of his production schedule in the early 1950s, he churned out an average of seventeen features and three serials a year, none of which lost money or cost over $500,000.

Katzman specialized in disposable low-budget fare with modest but certain profit margins. He is credited with—or blamed for—dozens of negligible productions, of which any random sampling is representative of the whole. In 1953, for example, cued by the popularity of biblical blockbusters, Katzman went through a prolific Middle Eastern phase, supplying exhibitors with (successively) *Siren of Baghdad*, *Flame of Calcutta*, *Serpent of the Nile*, *Slaves of Babylon*, and *Prisoners of the Casbah*. His production of the profitable Jungle Jim series, featuring Johnny Weissmuller, earned him the moniker "Jungle Sam," but the nickname could just as well have been a tribute to Katzman's knack for survival in a treacherous industry. Unfettered by artistic or professional pretensions, Katzman reveled in his reputation as the definitive commercial moviemaker. "His chief concern aside from making consistent profit," noted his studio biographer, "is to entertain the masses with simple, up-to-the-minute, topical, fast-moving fare. 'Let the arty guys get the ulcers,' he says." Or, as he bragged to *Life* magazine in 1953, "Lord knows, I'll never make an Academy Award movie, but then I'm just as happy to get my achievement plaque from the bank every year."

Early on, Katzman saw the box office importance of tailoring filmic subject matter to fit a specific audience. At Monogram in the 1940s, and later with Columbia, he specialized in B-movie matinee fare pitched alternately to the preteen "cap pistol set" (the serials *Atom Man vs. Superman* [1950] and *Captain Video* [1951]) or to a slightly older group comprising mostly adolescent males (the Bowery Boys and Jungle Jim series). As early as 1946, he had become especially attuned to the latter group, billing himself in Monogram trade ads as a producer for "Teen Agers" and proving it in *Junior Prom, Freddie Steps Out, High School Hero,* and *Betty Co-ed* (all 1946, the last for Columbia). After television became suburbia's most popular babysitter, Katzman devoted himself almost exclusively to films with a particularly pubescent appeal. "We got a new generation," he said in 1952, "but they got the same old glands."

Katzman stimulated the adolescent glands with disheveled actresses, exotic locales (filmed in California), and freakish bipeds (apes, dwarves, and monsters). Grafted onto a flimsy story line, these elements possessed a perennial attraction for pubescent audience and publicity department alike. Given his strenuous production schedule, though, not even Katzman could rely exclusively on the same half-dozen dependably exploitable ingredients for every film. For new and exciting ideas, he was guided by contemporary journalism: Katzman turned newspaper headlines into film titles.

In this, the producer was hardly breaking new ground. Since the fast-paced days of early silent cinema, "as timely as today's headlines" has been a thrifty source of inspiration and a juicy publicity hook. In 1901, Edwin S. Porter had done little more than visually render newspaper accounts of contemporary events in *The Execution of Czolgosz, Terrible Teddy the Grizzly King,* and *The Sampson-Schley Controversy.* Even at a time when the miracle of persistence of vision was attraction itself, filmmakers realized that cranking out dramatizations of front-page events paid special dividends. They could take advantage of the transitory public curiosity about a current event and reap maximum publicity value from the newspapers' continued coverage of the original. With the rise of classical Hollywood cinema, such speed was no longer possible—nor, as long as the studios had guaranteed exhibition outlets, was it necessary. But in the 1950s, with the old system faltering and competition for a dwindling audience intensifying, movie-makers were forced to reinvent their industry. Katzman's special contribution was to reintroduce something of the hustle of early silent production to postclassical Hollywood, demonstrating anew the profitability of speed and topicality.

By minimizing the time between an event and the film that exploited it, Katzman, like Porter before him, was assured of an avid audience and some free publicity. The success of his quickie productions bore out an exploitation truism: be the first, not the best. Katzman began work on an atomic thriller the very day he heard the news of the first H-bomb explosion. A few days after the outbreak of hostilities in Korea, Columbia Pictures solicited a Korean War movie. Katzman quickly came up with a title—*A Yank in Korea*—and delivered the completed film six weeks and two days later.

Given his background and modus operandi, Katzman's decision to make a rock 'n' roll exploitation film in early 1956 accorded with established practice. Timely, controversial, and the special province of teenagers, rock 'n' roll music was obvious grist for his production mill. Less obvious was the profound and long-range effect this assembly-line quickie was to have on the motion picture industry. *Rock Around the Clock* became the first hugely successful film marketed to teenagers *to the pointed exclusion of their elders*. By showing that teenagers *alone* could sustain a box office hit, *Rock Around the Clock* pushed motion picture production strategy toward the teenpic. Its own history and promotional campaign provided a model fit to be imitated.

Teenpic Antecedents

Like most exploitation movies, *Rock Around the Clock* was not a move into uncharted territory. Exploitation moviemakers are careful businessmen, generally too careful to risk a radically new formula. More often than not, they capitalize on successful gambits by the major motion picture companies. In 1955, the profit margins and the controversy generated by MGM's *Blackboard Jungle* and Warner Bros.' *Rebel Without a Cause* cued Katzman and several other savvy moviemakers to the theatrical attraction rebellious youth held for teenage moviegoers. Although purportedly adult films, *Jungle* and *Rebel* immediately found their own level and were embraced enthusiastically by the nation's young. (A 1956 survey by Gilbert Youth Research Reports found that *Blackboard Jungle* was the favorite film of high school students, and

Rebel Without a Cause star James Dean the favorite actor.) Not teenpics themselves, both *Jungle* and *Rebel* nonetheless offered convincing evidence that teenagers were becoming the most populous segment of the moviegoing audience.

In the tradition of Hollywood social problem films such as *Gentlemen's Agreement* (1947) and *Pinky* (1949), *Blackboard Jungle* was a well-budgeted mainstream melodrama about a "serious modern problem": juvenile delinquency. Glenn Ford played an excruciatingly earnest English teacher ("Daddy-O" to the homeroom hoods) sent to minister to a tribe of primitive ethnic types in an inner-city high school. The students spend most of their class time abusing adult authority. The film's signature scene, a wonderful foreshadowing of the shape of things to come, occurs when the kids erupt in an orgy of destruction and play Frisbee with their music instructor's priceless collection of Bix Beiderbecke 78s. Daddy-O perseveres, beating up a would-be student rapist, ducking deadly projectiles from the back row, overcoming his own latent racism, and practicing the best in modern pedagogy before finally establishing an atmosphere conducive to learning.

Despite its reassuring conclusion, *Blackboard Jungle* generated enormous controversy in its time. The most celebrated negative reaction came from Claire Booth Luce, the ambassador to Italy, who became so angered by the violent New York–realist portrait of American adults under siege that she forced the picture's withdrawal from the Venice Film Festival. She also helped catapult it to international notoriety— and, increasingly, controversy was a commodity to be cultivated, not avoided. On the domestic front, denunciations of *Blackboard Jungle* by educational groups only added to its box office take: Luce's action made it "the most highly publicized film on the worldwide market." At the time, that kind of furor could mean an extra $1 million in box office take. None of this was lost on exploitation moviemakers.

Although its shock value has diminished with time, *Blackboard Jungle* remains a harsh testimony to how wide the gulf between parents and teenagers had become by the mid-1950s. The unfocused sociopathic violence of teenage hood Artie West (Vic Morrow, wielding the obligatory switchblade) is different in degree and kind from the petty infractions of the Dead End Kids or of the troubled youngsters at MGM's *Boys Town* (1938). Throughout *Blackboard Jungle* was a real sense that the terms of the social contract between young and old had changed. On film at least, the relationship had never been so frightening, ambivalent, or antagonistic. In the end, teacher Glenn Ford re-

Bix Beiderbecke bows to Bill Haley: the famous record-breaking scene in *Black-board Jungle* (1955). (Museum of Modern Art Film Stills Archive: Courtesy of Turner Entertainment)

asserts adult authority in the classroom only through superior force of arms. Unlike so many of his predecessors in the 1930s and 1940s, Morrow's young punk never acknowledges the moral superiority of the social order. He's just beaten down.

Over the title sequence and end credits of *Blackboard Jungle*, director Richard Brooks made an audacious choice in background music: "Rock Around the Clock," a minor hit by a little-known dance band called Bill Haley and the Comets. An amalgam of country music and rhythm and blues done to nursery-rhyme lyrics, the tune marked the first appearance of rock 'n' roll in a major motion picture, and the impact was phenomenal. Largely on the strength of its soundtrack exposure, "Rock Around the Clock" gained new life on the pop charts. By the end of the year, it had sold 2 million copies and provided Bill Haley with a lifetime meal ticket.

Although the scale of Haley's show business success was impressive, there was nothing, at least in the very early days, to indicate that something more than entertainment as usual was going on. Shrieking, swooning, and other manifestations of (often well-staged) audience hysteria had been a part of pop music performances since the 1920s. Rudy Vallee, Frank Sinatra, and, most recently, "nabob of sob" Johnny Ray had each in his turn inspired progressively demonstrative reactions from claques of devoted fans. Few imagined that "Rock Around the Clock" would become, in rock historian Lillian Roxon's phrase, "the Marseillaise of the teenage revolution . . . the first inkling teenagers had that they might be a force to be reckoned with in numbers alone." At the close of 1955, the song, Haley, and the attendant rock 'n' roll hoopla had all the markings of the usual musical fad—and, as a fad, it had evident exploitation possibilities for "Jungle Sam" Katzman.

In mid-January 1956, Katzman started production on *Rock Around the Clock;* by the end of the month, he had completed shooting. Columbia, the usual distributor for Clover, Katzman's production company, released the first rock 'n' roll musical that March. Directed by Fred F. Sears and featuring Bill Haley and the Comets, the Platters, and disc jockey Alan Freed, the film was a variation on the Big Band musicals of the 1940s, a form then undergoing something of a resurgence with *The Glenn Miller Story* (1954) and *The Benny Goodman Story* (1955). In terms of production strategy and narrative content, the film wasn't discernibly different from the material Katzman had been making for years: mildly controversial, timely, pitched to teenagers, and relatively inexpensive (under $300,000). A forewarning of future trends and a preparation for exploiting them, however, may have been gleaned from Clover's "in-house" experience with a prior production, *Teenage Crime Wave* (October 1955). With the same director, demographics, and source of filmic inspiration as *Rock Around the Clock,* the earlier film seems to have mapped out both an exploitation path and a narrative direction for the production next in line.

A tale of the "sidewalk jungle," *Teenage Crime Wave* concerns the inadvertent involvement of nice-girl Jane (Sue England) with the wild and dangerous teenage couple Mike and Terry (Tommy Cook and Mollie McCart). Gunplay, car chases, a juvenile correction house, kidnapping, catfights, home invasion, murder, and death in a hail of police bullets follow. Although opportunities to deploy rock 'n' roll as background music abound (as opposed to its nonmotivated soundtrack appearance in *Blackboard Jungle)*, this pioneer juvenile delinquency (j.d.) teenpic in the end banked on melodrama, not music, and consequently failed to accrue the financial rewards or culturewide notoriety of its successor. But, though depreciated in the narrative, rock 'n' roll was

Don't touch that dial: exploitation fare such as *Teenage Crime Wave* (1955) showed exhibitors how to lure audiences away from television. (Museum of Modern Art Film Stills Archive: Courtesy of Columbia Pictures)

accentuated in the publicity campaign for *Teenage Crime Wave*. In what was probably the first extensive exploitation of rock 'n' roll for the avowed purpose of luring teenagers to the movies, the advertising kit for the film offered expansive advice to exhibitors on rock 'n' roll tie-ins:

ROCK-AND-ROLL BALLY!
Latest music craze among teen-agers is the rock-and-roll type music. Use rock-and-roll to call teen-age attention to your picture!

ROCK-AND-ROLL IN THE STREETS!
If your situation permits, use a sound truck or car featuring current rock-and-roll tunes. Highlight blowups of teenage crime headlines and picture credits for maximum effect.

GO AFTER DISC JOCKEYS!

Interest disc jockeys with rock-and-roll following in the problem of teenage crime. Seek out favorable comment on your picture from them on the air!

DO-IT-YOURSELF!

Put rock-and-roll on your own p.a. system during show breaks, with frequent picture credits. Get a lobby juke box playing recordings of latest rock-and-roll.

Teenage Crime Wave was no spectacular success, but the rock 'n' roll exploitation angle performed well enough to lend experience and provide encouragement for the subsequent production. Minimizing the financial risk still further, *Rock Around the Clock* was a model of exploitation marketing in two important ways: it was the first out of the gate, and it had the best title. Katzman's nominal competition in quickie, low-budget production had been caught napping on the rock 'n' roll craze. American International Pictures, Distributors Corporation of America, Allied Artists, and Universal-International took months to fabricate their own rock 'n' roll films.

Foresight was evident in the film's very title: by beating his rivals to the MPAA's Title Registration Bureau and procuring the rights to the immediately recognizable catchphrase "Rock Around the Clock," Katzman secured thousands of dollars in free radio advertising. Although under U.S. copyright law a moviemaker, like a songwriter or book publisher, could not legally keep others from using the same title, since 1936 the Title Registration Bureau had protected "those who first conceived certain distinctive titles" with a "voluntary method of title registration." The bureau determined priority rights to valued titles, and its mediating decisions were generally honored by major companies and independent signatories alike. Coming up with an engaging "high-concept" title may actually be an exploitation moviemaker's most important creative decision.

Articulating another exploitation commandment, Katzman defined his creative process: "We don't get stories. We get titles and then write stories around them or to fit them." Not even a businessman as prescient as he, however, could have realized how big a score he had on his hands with *Rock Around the Clock*, or how powerful an influence it was to have on the motion picture industry.

Reviewers for mainstream periodicals ignored the film's initial release, but the trade press sensed possibilities from the beginning. *Billboard* spoke for the consensus: "*[Rock Around the Clock* is] certain to meet with better than average reception by the teenage set and the legion of fans who worship at the shrine of rock and roll. Though it may not come up for an Academy Award next December, its entertainment value alone will endear [its] stars . . . to their cult even more." *Variety* enthusiastically predicted that it would "prove a handy entry for exhibitors packaging a show aimed at the sweater-levi crowd." And handy it was. In relation to production costs, the film's financial returns were astonishing. With reported worldwide grosses of $2.4 million, or eight times the initial production costs, it was easily "one of the most spectacularly successful pictures of the year." For Hollywood accountants, a picture's total gross receipts are less important than its profit margin, the ratio between box office take and the film's negative costs. By these terms, *Rock Around the Clock* was as impressive as larger-grossing but far more expensive productions such as *Guys and Dolls* and *The King and I*, the box office champions of 1956. In an era in which Hollywood was banking more and more on fewer and fewer films, *Rock Around the Clock* showed that with the right kind of project, filmmakers might gain much while risking little.

There was one worrisome marketing problem, however: the possibility that the controversy over rock 'n' roll would reach a flash point. In late 1955 and early 1956, minor incidents of violence had erupted during live rock 'n' roll shows and at theaters during the "Rock Around the Clock" title sequence for *Blackboard Jungle*. Columbia's release of *Rock Around the Clock* exacerbated an already emotionally charged dispute concerning the music's alleged connection to violence and juvenile delinquency.

Although the average 1950s parent was probably more anxious about fluoridation of the drinking water than teenage music on the radio, the national media found the "rock 'n' roll phenomenon" natural fodder and devoted reams of copy to its colorful stars, fans, and detractors. In retrospect, the intensity of the controversy over rock 'n' roll is easy to overestimate, especially given the delight rock historians take in citing the most extremist pronouncements from the least level-headed of Cold War commentators. But if hysteria was not exactly rampant, neither was public discourse noticeably calm and reasoned.

The racism lurking beneath much anti–rock 'n' roll sentiment was brought to the surface by Asa Carter, executive secretary of the North Alabama White Citizens' Council, who condemned the music as an NAACP conspiracy to infect white teenagers via the nation's jukeboxes. More in line with the Freudian temper of the times was psychiatrist Francis Braceland, who called rock 'n' roll a "cannibalistic and tribalistic form of music" and explained somewhat anachronistically that "it is insecurity and rebellion that impels teenagers to affect 'ducktail' haircuts, wear zoot suits, and carry on boisterously at rock 'n' roll affairs." To the Massachusetts Public Health Department, rock 'n' roll was responsible for increases in venereal disease and juvenile delinquency. Although the attitude of the parent culture toward rock 'n' roll was as often condescending as alarmist, the new teenage music had become a dramatic arena in which to play out generational conflict. In this sense it was one of the most fiercely debated items on the nation's cultural agenda.

Rock Around the Clock was launched directly into the maelstrom. Soon after the picture's release, a front-page story in *Variety* warned, "Rock 'n' roll—the most explosive show biz phenomenon of the decade—may be getting too hot to handle. While its money-making potential has made it all but irresistible, its Svengali grip on the teenagers has produced a staggering wave of juvenile violence and mayhem." By the terms of later decades, the juvenile mayhem—screaming, foot stomping, and the occasional scuffle—has an almost nostalgic flavor. After a screening of *Rock Around the Clock* in one Midwest city, for example, teenagers snake-danced downtown and broke store windows before "police quelled the youthful rioters." At one live rock 'n' roll show, police were reportedly so jumpy that "they even frowned when the kids applauded the acts."

Overseas the juvenile audiences were less restrained, and the possibility that American teenagers might begin to imitate them gravely concerned Stateside exhibitors. As the film had its first European play dates in late 1956, the American press recorded a rising crescendo of teenage violence. In England, police arrested more than "100 youths, boys, and girls" driven to violence by the "hypnotic rhythm" and "primitive tom-tom thumping" of *Rock Around the Clock*, in what was called "the most impressive aftermath of any film ever shown in Britain." The queen herself requested a private screening to see what the fuss was about, while on the Continent the film was met with riots in Oslo and banning in Belgium.

American exhibitors were caught between desire for teenage dollars and dread of teenage violence. In a delicate balancing act, Columbia's publicity campaign exploited the controversy—"Now's the time to book Columbia's *Rock Around the Clock* while it's headline news in the USA"—at the same time that it tried to allay exhibitor fears. "Except for minor incidents, we've had no trouble so far," said a theater manager. "It's doing fantastic business." Reflecting the industry's two minds about the teenage audience, the trade press told exhibitors to temper the usual ballyhoo with sound judgment. "All these rock 'n' roll stars mean something to rock 'n' roll addicts, and they are very numerous. It's the most! They'll be dancing in the street, in the lobby, and in the aisle," exulted *Motion Picture Herald*'s adviser on selling approaches, who was cautious enough to conclude his pitch with the warning: "Don't let them dance all-night. The all-night dance-a-thons can get out of control—and do you more harm than good." Many exhibitors who played the film had an additional worry in resistance from local law enforcement officials, newspaper editorialists, and civic groups.

Exhibitor misgivings aside, the financial success of *Rock Around the Clock* sent the unmistakable message that there was money to be made from teenagers by capturing the rock 'n' roll craze on film. By the end of 1956, a half-dozen rock 'n' roll (or ersatz rock 'n' roll) pictures had completed production. The recently reorganized American International Pictures (AIP) showed the acumen that was presently to make it the dominant force in teenpics, leading the pack with *Shake, Rattle, and Rock!* (released October 1956); Twentieth Century-Fox had Elvis Presley ready by Thanksgiving vacation in *Love Me Tender* (released November 1956), and for the Christmas holidays the company was busily promoting its second rock 'n' roll offering, *The Girl Can't Help It* (released December 1956). Distributors Corporation of America weighed in with Vanguard's *Rock, Rock, Rock!* (released December 1956), and Universal-International (UI) submitted *Rock, Pretty Baby* (released January 1957). Even the Abbott and Costello series tried to muscle in with the deceptively titled *Dance with Me Henry* (released December 1956). Katzman himself hoped lightning would strike twice with a sequel, *Don't Knock the Rock* (released January 1957).

Narrative Meanings, Ritual Occasions

Even before Bebe Daniels looked at Ruby Keeler in *42nd Street* (1933) and exclaimed, "Youth! Beauty! Talent! You've got so much to give!" plucky kids with a hot new sound went out on stage nobodies and came back stars: for film musicals of whatever stripe, it is a formula etched in granite. Likewise, the cultural conflict between the music of propriety—classical, symphony stuff—and of popular taste—jazz, Tin Pan Alley—is a perennial that predates movie sound itself. As early as *Jazz Mad* (1928), a neglected gem of the silent screen, a respected Old World conductor/composer is humiliated to find his symphonic masterpiece has no commercial potential with New World music publishers. In the 1940s, jazz and swing musicals such as *Blues in the Night* (1941) and *The Fabulous Dorseys* (1947) continued in the tradition, emphasizing a telling plot complication. In these films, entrenched cigar-chomping showbiz professionals don't deny the performers' talent as much as they resist the musical style, a "sound" that is too personal, uncommercial, or just plain different. In *The Benny Goodman Story*, for example, the young clarinetist displays his virtuosity at a classical recital and easily finds work with a straight popular orchestra, but he dreams instead of making a living playing his personal brand of swing.

The rock 'n' roll cycle contributed its own permutation by building the drama around generational as well as musical differences. Some of the early rock 'n' roll pictures, such as *Don't Knock the Rock*; *Shake, Rattle, and Rock!*; and *Rock, Pretty Baby*, do this directly, structuring themselves unequivocally around the generational conflict over rock 'n' roll. Others, such as *Rock Around the Clock*, *Loving You*, and *Jailhouse Rock*, do it implicitly, portraying rock 'n' roll as a valid teenage activity without undue discussion or inquiry. Even in the later films, however, the rock 'n' roll controversy is never far from the surface: all include at least one pro forma defense of the music in the face of adult opposition.

Despite being the film that spurred much of the original controversy, *Rock Around the Clock* is itself fairly oblivious to the dramatic potential of pitting the generations against each other: this was left to its sequel, *Don't Knock the Rock*. But in providing a stage to showcase the rock 'n' roll performances that are the film's best draw, the narrative—no matter how laughably contrived or boringly predictable—is no mere filler: it provides at least a recognition, at most a validation, of the subcultural ways of the target audience.

Although rock historian Nik Cohn has a point when he says the main plot of *Rock Around the Clock* is "that Bill Haley grinned," the story line is (marginally) more complicated. Frustrated manager Steve Hollis (Johnny Johnston) tries in vain to convince his Big Band client to switch to a more commercial musical style. "The public's going in for sounds, Georgie—they want to hear small groups, vocalists, novelty combos," he argues. "The only thing that's stayed up to date in this band of yours is your watch." When the band refuses to move with the times, Steve quits: in contrast to the Big Band musicals, the bandleader's refusal to adapt to popular tastes, his elevation of artistic integrity over commercial compromise, is foolishly hard-headed. Motoring through the small town of Strawberry Springs, Steve stumbles upon a Saturday-night dance that has all the customers and enthusiasm his former bookings lacked. Onstage, Bill Haley and the Comets are playing "See You Later, Alligator." A signature exchange occurs between Steve and an ecstatic female dancer:

> *Steve:* What's that outfit playing up there? . . . It isn't boogie, it isn't jive, and it isn't swing. It's kind of all of them.
>
> *Dancer:* It's rock 'n' roll, brother, and we're rocking tonight!

Steve proposes to manage the band, which includes a brother-sister act, Lisa (Lisa Gaye) and Jimmy (Earl Barton). Lisa calls the shots for the act and strikes a business-wise bargain for Steve's management services. In what would become a rock 'n' roll cycle commonplace, Haley, the musical talent, defers his career decisions to a professional. "Don't look at me, Mr. Hollis," says the compliant Haley. "If Lisa won't go for 60–40 [percent], there's nothing I can do about it." By placing the ultimate reins of rock 'n' roll power in the hands of straight business types (for reasons of dramatic economy and romantic subplotting, usually female), the teenpic deflates whatever uncomfortable portents of evil influence the rock 'n' roll talent itself conjures in the musical performances.

Lisa and Steve fall in love, and much screen time is spent on Steve dodging the attentions of his former, vengeful lover Corrine (Alix Talton), who happens to be the top dance-band booker in the country. Aggressive, sharp, and coiffured in a short, masculine haircut, Corrine is so blinded by jealousy she fails to see the Comets' commercial possibilities. She tries to sabotage the band's professional debut by booking them for the high school prom at the upper-crust Mansfield School for Girls ("Steve, I'm worried," confides Lisa. "This doesn't look like a rock 'n' roll crowd to me."). The adult chaperons are appalled ("Infamous! Barbaric!"), but the promgoers go wild when Haley and the Comets appear in jive outfits and launch into a rave-up version of "Razzle Dazzle."

Corrine is unimpressed with the comeback ("Excellent. You've succeeded in making a bunch of whirling dervishes out of girls who were brought up to be ladies."), but real-life disc jockey Alan Freed makes a fortuitous entry and offers the group guidance and bookings. A montage sequence done to "Rock Around the Clock" then traces the Comets' meteoric rise. An end-reel grand finale features a live television coast-to-coast hook-up with the Platters ("The Great Pretender") and, closing the show, "one of the most phenomenal acts in the history of show business," Haley and the Comets ("Rudy's Rock"). Like so much else in this landmark teenpic, the live TV climax was to become a staple of the first rock 'n' roll cycle. A testimony both to the powerful role the new medium played in the popularization of rock 'n' roll and to TV's centrality for the new generation, the televised finale was an often-used means of narrative closure: *Shake, Rattle, and Rock!*; *Loving You*; *Jailhouse Rock*; and *Rock, Pretty Baby* all conclude with telecast extravaganzas.

Taking dramatic advantage of the rock 'n' roll controversy that *Rock Around the Clock* had helped foment, subsequent teenpics used the uproar as a narrative frame for their musical presentations, addressing the intergenerational squabble with didactic dialogue and transparent sympathies. In AIP's *Shake, Rattle, and Rock!* a busybody citizen's group called SPRARCAY (Society for the Prevention of Rock and Roll Corruption of American Youth) battles with an Alan Freed–by-way-of–Dick Clark television deejay charged with musically inciting violence ("a rock 'n' roll orgy") at the local Teen Town. In the film's emotional conclusion, rock 'n' roll is put on trial on live television. SPRARCAY and the deejay debate the merits of what is alternately described as "cannibalistic celebrations" or "five thousand kids held together by a common interest." In line with the sentiments of the White Citizens' Council, SPRARCAY exhibits a travelogue clip of native Africans dancing to drumbeats and announces victoriously, "You see the disgusting source of this cultural form, rock 'n' roll—look at the utter depravity!"

The deejay responds with a familiar counterpoint, namely, that rock 'n' roll is no more significant or harmful than the turkey trot, the Charleston, or the black bottom—whereupon he screens his own film clips from the 1920s and 1930s. When the opposition (which includes Groucho Marx's old nemesis, Margaret Dumont) claims that "we never participated in those decadent antics," someone spots a SPRARCAY member whirling away in the old newsreel clip. In the end, everyone agrees that adults should "give the kids a chance to work their own way out of their teens." Besides, as a supportive newspaper editorial put it earlier in the film, "better on the dance floors than in the alleys, better around a jukebox than a pool table."

As the title telegraphs, *Don't Knock the Rock* is also built around generational animosities aroused by rock 'n' roll music. Alan Freed again appears as the avuncular mediating figure between intolerant parents and frolicking teens. A now-forgotten singer named Alan Dale plays Arnie Haines, a performer happy to go with the tide and cash in on the rock 'n' roll craze. (Arnie has a weak rock 'n' roll heart. When someone asks him, "What happens to you when the public gets over rock 'n' roll?" he blithely echoes Elvis's snide remark, "If they ever do, I'll go back to ballads.") In bucolic, small-town Melandale, a group of old fogies described as "Carrie Nations with their hatchets" oppose a local rock 'n' roll show. To allay the town elders' misgivings, Freed and the kids put things in context by presenting a historical tableau ("The Pageant of Art and Culture of the Young Players of Melandale"). The pageant moves briskly from George Washington to the Charleston and the lindy hop, persuading everyone that rock 'n' roll is, in the oft-quoted phrase, just "a harmless outlet for today's kids." "If parents could only realize that the kids are no different than they were," pleads Freed. "Parents need not worry about today's generation. They'll grow up to be the same fine sort."

Given the superb lineup of rock 'n' roll talent and the splendid showcase accorded it (Fats Domino and Joe Turner in *Shake, Rattle, and Rock!* and Little Richard in *Don't Knock the Rock*), these films, whatever the final verdict of the rock 'n' roll courtroom drama, may well have scored with the teenage audience even had their reels been projected out of sequence. But the financial success of Universal-International's *Rock, Pretty Baby*, one of the first and most profitable of the post-Katzman wave, argues against a formulation of the rock 'n' roll teenpic that subordinates narrative meanings to musical presentation. The film does not boast one authentic rock 'n' roll act, and the fabricated soundtrack pantomimed by the actors found no home on the *Billboard* charts. UI's astute marketing campaign spurred *Rock, Pretty Baby*'s popularity, but its teen-level story seems to have struck a responsive chord in the target audience and inspired the kind of favorable word-of-mouth advertising that is more valuable than any contrived publicity.

The story concerns Jimmy Daley (borderline teen idol John Saxon), a handsome youngster with a goodly share of Presley's dark androgyny.

Jimmy wants to play rock 'n' roll with fellow enthusiasts Ox, Fingers, Sax and Half-Note, a combo that includes Sal Mineo on drums and Rod McKuen on upright bass. But Jimmy's father (*Rebel Without a Cause* social worker Ed Platt) wants the boy to follow in his footsteps and become a doctor. Punctuated by an exceptionally bland score, composed in part by Henry Mancini and sung mostly by McKuen (curiously, Saxon, the nominal leader of the Jimmy Daley Combo, has no vocal solo), the film puts more fervor into melodrama than music: Jim pawns his medical books to buy an electric guitar, wrecks his parents' home during a teenage party, and smashes his guitar in adolescent anger. Coaxed along by his understanding wife (Fay Wray), Dad ultimately sees the error of his authoritarian ways and acquiesces to Jimmy's ambitions. Mom reminds him that their son "is so hurt and confused he doesn't know what he's doing." After all, "an adolescent is only a part-time adult." Dad proves his conversion by getting five traffic citations rushing Jimmy to his band's live TV performance in an amateur show.

On its face, the plot already seems a teenpic cliché, but *Rock, Pretty Baby* is very careful to tell a teenage story from a teenage perspective. Dated as the material now is, the depictions were probably meaningful, certainly identifiable, to the target audience. The scenes are set in familiar middle-class teenage haunts: record-store listening booths, pizza shops, beat-up vehicles, and well-furnished homes. The film's distinctively teenage allegiance is dramatized in an early sequence featuring the Jimmy Daley Combo playing a gig at a fraternity house party. College-age make-out artists hope to entice nice high school girls into necking on the veranda; their seductions are short-circuited when the band plays rock 'n' roll and the girls rush to the dance floor. "Start playing square," orders a big man on campus. "Drive them away from the dance floor." Jimmy refuses and ends up taking the frat man's would-be victim, Joan (Luanna Patten), for a malt.

The appreciation of the gulf between high school teen and collegiate young adult life, and the bestowing of moral and stylistic superiority on the former, is a shrewd narrative move, as is the nature of the romance that develops between Jim and Joan, a relationship far more intense and emotionally complex than most teenage pairings on screen. Much of their spatting is the usual breakup-to-makeup calculation, but Joan, career minded and wary of boys, has a genuine problem coming to terms with her budding sexuality: when a gaggle of girls playfully plant kisses on Jim, Joan finds herself unable to join in the game. No

Pretend to rock, pretty baby: story, not song, accounted for the success of *Rock, Pretty Baby* (1956). (Museum of Modern Art Film Stills Archive: Courtesy of Universal Pictures)

masher himself, Jim is the perfect gentleman with her until, in a highly sexy beach scene at night, the two teens, bodies glistening, finally embrace and kiss. Joan is momentarily overcome with passion and then quickly pulls back, confused and frightened. "All I think about is necking and petting," she confesses desperately, an admission sympathetically capturing the 1950s adolescent poised between passion and propriety.

Two other teen-centered details in *Rock, Pretty Baby* are noteworthy. First, at age thirteen, Jim's younger sister Twinky (future teen idol Shelley Fabares) is on the brink of entry into teenage subculture. Her initiations, especially the unfurling of a training bra, are the subject of some genuinely amusing familial banter. Second, in the climactic amateur show, Jim arrives for the talent competition with only moments to spare. He snaps on his guitar and the combo rocks out the largely teenage studio audience. Offstage, Dad proudly congratulates Jim (Jim: "You don't know how long I waited to hear that." Dad: "Sometimes it takes a father longer to grow up than his son.") The winner of the talent contest is then announced—and Jim's band loses. The oldster judges have failed to appreciate his music; the teenagers in the crowd moan, mystified at this miscarriage of justice. Happily, the combo is still offered a booking for the duration of the summer, but the film's departure from the traditional musical happy ending is a cagey turn made palatable and convincing by placing the onus not on the combo but on the straight-laced old-timers who lack the discernment of the teenage audience, on screen and off.

Perhaps the only "old-timer" truly graced with teenage discernment —and trust—was the famous entertainer/entrepreneur Alan Freed. As much as any of the featured acts, Freed was an integral part of the first rock 'n' roll pictures; his dramatic function, duplicating his real-life avocation, is crucial to one meaning of the rock 'n' roll teenpic. As a Cleveland disc jockey in the early 1950s, he acquired both a passion for rhythm and blues and a faith in its crossover potential. His experience on radio and as a concert emcee soon convinced him that much of the growing audience for "race music" was in fact white. Perhaps to avoid the racial connotations attached to rhythm and blues and thereby to expand the potential audience, he took to calling it "rock 'n' roll," a popular euphemism for sexual intercourse in black English vernacular but one that had not entered standard usage. The phrase—and the music it described—made him famous. By 1956, he was one of the music industry's most successful showmen, host of a nationally syndicated *Rock 'n' Roll Dance Party* on CBS Radio and promoter of a now-legendary package of rock 'n' roll shows at Brooklyn's Paramount Theatre.

Freed was quick to discern the box office potential of rock 'n' roll movies. As a disc jockey, he knew that cooperation between the motion picture and music industries was not without mutual rewards. The new long-playing record had expanded the market for film soundtracks; a soundtrack played on the radio could boost sales at the ticket window. In late 1956, *Billboard* commented that "never before in the history of the film business has the disc jockey and the value of recorded music been so graphically evident or so vitally important." Freed pioneered the now-standard practice of the multiple tie-in. He publicized the films he appeared in by playing their songs on his radio show; he'd often use one of his films as an audience warm-up in the rock 'n' roll packages he promoted; theater lobbies were encouraged to display copies of soundtrack records, and in turn, record stores put up posters for the movie theater. Occasionally, Freed might have a piece of the publishing rights as well.

Freed marketed rock 'n' roll with entrepreneurial fervor, but his affinity for the music was genuine and he proselytized for it with a true believer's zeal. Both activities made him a natural target for repressive civic and editorial forces. In April 1956, after a spate of hysterical anti–rock 'n' roll articles in the *New York Daily News*, Freed went on his WINS radio show in New York and defended the music in an emotional plea to the moms and dads listening in. He reminded parents of what Benny Goodman and Glenn Miller had meant to them (and to himself). He told them of the eleven thousand rock fans who helped him raise funds for the childhood disease nephrosis on a rainy Saturday morning. Finally, he promised, "As long as there are radio stations in America, and as long as there are people who like me around, we're going to rock 'n' roll until you don't want to rock 'n' roll any more and then when you don't want to rock 'n' roll any more, I'll give you what you want."

Freed played variations on this appeal in *Rock Around the Clock; Don't Knock the Rock; Rock, Rock, Rock!; Mister Rock and Roll* (1957), and *Go, Johnny, Go!* (1959). An adult who "dug" rock 'n' roll, who could allay parental concerns at the same time that he participated in their off-springs' most rebellious gesture, he was a natural mediator between teenage subculture and parent culture. In his rock 'n' roll films, Freed was never a pied piper; he was an embodiment of the mutual desire for accommodation. Straddling the generations, he played the sympathetic emissary for both sides, offering parents politeness and rational discourse and offering teenagers fatherly concern and unconditional support.

The presence of the Freedian envoy betrays an essential duplicity in the teenpic. A product of parent culture peddled to teenage subculture, it receives its marketplace validity only from the latter but its textual values mainly from the former. To the extent that the solid ground of cinema can be said at all to "express," "reflect," or "represent" the cloudy realm of ideology, the narrative of the teenpic typically advances the values of the creator, not the consumer culture. Appearances to the contrary, there can be few illusions about who controls the means of filmic production and for whose ends those means are ultimately marshaled. Certainly, any reading of the narratives of the rock 'n' roll teenpics reveals that although they may traffic in generational conflict, they deliver generational reconciliation, the cultural challenge introduced in the opening happily defused by the finale.

In *Coming of Age in America* (1963), Edgar Z. Friedenberg employed a modified colonial metaphor to describe that dynamic intergenerational relationship: parents play the imperial rulers, sometimes benign, sometimes oppressive, and teenagers play the natives, sometimes acquiescent, sometimes rebellious. Like any metaphor, the colonial comparison breaks down if carried too far. As Friedenberg recognizes, the essential difference is that teenagers, unlike natives, are constantly being groomed to assume the position of the imperial rulers and to reenact the colonial relationship. Still, as a way to categorize teenpics and to evaluate their ritual purpose for subculture and culture alike, the colonial metaphor has a certain usefulness. For teenpics fall readily between two pillars that might be labeled "imperial" and "indigenous," aligning themselves with either parent culture or teenage subculture.

Two examples may clarify the model's applicability to teenpics. Frank Tashlin's *The Girl Can't Help It* is nominally a rock 'n' roll teenpic boasting a top-notch lineup of teen-favored talent set against a narrative background of the popular music industry and the marketing precedent of *Rock Around the Clock*. Perhaps half of the featured performers—Little Richard, Gene Vincent, Eddie Cochran, and the Coasters—are concessions to the teenage audience; the remainder— Ray Anthony, Julie London, and Abby Lincoln—are for adult tastes. In one sense, elevating teen tastes to equal footing with adult preferences is itself an impressive tribute to teenage subculture. Narrative considerations aside, teenpics, merely by being about teenagers, serve as a recognition of their subculture and hence a kind of validation and reinforcement. At the same time, however, director Tashlin displays something less than sensitivity to, respect for, or understanding of the teenage subcultural preference (rock 'n' roll music) that is, in tandem with Jayne Mansfield, one of the film's three main exploitation angles.

Built from a parental frame of reference, *The Girl Can't Help It* is an imperial product from top to bottom. Beginning with its famous pre-credit sequence, when Tom Ewell sarcastically announces that the upcoming entertainment is not about old-fashioned music but about "the music that expresses the refinement and polite grace of the present day," only to have the last words drowned out by Little Richard's dissonant title tune, the film refuses to take teenage subculture on its own

Not featured up front: even Jayne Mansfield can score a hit in Frank Tashlin's imperial teenpic *The Girl Can't Help It* (1956). (Museum of Modern Art Film Stills Archive: Courtesy of Twentieth Century-Fox)

terms. The story line follows the vintage scenario of a backstage musical: boozed-down and washed-up agent Tom Miller (Ewell) is ordered by former mob kingpin Fats Murdoch (Edmond O'Brien) to turn girlfriend Jerry Ann (Mansfield) into a pop music sensation. Mansfield's cartoonish proportions serve former Looney Tunes auteur Tashlin in good stead, an irresistible occasion for Production Code–cracking double entendres and outrageous sight gags (in the trademark sequence tracking her sashaying perambulations, ice melts, milk boils, and eyeglasses crack as gaga males ogle her 40-21-35–inch frame). Mansfield gets added exposure when Ewell takes her to a round of nightclubs to generate publicity. The nightclubs are typical Hollywood establishments—formal attire, cigarette girls, elaborate sets in blinding Technicolor—only the acts are Little Richard and the Coasters.

Thus, at around the same time that Elvis Presley was bombing in Vegas in these very settings, *The Girl Can't Help It* presents teenage rock 'n' roll in adults-only venues. In a kind of variety-show format, the rock 'n' rollers are inserted into the narrative, given their moment on screen, and banished. None are integrated into the plot or given one line of dialogue—a sharp contrast to the Freed films, which always presented the rock 'n' rollers as fellow high schoolers or personable older brothers. (In *Go, Johnny, Go!* Chuck Berry plays sidekick to Freed-as-himself.) The musical performer granted the most elaborate cinematic presentation is Julie London, who sings "Cry Me a River" as a recurring "gorgeous Technicolor" apparition to the lovelorn Tom Ewell. The film offers a few moments that recognize the existence of teenage subculture—Eddie Cochran doing "Twenty Flight Rock" on a television show—but its overall outlook is smugly condescending or simply misinformed, as in its choreography of a "rock 'n' roll jamboree" that is really a 1940s dance-band performance. Like so many imperial treatments of rock 'n' roll music, teenage tastes are considered crass and bewildering, unaccountable yet amenable to cynical adult manipulation. Through guile and intimidation (in a cynical acknowledgment of mob influence in the record business, former slot-machine king Murdoch corners the jukebox market), the talentless Mansfield gets a manufactured hit record, complete with banner headlines in *Billboard* confirming the million-dollar sales. The film's imperial depiction is aptly concluded in a musical finale wherein Edmond O'Brien performs an intentionally horrible vocal on an intentionally awful send-up of "Rock Around the Clock" called "Rock Around the Rock Pile Blues"—and wows his teenage audience.

By way of comparison, Richard Thorpe's *Jailhouse Rock* (1957), Elvis Presley's third and best film, consistently assumes an indigenous attitude toward its target subculture. In narrative content and visual presentation, the film does not simply recognize teenage subculture (all teenpics, after a fashion, do that) but displays the inside knowledge and tacit respect that is the mark of the informed observer. The fortuitous preservation of classic performances by Vincent, Cochran, and Little Richard notwithstanding, the makers of *The Girl Can't Help It* know little and care less about rock 'n' roll music and teenagers. *Jailhouse Rock* presents a rock 'n' roll icon in a format that permits Presley full display of his talent and subcultural sensibility. As an unapologetic vehicle for rock 'n' roll's premier performer, *Jailhouse Rock* can do nothing but aggrandize its subject; what marks it as indigenous is that, like the teenage audience, it accords validity to the man and his music.

The opening sequence introduces a nice young man at the local bar on payday. In what is apparently a weekly ritual, he challenges the barkeeper to an arm-wrestling contest. Displaying a secure sense of self he was never again to regain, Presley loses the contest and good-naturedly buys a round for the house: the loss has built up his character more effectively than any victory. But Presley shortly proves his true mettle by inadvertently beating to death an obnoxious barfly. In the jailhouse, he turns mean after getting from the prison authorities the parent culture's punishment of choice: a severe and erotically charged whipping. Having mastered guitar and received professional encouragement from his bunkmate and a talent-show audience, Presley makes for the record biz upon release. A female impresario takes him under her not-disinterested wing, but as Presley attains the stardom that is his inevitable due, he reverses the customary Svengali-Trilby relationship and takes the managerial reins. On screen, if not in life, Presley calls the shots in his career.

In *Jailhouse Rock*, the treatment of rock 'n' roll music, both as narrative content and as cinematic performance, is knowing and respectful. The music is enthusiastically embraced by the record industry and Presley's raw talent is sympathetically rendered, especially in a scene in a recording studio that duplicates his well-known Damascus moment at Sun Records. Significantly, it is a mark of taste and discernment, not gullibility and immaturity, when teenagers, not record company executives or disc jockeys, discover his music, tracking it down in record stores and barraging radio stations with requests. The elaborate choreography for the title tune, the long takes and uninterrupted screen time given to the other numbers, and the musical pacing—the rock 'n' roll builds in quality and intensity—all show an indigenous appreciation of Presley and rock 'n' roll.

To many rock critics, a narrative analysis of the rock 'n' roll cycle may be beside the point. In their comprehensive study *Rock on Film*, David Ehrenstein and Bill Reed maintain that the sole purpose of the cycle was "to squeeze in as much music as possible into their ninety minutes (or less) of running time-with the 'dramatic' filler consisting of such will-o'-the-wisp concerns as the havoc wreaked by a teen vamp, a band's struggle for stardom, or being allowed to attend the big dance." "The intrusion of the dopey plot," in fact, may have been something of a calculated strategy, providing "the perfect opportunity to prowl the theater, chat with friends, and make dates after the show." Or as film historian Richard Thompson said of Sam Katzman's *oeuvre*: "[It] makes ideal drive-in fare, because you can look up at any point and comprehend it without prior knowledge of the plot."

From this vantage, what happens in front of the screen is as important as what happens on it. A purely narrative reading of the rock 'n' roll musical, or even an appreciation of the rock 'n' roll performances,

Small screen/widescreen: Elvis is doubly showcased in *Loving You* (1957).
(Museum of Modern Art Film Stills Archive: Courtesy of the Presley Estate)

misses its subcultural function as a ritual occasion for the congregation. Teenpics foster public demonstrations of teenage presence, identity, and solidarity. They provide an explicit recognition that lends a degree of implicit validation to teenagers as a subcultural group. Through the simple appearance of a teenpic at a downtown venue, the parent culture validates and reinforces, in its own citadel, the teenage subculture. Whether the teenpic's affinities lean toward parent culture or teenage subculture, the prime subcultural value—legitimacy—has already been conferred by the product itself. Hence the ease with which teenagers hijack the characters and meanings for their own ends: Artie West becomes the hero of *Blackboard Jungle*, and the rebellious exhilaration of rock 'n' roll is the message gleaned from the conciliatory musical. Even when the content of the imperialist teenpic is inimical to teenage values (however defined) and fraudulent in their presentation, the teenpic lends legitimacy and encouragement to the group.

Teenpic advertisers contributed mightily to the ritualistic power of the teenpic by hyping films "for teenagers only." The success of the rock 'n' roll–less *Rock, Pretty Baby* was spurred by its clever for-and-about-teens exploitation campaign ("the wonderful story of today's rock 'n' roll generation the way they want it to be told!") and the short-lived heartthrob appeal of its lead actor ("that new teenage sensation"). Reverse psychology was an especially reliable, if transparent, marketing technique. *A Room Full of Roses*, a mild play about the problems divorce makes for children, was filmed as *Teenage Rebel* (1956) and exploited as a licentious teenpic. "Don't talk about *Teenage Rebel* in front of teenagers," warned the ads. "There are some things better left unsaid . . . others that can be spoken in whispers only." Lest the true target audience miss the point, the copy also noted: "If you're 16, you're old enough to see it." In keeping with a typical teenpic pattern of deceptive advertising, *Teenage Rebel* promised more than it delivered. "The teenagers seen here," one reviewer observed, "are orderly, mannerly, convention-abiding young folks who behave perfectly, maybe even more perfectly, than the teenagers in the Hardy family."

With the exception of the big-budget crossover experiment *The Girl Can't Help It*, the early rock 'n' roll cycle, like teenpics in general, willfully banished adults from their ceremonies on and off screen. Reviewer after reviewer noted that these were films only a teenager would want to endure. The plot of *Rock Around the Clock*, sniffed Louise L. Bucklin in *National Parent Teacher*, "stresses its appeal to young people. Those not so young may have trouble distinguishing one number from another." "It'll make adults squirm and probably drive 'em out of the theatre," wrote *Variety* of *Rock, Pretty Baby*. The "comparatively middle-aged" *New York Times* reporter "who made the awful mistake of grabbing a seat down front" at *Don't Knock the Rock* warned that "anybody above 30 who elects to brave Paramount's new program may find himself amid a composite of a teenage revival meeting and the Battle of the Bulge." Of course, the carping from adults only enhanced the cycle's popularity with teenagers.

Calypsomania

Katzman's *Don't Knock the Rock* is worth further note as an example of how exploitation filmmaking feeds on itself. In a cost-efficient wheels-within-wheels circularity, the film exploits not only the rock 'n' roll controversy but its parent film, *Rock Around the Clock*, hence milking exploitation value out of the previous successful exploitation. Discussing his methodology, Katzman confided that he "never work[ed] too far ahead" of a trend and never made more than two or three exploitation pictures on the same subject "unless something very unusual present[ed] itself." The second exploitation picture usually did about 75 percent of the business of the first, while "the third begins to level off to the point it's advisable to search for something new."

The trick is to hit the crest of the wave, ride it, and jump off before wiping out. The attempts by Katzman and several other producers to cash in on calypso music illustrate the advisability of also catching the right wave. Generations removed from their target audience, moviemakers in the 1950s struggled to anticipate teenage tastes. In early 1957, soon after his success with two rock 'n' roll exploitation pictures, Katzman was reported to be biding his time, "waiting for something to happen" on which "to base future production." He opted for calypso music, a new and provocative rhythm that in late 1956 and early 1957 enjoyed a brief vogue on the *Billboard* charts. The "calypso invasion" was spearheaded by Harry Belafonte's "The Banana Boat Song" and the Easyriders' much-covered "Marianne." Like all musical crazes, it inspired dances, fashions, and public curiosity. Having seen rock 'n' roll as a temporary affliction anyway, some in the entertainment industry assumed calypso would displace rock 'n' roll and become the next teenage music sensation. In a widely quoted pronouncement, "recognized jazz authority" the Reverend Norman O'Connor averred that rock 'n' roll was fading fast. "Rock 'n' roll is a stage in popular music similar to the Charleston, jazz, swing, and the jitterbug of the past two generations and is on its way out. . . . The present fad is now giving way to calypso music."

Low-budget film producers, the precedent of *Rock Around the Clock* fresh in mind, stampeded to the MPAA Title Registration Bureau to get first crack at such names as *Calypso Holiday, Calypso Nights, Calypso Rhythm, Bop Girl Goes Calypso, Calypso-Gripso, Calypsomania, Banana Boat Calypso, Calypso Kid,* and *Mad Craze from Trinidad.* An Allied Artists entry, *Calypso Joe,* and a Sam Katzman production, *Calypso Heat Wave,* were soon neck and neck in a race to cash in on the (presumed) calypso market. In May 1957, Allied Artists won: *Calypso Joe,* promised the ads, was "ready right now for a calypso crazy nation." *Calypso Heat Wave* descended a couple of weeks later.

Alas, the craze was a showbiz flash in the pan and an exploitation false alarm. There being no payoff in the calypso sweepstakes, the "calypso cycle" was short-lived. Weighing the prospects of *Calypso Heat Wave*, *Variety*'s reviewer noted: "It's none-too-subtly aimed at the teenage market and there will have to find its greatest appeal. Against it is the fact that the calypso song craze is on the wane and some say already dead." By the time *Bop Girl Goes Calypso* appeared several weeks later, it could confidently be pronounced dead on arrival, a "mild musical badly outguessed by events . . . vitiating the potential it might have had earlier as a musical programmer." The plot of *Bop Girl Goes Calypso* mirrors the misjudgment of its producers: Bobby Troup (composer of "Route 66") plays a psychologist whose thesis research ("Mass Hysteria and the Popular Singer") leads him to conclude that rock 'n' roll will soon succumb to West Indian kettle drums. He convinces rocker Judy Tyler to switch to calypso and she becomes a big star. (The remaining calypso movie titles went unused.)

Despite the calypso cycle's failure, the quick and substantial profits from the first wave of rock 'n' roll pictures had proven the box office power of the teenage filmgoer. (Many of Harry Belafonte's fans were adults, and the motion picture industry was learning that record sales might not translate into ticket sales unless teenagers were buying the records.) *Rock, Pretty Baby*; *Rock, Rock, Rock!*; and *Don't Knock the Rock* were all extraordinarily profitable in relation to their costs.

The success of the Elvis Presley vehicle *Love Me Tender*, however, was downright phenomenal. Timed to coincide with the Thanksgiving school break, it immediately set box office records across the country. A perfunctory western that featured no overt rock 'n' roll, *Love Me Tender* was titled *The Brothers Reno* until someone realized the tie-in value of Elvis's change-of-pace ballad. At one theater in San Francisco, two hundred teenagers lined up for tickets at 10:00 A.M. "despite the fact classes were not excused until 3:00 P.M."—at which time the deluge began. In release for less than six weeks, *Love Me Tender* was number twenty-two on *Variety*'s year-end list for 1956, grossing $3.75 million. The first of a decade-long series of sequels followed with the rock-oriented *Loving You* (released August 1957) and *Jailhouse Rock* (released November 1957). With *Love Me Tender* still going strong, Presley finished 1957 with three pictures in the top twenty: *Love Me Tender* (number ten, grossing a cumulative $4.5 million), *Jailhouse Rock* (number fifteen, grossing $4 million), and *Loving You* (number nineteen, grossing $3.7 million). Pat Boone, Presley's chief rival for teenage affections, achieved comparable success in his two 1957 vehicles, *Bernardine* (number fourteen, grossing $4 million) and *April Love* (number eighteen, grossing $3.7 million). Frank Tashlin's *The Girl Can't Help It* had a heftier budget and higher ambitions than most of the field, and Jayne Mansfield's presence up front provided broader demographic appeal, but its formidable lineup of classic rock 'n' roll talent was certainly responsible for much of the $2.8 million it accrued.

A new genre and a new audience had rocked Hollywood. At the close of 1957, for the first time, *Variety*'s year-end list of box office hits included a goodly number of what could only be called "teenpics," movies made specifically for the teenage audience to the pointed exclusion of other patrons.

5

Dangerous Youth

Somehow we must get at the causes, must clean up the conditions, which breed criminals. We will find them, I think, in the slums, where the kids don't have a place to play; in social conditions, where the young feel that society is their enemy; in economic conditions which breed hunger and despair; in lack of parental interest and supervision; and, perhaps, even in a lack of understanding on the part of some of our correctional institutions.

Senator Estes Kefauver, 1953

"The Right to Professional Help Whenever Necessary": The teenager is growing fast in mind and body. When something interferes with that growth or his personality adjustment or with his health, the necessary professional help should be available to him either through his parents or from community resources.

New York Federation of Jewish Philanthropers' "A Teenage Bill of Rights," article 10, 1945

What *Blackboard Jungle* did for rock 'n' roll, *Rebel Without a Cause* did for drag racing. Released shortly after James Dean plowed his Spyder Porsche into a Ford at a California intersection on September 30, 1955, *Rebel* remains the touchstone for generational strife in the 1950s. From Dean's opening cry of animal pain ("You're tearing me apart!") to

83

Sal Mineo's sacrificial snuff-out, the film is awash in soon-to-be arche-
typal images of teenage angst. Depression-hardened parents who spent
their youth at war may have wondered what these well-fed youngsters
had to wail about, but for teenagers, the film's plaintive expression of
adolescent unrest sounded just the right note. In *Rebel*, inarticulateness
was a virtue: it said much about the confusions, doubts, and fears of
both generations.

Unlike the natives of *Blackboard Jungle*, the teenagers of *Rebel* are
affluent suburbanites inhabiting a world similar to that of the middle-class audience so valued by Hollywood. Little in this environment
seems to encourage knife fights and "chickee runs." But as in his subsequent film, *Bigger Than Life* (1956), director Nicholas Ray uses the
familiar 1950s milieu of well-appointed households and disciplined
high schools to dramatize the tensions behind the tranquillity. External (societal) order is continually juxtaposed with internal (individual)
havoc; public face contradicts private self. Jim Stark, the protagonist,
can't seem to get his categories straight, and the adults around him offer little guidance. Although much of the film's pop Freudianism has
dated badly (castrated patriarch Jim Backus tiptoeing around his house
in an apron, harridan Mom going for the guilt jugular with lines like "I
almost died giving birth to him!"), *Rebel* has been consistently popular
with successive generations for its on-the-mark rendering of what it's
like to grow up dazed and confused in America.

Ninety percent of the film's evocative power comes from the cha-
rismatic performance of James Dean, the young method actor who
achieved instant icon status as the personification of the moody, unfocused 1950s teen. Though purportedly more sensitive and less sure of
himself than his John Wayne–Gary Cooper predecessors, Dean's character was a recognizable hero in the old-fashioned Hollywood sense—
winning the showdown, getting the girl. No wonder Plato (Sal Mineo)
looks up to him and rival Buzz Gunderson (Corey Allen) shows a
knightly deference during the chickee-run duel. What was new about
the heroics of *Rebel Without a Cause* was that the cool-but-caring, strong-
but-sensitive combination was put at the service of youth. In 1975, a
British documentary on Dean's life expressed it another way: on film, at
least, he was "the first American teenager."

Jim Stark's instinctive allegiance to the values of peers over parents
marks an important departure from previous filmic dilemmas of dual
loyalty. In the classical western or gangster genre, the reformed outlaw

"You gotta do something, doncha?": Jim Stark (James Dean) and Buzz Gunderson (Corey Allen) share an automotive moment of male bonding before the chickee run in *Rebel Without a Cause* (1955). (Museum of Modern Art Film Stills Archive: Courtesy of Warner Bros.)

must break with his fellows and accept society's law or face the end-reel consequences. Jim Stark's social order, as represented by his father, is impotent, unable to provide the "direct answer" that Stark longs for. Challenged to an illegal chickee run by leather-clad tough guy Buzz Gunderson, Stark has apprehensions, but no doubts, about participating. As he later explains to his father, "They called me 'chicken,' y'-know, chicken. I had to go. If I didn't, I'd never be able to face those kids again." Throughout, Stark and his alternative "family" (surrogate wife Judy, played by Natalie Wood, and surrogate son Plato) lead an autonomous existence; the adult world is peripheral. Father Jim Backus has no idea what his son does outside the home, much less what his inner life is like.

Significantly, it wasn't Dean's sex appeal that made him the movies' first authentic cult figure since Rudolph Valentino; it was his stance, his representative power as a teenager. An image frozen by death, it made sense that leaving a beautiful corpse enhanced his popularity with fans, the obsessive "Dean-agers." Through him, *Rebel* did more than depict the style and autonomy of teenage life in the 1950s: attractive in his alienation, self-assured even in his confusion, Dean validated it. In locking the audience into Jim Stark's upside-down viewpoint, director Ray offered a critical perspective on an adult world far less exhilarating or rewarding than the world of Jim, Buzz, Julie, and Plato. Ray's dynamic use of CinemaScope space visually renders the emotional distance between the generations: for once, Hollywood's new aspect ratio paid off with dramatic meaning.

The action centerpiece of *Rebel* is its famous chickee run, a nighttime automotive duel between Stark, Gunderson, and the abyss. Their attendants fix up two jalopies for the contestants to drive over an ocean-front cliff. First one to leap out of the car is "chicken." Before takeoff, Jim and Buzz share a comradely cigarette and express their existential ethos. "Why do we do this?" asks Jim. "You gotta do something, doncha?" comes the edgy reply. The erotically radiant Judy, Buzz's present and Jim's future girl, signals the start, and the two cars zoom for the edge. A strap from Buzz's leather jacket catches on the door handle and he's unable to jump out. While Jim ditches, Buzz plunges over the cliff, accompanied by Nicholas Ray's CinemaScope lens.

This one scene from *Rebel* inspired a souped-up series of teenage drag-racing films. Motor-mad 1950s youth had made its first noteworthy appearance on screen in the Stanley Kramer–produced, Laslo Benedek–directed *The Wild One* (1954), the popular Marlon Brando film about a motorcycle gang terrorizing a small California town. (Few montages of teenage life in the 1950s can resist the iconographic shorthand of the flippant exchange between Brando and a flirty townie: "So what are you rebelling against?" she asks. "What d'ya got?" he answers.) Although the earlier film inspired a teenpic or two itself (AIP's *Motorcycle Gang* [1957], a virtual remake, and one-half of the same company's *Dragstrip Riot* [1958], which had a cycles–versus–hot rods premise), motorcyclists still had too much of a deranged outlaw image to capture the sensibilities of suburban teenage Americans. Not until Roger Corman's *The Wild Angels* (1966) would the "cycle cycle" come into its own. For a 1950s filmmaker, enthusiasm for six cylinders was more easily appropriated. American International Pictures set the pace for automotive exploitation, but all the usual suppliers of low-budget programmers launched vehicular vehicles in the spirit of *Rebel*'s dramatic chickee run and Dean's poetic end.

Like rock 'n' roll, drag racing in the mid-1950s was a controversial, confrontational teenage activity, as much an occasion for subcultural consolidation as an expression of subcultural values. The "meaning" of drag racing (a behavior) is perhaps less amenable to interpretation than rock 'n' roll (a text), but the appeal for adolescent boys is evident enough: an opportunity to display mechanical aptitude and physical courage, a literal vehicle for independence and potency. Put against the background of the sinister overtones attached to rock 'n' roll music, however, drag racing seems very much in tune with parent culture norms. It earned official censure for two reasons. First, by drag racing, teenagers adopted adult values, to be sure, but they did so prematurely and without permission. It was for parent culture to bestow independence and power, not for teenage subculture to usurp it. Second, teenagers were young and foolish enough to call in the promise of gratification that parent culture was content to defer. In their reckless pursuit of happiness behind the wheel, a defiant and suicidal courtship of death was a bracing rejection of the life and liberties of American culture. Parent culture had good reason for concern.

"Scarcely a city in the country has not been bedeviled by the problem," reported *Newsweek*, which also noted the popular "association between drag-racing and any kind of wild, or drunken driving, or with crowds of riotous teenagers mocking the forces of law and order." Where the rock 'n' roll debate was polarized into the "incitement to violence" and "harmless outlet" arguments, the two sides on the drag-racing question debated the issue of safety. Compared with the public uproar over rock 'n' roll, the "controversy" over drag racing was pretty mild, especially considering its decidedly deadlier consequences. Everyone agreed that unsupervised drag racing was a menace. The debate, such as it was, concerned regulation. If the kids were going to drag race anyway, said proponents, let them do it under professional adult supervision, away from terrified motorists. A few critics, such as the Pittsburgh superintendent of police, demurred: "You're just giving the kids a place to kill themselves. We don't want any part of it." But rare was the American who could with a clear conscience condemn the national mania for automotive speed. By spring 1957, *Life* had anointed drag racing an alternative national pastime: "Drag racing started out as a postwar teenage infatuation with souped-up cars in which speed-crazy kids raced surreptitiously at 80 or 90 miles per hour over lonely roads scaring ordinary drivers to death. Now in many places in the U.S. it has come out into the open as a respectable—and controlled—sport.

Life's imprimatur to the contrary, the sport had enough distinctly teenage associations to find its way into *Rebel* and then to inspire a modest and mildly profitable group of teenpics. Calling drag racing "the racket that sweeps the country," a promotion for one of the earliest entries, United Artists' *Hot Cars* (1956), played up its immediacy and topicality: "We noticed in our home town newspapers the other day, big news stories of 'hot cars' on our own small town streets. . . . [This film has] a timely story that may be of bitter interest to your public." Like the early rock 'n' roll teenpics, the drag-strip cycle both validates and domesticates a controversial teenage activity. A Freed-like mediating agent, often a sympathetic cop, is the buffer between worrywart town elders and grease-monkey kids. Complicating matters is a chicken race for honor and, usually, an accidental automotive death, often instigated by a speed-crazy female hellcat. Inevitably, resolution means the containment of teenage energies within a limited, supervised arena.

AIP's *Hot Rod Girl* (1956) enacts the process of domestication. Enclosure begins at once: the title credits note "technical supervision" from the San Fernando Drag Strip and offer thanks to the National Hot Rod Association. An introductory montage of actual drag racing at a supervised forum and main location site, the San Fernando Drag Strip, puts a sound amplifier center-screen and mixes in a series of announcements over roaring engines and screeching tires. The public address system doubles as the voice of parents who appear nowhere in the film. "Please observe our safety regulations," cautions the strip announcer, and periodic advisories follow ("Take it easy going home. Play it safe on the road, the same as you do here on the strip."). The plot concerns the efforts of Officer Ben Merrill (Chuck Connors) to establish a community drag strip so that teenagers will have a safe, supervised environment for their hot-rodding. In spite of opposition from "the city council and other soreheads," Merrill tells his sympathetic captain that "more kids on the drag strip means fewer on the street."

Alternately aiding and resisting Merrill's ministrations is Jeff Northrup (John Smith), a slightly older hot-rodder and garage mechanic who is the natural leader of a cast of supporting players that includes mimic Frank Gorshin as a cutup named Flat-Top. Jeff and his younger brother Steve are responsibly driving home from the strip when Steve, at the wheel, is baited into a drag race by an anonymous driver who bumps his car and taunts him on the city streets. Probably for financial and technical reasons, the crack-up is rendered off screen, but at the accident site, the consequences of unbridled speed are immediate and unforgiving. Suddenly and shockingly, the young and innocent Steve, a handsome, fresh-faced teenager, is dead. Tormented by grief and guilt, Jeff cuts himself off from the drag strip and his hot-rod girl, Lisa (Lori Nelson). The film's title notwithstanding, Lisa is on the periphery of the dramatic action, which mainly treats Jeff's participation in Officer Merrill's efforts "to save the strip" and combat the evil influence of a stranger named Bronc Talbot, a leather-jacketed hot-rodder who, despite "dreamy" good looks, is also quite clearly "crazy."

Although *Hot Rod Girl* deploys the stock elements of the 1950s teen-pic—the teenage juke-joint hangout (playing bad jazz, not rock 'n' roll, on the jukebox); strained jive talk (this being a hot-rod picture, the teenage slang tends toward motor metaphors such as "Your fuel mixture's too rich"); the displacement of parents by uniformly friendly and unthreatening surrogate authority (Officer Merrill, the wisecracking proprietor of the teenage hangout, and Jeff's solicitous boss at the garage); and pandering barbs aimed at recalcitrant oldsters ("Teaching those solid loud-mouthed citizens to respect the hot-rodders who *are* law-abiding is rougher than educating kids!" says Officer Ben)—it is really a parental road sign for restraint and caution. Nowhere does the thrill of "behind the wheel" cinema, the exhilaration of a well-shot race sequence from the point of view of the grinning driver, give the lie to safety-first dialogue. In *Hot Rod Girl*, drag racing off the strip is dangerous, dumb, and unnerving, while on the strip it is safe, smart, and predictable. Jeff accrues status through his prowess under the hood, not behind the wheel. As garage mechanic and inspector for the drag strip, he displays automotive skills that are mechanical/intellectual, not athletic/physical—skills of steady maturity, not daring youth.

The *de rigueur* chicken race in *Hot Rod Girl* bears comparison by way of contrast with its source scene in *Rebel Without a Cause*. In *Rebel*, the danger makes the race thrilling; Judy is sexually ecstatic when she flags off the cars. *Hot Rod Girl's* version is deadlier and more terrifying: two cars drive *at* each other until one driver loses his nerve and veers off. Unlike Jim Stark, who acquiesces readily to Buzz's suggestion, Flat-Top accepts the challenge of the maniacal Bronc under compulsion. He is clearly terrified, as is his girlfriend. Facing Bronc's relentlessly oncoming car, Flat-Top ditches—chickens out. His cowardice is portrayed as preferable to the insanity of his antagonist, who had no plans of turning off whatever the consequences. "He's crazy, completely crazy," says a female onlooker who had heretofore admired Bronc's reckless swagger. Still behind the wheel, Flat-Top reaches out the car window to embrace his girlfriend around the waist, laying his head, childlike, on her stomach. "From now on, yours truly is going to be one fat coward," he nearly whimpers—presumably to defensive jeering from teenage spectators.

To publicize the dragpics, exploitation in its root sense was not neglected. Press books encouraged exhibitors to find a colorful hot rod to display in theater parking lots. For drive-ins the dragpic was a ballyhoo natural; teenage patrons were urged to parade machines that might outshine the vehicles on the open-air screen.

Neither as tightly concentrated nor as clearly defined as the early rock 'n' roll cycle, the drag-strip cycle inspired no mad flurry of production during any one period (as with rock 'n' roll teenpics toward the end of 1956) and no through-the-roof drag-strip hit comparable to *Rock Around the Clock*. It generated modestly profitable "programmers" that fed exhibitor demand for new titles and teenage product. Allied Artists (AA) and AIP offered virtually indistinguishable drag-racing fare, AA's *Hot Car Girl* (1958) and AIP's *Hot Rod Girl* being typical of what insiders called "well-knit programmer[s] which may be exploited for satisfactory returns, especially with the juve trade." Likewise, AA's *Hot Rod Rumble* (1957) and AIP's *Dragstrip Girl* (1957) were "stacked with juve appeal" and "aimed at the levi and leather jacket crowd," each containing what was already being referred to as "the inevitable chicken race."

As an exploitation hook, drag racing had less going for it than rock 'n' roll. Whereas even the lamest rock 'n' roll film usually boasted at least one authentic hit from a top music act, the low-budget drag-strip film couldn't deliver on its action promise of death-defying races and thunderous crashes. After all, souped-up vehicles, special effects choreography, and top stunt men were expensive. The standard (and over-used) way around production costs was to incorporate real-life racing footage from the nation's speedways, as in AA's *Speed Crazy* (1959). With hot-rodders organizing themselves into well-regulated regional clubs, the controversy over the "drag-strip menace" diminished proportionately. Paramount's *The Devil's Hairpin* (1957), for example, blended the heavy breathing of advertising tag lines ("Fast, stream-lined, and low-down—that's the way 'the King' liked his women and his cars!")

with prim endorsements from regional car clubs. Typical of the era's teen-oriented exploitation fare, the drag-racing picture depended on an exhibition practice that became increasingly common during the last half of the 1950s: the teenpic double bill.

Teenpic Double Bills

Unlike classic Hollywood's double bills, which served up a short, cheap B movie for dessert after the main-course A production, the teenpic double bill paired two films similar in budget, length, and kind. Surveys had found that "teens tended to double bills," and by booking two different kinds of exploitation teenpics, exhibitors could appeal to two different (or, just as frequently, overlapping) teenage markets. Thus, Howco paired Jacques Marquette's dragpic *Teenage Thunder* (1957) with a rock 'n' roll quickie *Carnival Rock* (1957); Twentieth Century-Fox teamed *Young and Dangerous* (1957) with *Rockabilly Baby* (1957); and Allied Artists tried to boost *Calypso Joe* (1957) by linking it to *Hot Rod Rumble* (1957). Teenage couples were lured with boy-girl pairings, each half of the bill relying on a sex-specific exploitation appeal. In popular double features like Allied Artists' *Unwed Mother* (1958)/*Joy Ride* (1958) and AIP's *Sorority Girl* (1957)/*Motorcycle Gang* (1957) and *Diary of a High School Bride* (1959)/*Ghost of Dragstrip Hollow* (1959), the first film was "aimed at the femme teenage market" and the second conceived "as a sop to the male side."

The double-bill strategy was especially attractive to operators of drive-in theaters. In 1950, there were fewer than five hundred "ozoners" in the country; by 1957, they had increased tenfold, multiplying almost in direct proportion to the demise of conventional four-wall "hardtops." By 1959, attendance at drive-ins matched that at four-wallers. *Variety* concluded the obvious in calling the growth and acceptance of drive-ins as "respectable family emporiums" the decade's greatest development from the standpoint of exhibition. Exhibitors touted drive-ins as "the answer to the family's night out," a way for a young married couple with toddlers to avoid the expense of babysitters and downtown parking. To sweeten the lure, they admitted children under age twelve free and installed playgrounds, amusement park rides, laundries, and swimming pools as sidelines.

Ozoner operators courted teenagers with open-air dance floors and fixed-price-per-carload admission. They also innovated special teen-targeted double (or triple or quadruple) late-show bills, a tactic that first became standard exhibition practice during the 1950s for drive-ins and hardtops alike. The exact origin of "midnight movie" or "dusk-to-dawn" shows is obscure, but if the Moonglows' hit "We Go Together" is any indication, it was a widespread teenage ritual as early as 1956: "We like the same things / That make living sweet / Love midnight movies / And balcony seats." By 1958, the practice was familiar enough for the title creature of *The Blob* to know immediately where to seek out teenage victims in the early morning hours: entering through the theater's air vents, it disrupts the necking during a midnight movie horror show.

Suburban parents found that a night out with the kids wasn't much of a night out, but for "the postpubescent set" the privacy of drive-in seating held tantalizing possibilities. Obviously, the romantic allure of a drive-in date was the most powerful inducement to regular patronage. Among 1950s teenagers, the back rows of any drive-in lot had a deserved reputation as the local "passion pit." To appease worried parents and discourage shenanigans, theater managers sent out surveillance "flashlight patrols" and stationed attendants in restrooms to prevent spiking of soft drinks. With this kind of rigorous supervision in place, Standford Kohlberg, a vigilant founding father of the drive-in business, seriously maintained that "the drive-in is the answer for wholesome amusement for teenagers."

Teenagers were worth the trouble. The intermission at a teenpic double bill could be more profitable than the box office receipts because refreshment receipts didn't have to be shared with the distributor. Ozoner and hardtop exhibitors alike made their real money at the concession stand, a part of the business as important as what was on the screen. (Some drive-in owners calculated that every dollar taken in at the entry gate was matched by one spent on overpriced drinks, popcorn, and candy.) Throughout the 1950s, concession-stand profits rose with the development of fast-food technology, jumping from an estimated $15 million in 1949 to $108 million in 1959. The growth was largely attributable to the adolescent appetite for junk food, yet another reason for exhibitors to go after the teenage audience. One drive-in operator explained, "Let's say you're showing *The Nun's Story*. You'll get a lot of adults for that; they've had their dinner and your concession doesn't do much. But if you're running, say, *Some Like It Hot* or *Rio Bravo*, which is a real slam-bang western, you'll pack the place with kids and teenagers and your concessions really hum." When exhibitors offered teenagers special ticket prices, they knew that money lost at the box office would be recouped at the concession stand.

Teenage Crime Wave

Fast kids in cars remained a teenpic staple, but generally filmmakers blended the fast cars with other teen-oriented tastes. Few teenpics of the late 1950s relied on only one exploitation hook. Combining the double-bill strategy into one picture, they mixed two or more exploitation items—rock 'n' roll, drag racing, high school vice—in inventive hybrids. The result was a bizarre cross-pollination of gimmicks, a kind of exploitation overload.

Blackboard Jungle and *Rebel Without a Cause* had each suggested a distinctive exploitation cycle. Together they spawned a broader filmic category: the delinquent movie. "Dangerous youth" or "adolescent problem" pictures had been around, after a fashion, for decades. The Jazz Age saw *Our Dancing Daughters* (1928) and *The Wild Party* (1929); the 1930s had the Dead End Kids, collegiate "pigskin" pics, and a spate of germinal, non-Code exploitation films such as *Maniac* (1934) and *Reefer Madness* (1936); the late-1940s B movie had embraced violence-prone young misfits in stylish film noir such as *Gun Crazy* (1949) and *They Live by Night* (1949). The distinctive "dangerous youths" of the 1950s were juvenile delinquents, and like everything about the era's young people, they were more celebrated, better equipped, and in greater numbers than their predecessors. Moreover, judging from contemporary expressions of concern from parents, public officials, and the media, they were perceived as an authentic threat to the social order. As a subject for exploitation filmmaking, juvenile delinquency in itself wasn't controversial; all considered it a scourge. The controversy was over causes and cures and, in regard to the film industry, the role movies played in both.

The influence of motion pictures on impressionable young minds is a concern as old as the industry itself. Periodically, from the nickelodeon of one *fin de siècle* to the multiplex mall of another, an escalation in on-screen crime and violence focuses national attention on the cause-effect equation between film and social reality. In 1911, psychologist Emma Virginia Fish staked out the rhetorical boundaries of a perennial dispute between moviemakers and parents groups. Foreseeing that "the picture show is going to be a hard subject for parents to manage," Fish wrote:

> While in most cities the law forbids the attendance of youths under 16 unchaperoned by an adult, this law is often not enforced, and already boys have been arrested for crimes of burglary, etc., which they have confessed have been suggested by these pictures in such attractive form as to lead them to try their hands at picking locks, robbing safes, and even robbing trains. Recently, in one of our large cities, little girls, arrested for improper conduct, confessed to police authorities that under cover of the semi-darkness in the moving picture theaters men have said vile things to them and have attempted insults. It is a burning shame that an amusement with such immense possibilities for good as the kinetograph should be put to such vile uses. To prevent its harming irreparably the morals of our youths, parents must either keep their children entirely away from any but the absolutely moral exhibitions or take urgent means to prevent the display of the questionable pictures and see that the laws are enforced.

Subsequent inquiries into youth and movies tended to mix psycho-sociological jargon with a moral tone that was still recognizably Fish-like. By far the most rigorous and comprehensive of all the "impact" investigations was the famous series of twelve studies underwritten by the Payne Fund from 1929 to 1933. In the introduction to Henry James Forman's *Our Movie Made Children* (1933), a popularized abridgment of the findings, W. W. Charters, chairman of the Committee on Educational Research of the Payne Fund, summed up the academic consensus in tendentious tones and careful language: "The content of current commercial motion pictures constitutes a valid basis for apprehension about their influence upon children." Writing of the gangster cycle, however, Payne Fund sociologists Herbert Blumer and Philip M. Hauser were somewhat blunter, concluding that "motion pictures may create attitudes and furnish techniques conducive, quite unwittingly, to delinquent or criminal behavior." In like manner, the picturesque bloodletting of the splatter cycle in the 1970s and the pathological home pages of the World Wide Web in the 1990s have given rise to similar misgivings, though not yet to the same level of research funding.

Predictably, the well-publicized arrival of the postwar juvenile delinquent sparked renewed interest in the mass media's role in shaping young people's behavior. In early 1955, responding to a barrage of letters from worried parents, Senator Estes Kefauver (D–Tenn.) held hearings of the Senate Judiciary Subcommittee to investigate juvenile delinquency in the United States and to inquire into the "possible dele-

terious effect upon . . . children of certain of the media of mass communication." Kefauver's committee published three reports treating
the relationship between juvenile delinquency and crime and violence
in three media (comic books, television, and motion pictures). Issued
in March 1956, the committee's report *Motion Pictures and Juvenile
Delinquency* was an inconclusive document in which Congress both
praised the film industry and hedged its bets. "The subcommittee realizes that to say bad movies create additional delinquency is not in
keeping with present-day social-psychological thinking," it affirmed,
and then went on to note that social scientists "do feel that to allow the
indiscriminate showing of scenes depicting violence or brutality constitutes a threat to the development of healthy young personalities."

The committee astutely summarized its—and Hollywood's—dilemma
with the observation: "If crime and violence assume an upswing in our
social and national experience, it follows that the Hollywood movies reflect that upswing in a corresponding increase of screenplays featuring
violence. This may presently indicate a vicious circle in which the motion picture and television borrow criminal color from current circum-
stances and pass it on to society at some peril of increasing the momentum of the prevailing evil." *Blackboard Jungle* was singled out for
special comment:

> While the committee recognizes and appreciates the artistic excellence of
> this film, it feels there are valid reasons for concluding that the film will
> have effects on youth other than the beneficial ones described by its produc-
> ers. . . . It is felt that many of the type of delinquents portrayed in this pic-
> ture will derive satisfaction, support, and sanction from having made society
> sit up and take notice of them. Although the tough individual portrayed by
> Artie West is used to show the crime-does-not-pay requirement by the end
> of the film, even the producer, Dore Schary, agreed that the type of individ-
> ual portrayed by Artie West upon viewing this film will in no way receive
> the message purportedly presented in the picture and would identify with
> him no matter what the outcome of the film.

Although the caliber of Capitol Hill film criticism had improved
measurably since the HUAC hearings of 1947, the influence Congress
held over the motion picture industry had diminished proportionately.
The upshot of the hearings was little more than an assurance from
MPAA president Eric Johnston of the industry's good intentions. Johnston from time to time dutifully warned moviemakers "to consider
carefully the possible effects of pictures featuring crime, brutality, and
juvenile delinquency in order to counter the widespread criticism of

films of this type." But it was indicative of Hollywood's desperate financial straits and its increased awareness of the lucrative teenage market that, even in the wake of congressional hearings and amid sometimes vociferous public outcries, it persisted in supplying teenagers with films their parents could only find reprehensible.

The motorpsycho madmen played by Marlon Brando and Lee Marvin in *The Wild One* set an early style, but it was in the wake of *Blackboard Jungle* and *Rebel Without a Cause* that the j.d. pictures really flourished. The self-descriptive titles of *Running Wild* (1955), *Teenage Crime Wave* (1955), *Crime in the Streets* (1956), *The Delinquents* (1957), *Juvenile Jungle* (1958), *Dangerous Youth* (1958), *Young and Wild* (1958), and *The Rebel Breed* (1960) tell much of their stories. These are standard (or below-standard) crime melodramas in which the social depredations happen to be committed by young people. In his review of *Crime in the Streets*, venerable *New York Times* film critic Bosley Crowther interpreted the contemporary j.d. movies as a simple update of an old formula:

> Do you remember the Little Tough Guys and the Bowery Boys of a dozen or so years back? They were the hand-me-down brothers of the original Dead End Kids. Well, their collateral descendants may be seen in *Crime in the Streets*, a meager drama of juvenile delinquents. . . . The only difference between these present actors and the old ones that we can see is that they talk a more jivey lingo and dance to a rock and roll beat. They mutter such words as "Crazy!" and "Go, man!" to speak their ecstasies. And they wield switch blade knives—a kind of weapon the Little Tough Guys didn't have as we recall. But otherwise the juvenile misfits in this cheap little slum-pent film . . . are the same breed of pseudo-surly kids. And the picture itself looks exactly like some of those B-grade agonies of yore.

Crowther was right to point out the cycle's obvious filmic antecedents: little emerges from Hollywood *sui generis*. But if the juvenile delinquency picture often traveled familiar territory, it also broke new ground. The era's real juvenile delinquents were the most celebrated criminal class since the pioneering gangsters of the 1920s and 1930s; their crimes were as colorfully horrifying and their exploits as vigorously publicized. Consequently, the on-screen social disorder wrought by the 1950s delinquent outstrips the youthful hijinks of the Dead End Kids. In terms of filmic violence, Artie West and company are "collateral descendants" of public enemies like Scarface and Little Caesar, not back-street punks like the Bowery Boys and the Dead End Kids. J. Edgar Hoover himself made the association in one of his periodic tirades against the motion picture industry's "trash mills which spew out cel-luloid poison destroying the impressionable minds of youth." The FBI director asserted, "In the face of the nation's terrifying juvenile crime wave we are threatened with a flood of movies and television produc-tions which flaunt indecency and applaud lawlessness. Not since the days when thousands passed the bier of the infamous John Dillinger and made his home a virtual shrine have we witnessed such a brazen af-front to our national conscience."

More interesting than Hoover's routine attack on the motion pic-ture industry is his implied equivalence between 1950s juvenile delin-quents and 1930s gangsters as a societal threat. American International Pictures made the association explicit in *Machine Gun Kelly* (1958)/*The Bonnie Parker Story* (1958), a teenpic double bill that cast 1930s gang-sters as 1950s-style juvenile delinquents. Indeed, vintage gangsterism underwent a major revival, with "scripters poring over gangland his-tory to come up with fresh names heretofore unbiopicked." The years 1959–60 alone witnessed *Al Capone; The Rise and Fall of Legs Diamond; Guns, Girls and Gangsters; The Purple Gang; Underworld U.S.A.; I, Mob-ster; Anatomy of a Syndicate;* and *Some Like It Hot,* Billy Wilder's surpris-ingly violent comedy of sexual manners set in the Roaring Twenties. Such films played to the audience's fascination with contemporary criminality while offering temporal distance and the nostalgic assur-ance of traditional solutions.

To explain the violence of their featured characters, the classic gang-ster films characteristically offered a sort of social critique that came to be known as "Warner Bros. environmentalism." The poverty and neg-lect of slum life, the evil influences of bad companions, cruel reform schools, or the lack of honest work—in short, society—were blamed for adult criminality. Tom Powers in *The Public Enemy* (1931) and Tony Camonte in *Scarface* (1932) were products of the mean streets; Ma Powers and Mama Camonte bore no responsibility for the monsters who sprang up under their aprons. The temptations of the inner city ("an environment that exists today in a certain strata of American life," as an exculpating preface to *The Public Enemy* puts it) defeated consci-entious Old World child rearing.

An early scene from *The Public Enemy* is illustrative. When young Tom Powers steals a pair of skates, his stern father takes a strap to the unrepentant son. Far from implicating the parents in Tom's subsequent criminality, the act of discipline deflects criticism from them. In the context of the early 1930s, this is a punishment commensurate with the boy's crime; a father who spared the rod in this case wouldn't be fulfilling his parental duties. The point is that an urban backdrop of bars, poolhalls, and low companions is more formative than mom and pop.

The first of the postwar juvenile delinquency films, Maxwell Shane's *City Across the River* (1948), held fast to the old faith. Narrated in a you-are-there fashion by newspaper columnist Drew Pearson, the film, an adaptation of Irving Shulman's popular paperback *The Amboy Dukes*, initially promises an intermediate position between the slum-centered environmentalism of 1930s Warner Bros. and the suburban Freudianism later popularized by *Rebel Without a Cause*. At his work desk, stationed in front of a bookshelf and behind an ABC microphone, the authoritative Pearson eyes the audience steadily and intones:

> For most of us, the city where juvenile crime flourishes always seems to be "the city across the river." But don't kid yourself. It could be *your* city, *your* street, *your* house. Although this story happens in Brooklyn, it could just as well have happened in any other large city where slum conditions undermine personal security and take their toll in juvenile delinquency. You may be lucky. You may be living where such conditions don't exist. [The screen dissolves to a wide pan of the Brooklyn skyline—viewed from Manhattan.] But for the next eighty-nine minutes you're a kid named Frankie Cusak going down a confused road, toward gangsterdom, toward murder.

Despite Pearson's admonitions against complacency, the bulk of his monologue, and especially the distancing point-of-view shot that inaugurates the entry into Brooklyn, offers reassurance that juvenile delinquency is indeed something that happens elsewhere. Living in a squalid tenement apartment with his parents and kid sister, protagonist Frankie (Peter Fernandez) is a good boy who falls in with a bad gang called the Amboy Dukes. Again, the street and not the home breeds criminality in the young. Frankie's parents both work long hours—in the first sequence, Mom misses his birthday because she needs to get in some overtime—but they are mainly absolved from culpability. Although no postwar mom who spends time out of the house can be totally guiltless, Frankie's parents demonstrate proper concern and exemplary self-sacrifice. When Frankie becomes involved in petty crime, Mom and Dad resolve to remove their son from the evil environs; they take the family savings and buy a small house in the suburbs. Offering a social solution soon contradicted by historical experience, *City Across the River* presents a clean suburban home as the remedy for street-born

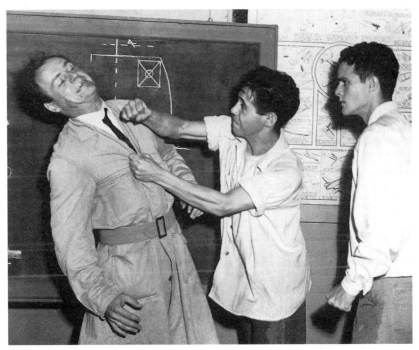

Early blackboard jungle: a shop teacher takes it on the chin in *City Across the River* (1949). (Museum of Modern Art Film Stills Archive: Courtesy of Universal Pictures)

delinquency. Ripe for recovery, Frankie proudly shows his gang around the empty house his parents have arranged to purchase. But when the hospital expenses for Mom's emergency appendectomy eat up the down payment for the mortgage, an angry, bitter Frankie is back on the streets and in the poolrooms. Neither a concerned community worker nor a nice girlfriend can turn him around.

In a scene that points ahead to the more violent classroom disruption in *Blackboard Jungle*, Frankie and his friend Benny instigate a rowdy disruption of shop class. This still being the 1940s, the overthrow of school authority is short-lived: the principal arrives, asserts control, and suspends the entire class. After school, Frankie and Benny confront the shop teacher, and in the ensuing scuffle Benny accidentally kills him with a zip gun. The pair avoids suspicion for a time, but the law comes down hard on the Amboy Dukes. As the police close in, Frankie's desperation is fed by his estrangement from his gang, his girl, and his partner in crime. Having squabbled with the Dukes and squealed on Benny, Frankie has isolated himself not only from the sanctioned institutions of parent culture—school, the community center, the family—but from his subcultural associations as well. For this juvenile, delinquency exacts a terribly high price.

As if unwilling to acknowledge the depressing consequences of its own observations, however, *City Across the River* wraps up by embracing the same complacency its opening lines cautioned against. After a climactic struggle in which Benny falls to his death from the roof of the tenement and Frankie is driven away in a police car through the grim, night-for-night streets, narrator Pearson returns on screen. "This is Drew Pearson again. Perhaps you'd like to meet the Dukes as they really are," he suggests from his well-lit office. With an obliging cut to the motion picture's soundstage and a bouncy tune on the soundtrack, Pearson introduces, one by one, the nice young actors who have played the mean street gang. Of the actor featured as the knife-wielding psychotic, Pearson confides, "He's not really crazy." Within a few years, in film fiction and in social fact, neither Hollywood nor the nation would be so confident about the containment of the juvenile menace.

The juvenile delinquent of the 1950s was a terrifying crime problem because he resisted a reassuring socioeconomic analysis, especially if (as was increasingly the case) he came from a fairly well-off background. In 1957, more in confusion than in anger, an editorial in the *Wall Street Journal* quoted the findings of the Kefauver committee: "For almost every case when you can demonstrate socio-economic depression in an area where a delinquent child lives, you can find a comparable child surrounded by luxury. . . . If poverty is the cause of delinquency, we should be singularly free of it. We are not."

An affluent culture demanded alternative explanations for delinquent behavior. Borrowing from the wider social discourse on the subject, and calling into service a pair of classic oppositions in Western political thought, the j.d. films improvised two answers, one soft, one hard; one rooted in the philosophical lineage of Jean-Jacques Rousseau, the other in Thomas Hobbes. The "softie" j.d. films have an "enlightened" liberal orientation that in filmic terms hark back to the social consciousness of *Dead End* (1937) and *Angels with Dirty Faces* (1938), though their immediate inspiration was the noble *Rebel Without a Cause*. In place of the curative power of socioeconomic reform, they substitute the era's dominant Freudianism. The "hard-nosed" j.d.

films are patterned after the nasty and brutish vision of *Blackboard Jungle*; these are Hobbesian melodramas that condemn the delinquent at the same time that they relish his antisocial energy.

The softie j.d. films feature young criminals more sinned against than sinning; these delinquents are cast as victims of a hostile home—not social—environment. The Freudian temper of the 1950s offered no prescription as formulaic as Warner Bros. environmentalism. Departing from values held even by the reputably "subversive" gangster films, they imply that there is something very wrong with the American family—or, more precisely, American parents. ("Better children," said the Senate, "can only come from better parents.") This outlook turns the moral universe of classical Hollywood cinema upside down. In the 1930s and 1940s, parents were more likely to be victims of their children than the other way around. The ungrateful brats spawned by the likes of Stella Dallas and Mildred Pierce supported a thriving two-hankie genre. For reasons that have as much to do with the popular dissemination of Freudian psychology as with the shift in audience, the softie j.d. films reverse the pattern. In an oft-cited scene from *The Wild One*, Marlon Brando is beat up by the citizens of the town his gang has besieged. Unimpressed with their blows, he mutters "My father hit harder than that." In *Rebel Without a Cause*, the parents are weak, awful, uptight, or absent. In *The Young Stranger* (1957), James MacArthur is neglected by his preoccupied father. In *Fear Strikes Out* (1957), Boston Red Sox fielder Jimmy Piersall (Tony Perkins) is driven to a nervous breakdown by his overbearing baseball dad. ("If it hadn't been for him standing behind me and pushing me and driving me, I wouldn't be where I am today!" Piersall blurts out to his sanitarium psychiatrist.)

No one turned more regularly to the theme of juvenile delinquency or better articulated the liberal line than writer Reginald Rose, three of whose teleplays on the subject were adapted for the big screen in one eight-month period: *Crime in the Streets* (November 1956), *Twelve Angry Men* (February 1957), and *Dino* (June 1957). Although the hugely popular *Twelve Angry Men* is only tangentially concerned with the j.d. problem (the defendant on trial is an adolescent charged with killing his abusive father), *Crime in the Streets* and *Dino*, both from Allied Artists, give full play to the actions of teenage criminals and the arguments over what Rose called "the motivations behind this strange, self-destructive, antisocial drive." *Crime in the Streets* favors sociology and *Dino* psychology, but disciplinary boundaries are crossed incessantly in the search for an explanation that squares doctrinaire liberalism with contemporary conditions. In both films, as in *Twelve Angry Men*, Rose's auteurist contribution to the debate over causality is child abuse (physical beating, not sexual violation). Even among the lower classes, environmentalism alone is not sufficient reason for an adolescent gone bad.

Bosley Crowther to the contrary, *Crime in the Streets*, directed by Don Siegel from a Rose teleplay originally broadcast by the *Elgin Hour* on March 8, 1955, is a first-rate urban melodrama. The mood is claustrophobic, the message passionate, and the look evocative at once of 1930s Warner Bros. melodrama and 1940s film noir. Virtually all the action occurs in a dead-end street lined with tenements and peopled by working-class ethnics, an inner-city landscape of darkened alleys, nighttime violence, and forbidding shadows. The opening set piece is a rollicking rumble between the Hornets and the Dukes, a nasty affair punctuated by blades, wrenches, and two-by-fours. The gang warfare serves to establish the j.d. credentials of three Hornets—leader Frank Dane (John Cassavetes), Lou Macklin (Mark Rydell), and tagalong Baby (Sal Mineo)—and to lend urgency to the mission of settlement-house worker Mr. Wagner (James Whitmore), a born Big Brother who is forever offering the boys dances, pool, and basketball as a substitute for zip guns, street hassles, and rumbles.

Wagner has a tough task of reclamation, his charges being decidedly more damaged psychically and dangerous socially than the teenage trio in *Rebel Without a Cause*. In the context of the times, the triangle is not merely disturbed but downright perverse: the homoerotic subtext of *Rebel* breaks to the surface with raw explicitness in *Crime in the Streets*. All toothy grin and limp wrist, Lou is an oily sociopath enamored of violence and given to single-entendre overtures to Frank ("I'm leaving now. Ain't you gonna kiss me good-bye?" or "You and me and Baby make three."). Frank, presumably the "salvageable" delinquent, is only slightly removed from the beyond-the-pale perversity of the weasel-faced Lou: it is he who proposes that the trio kill a bothersome old neighbor, to which Lou responds with almost sexual enthusiasm ("This is our first," says Frank. "How do you feel?" "Crazy, man," hisses Lou.).

The abnormality of the trio, their estrangement from peer as well as parent culture, is made clear when the rest of the Hornets balk at actually murdering someone. In teenpics, the true measure of maladjustment is the response of fellow teenagers. As outcasts from the gang no less than from adult society, Frank, Lou, and the impressionable Baby forfeit the representational possibilities of a Jim Stark or even an Artie West: the teenage audience embraces the stylish loner, not the creepy pariah. Frank has little to recommend him as a teen role model: a bundle of nerves, rotten to his mother and threatening to his younger brother, he behaves like an authentic head case, not a politely troubled "problem adolescent." He has a maddening (and symbolic) phobia about being touched. When Lou playfully smacks him, Frank throws a near-homicidal fit. The root cause, implied but not shown, is the physical abuse inflicted on Frank by a long-gone father.

Given the degree of delinquent derangement in *Crime in the Streets*, the proffered diagnosis and prescriptions seem less than reassuring. In a long dialogue with Baby's confused Old World father, Wagner, the appointed spokesman for Rose-colored liberalism, expounds at great length in tight close-up when Pops says the only way to cope with "these kids" is to beat them:

> *Wagner:* We're not talking about wild animals. We're talking about tough, angry kids. You can beat 'em up, they just get stronger and tougher. You send 'em to jail, maybe you wreck 'em for good. Those aren't the answers. . . .
>
> *Pops:* What are the answers?
>
> *Wagner:* We try to understand. We try to remember that kids don't get that way without good reason. We listen, we sympathize, and we talk. It's not easy, but it's the only way we can work. You can't tell a kid to be good. He's got too many reasons to be bad. So we're patient and every now and then we get to one of the really wild ones. Then we can do some good—maybe.

Wagner has his required heart-to-heart with Frank, but Frank gets the better of the sociological debate: "It's not because you want to help us," he notes reasonably. "It's because you're scared to death of us. It's because you shake in your pants every time you see us in the streets. . . . You're not coming up here to make things better for me." Frank is eventually reclaimed, but precisely how is left obscure. When the long-planned knifing of the neighbor is finally imminent, Frank hesitates only momentarily before resolving to plunge the blade in. Only the physical intercession of his little brother stops the murder. Immediately afterward, Frank is ready to accept the shoulder of the ever-present Mr. Wagner.

Rose's *Dino* (1957) delves into home-inspired delinquency in greater depth. Based on a successful *Studio One* teleplay and given crisply efficient direction by Thomas Carr, *Dino* reveals how far Hollywood criminology has come since the 1930s. Over the title sequence, thirteen-year-old Dino Manetti (Sal Mineo) helps murder an elderly warehouse guard who has stumbled on a nighttime heist. As the film proper begins, a hardened Dino awaits release from the state reformatory. Following a quick pro forma knife fight, some words of wisdom from his parole officer (Frank Faylon), and a meeting with an understanding settlement-house psychiatrist (Brian Keith), Dino returns home to find things much as he left them. Neither parent has bothered to take time off work to meet the long-absent son. Mom is a cold fish ("I guess you're too big to be kissed"); Dad is a louse who scolds Dino for the burden he's been and tells him to "behave like a decent citizen." Only younger brother Tony offers a sincere welcome home and a fraternal embrace. Dad goes back to reading his newspaper.

During sessions with "the skull doctor" ("Talking—that's how you learn about yourself"), Dino gradually reveals the source of his anger and violence: his father beat him. Immediately after this confession, Dino spots an elderly janitor outside the doctor's office and flashes on the murdered warehouse guard. The psychiatrist need not connect the Freudian dots for a 1950s audience: in killing the guard, Dino was merely acting out some well-founded Oedipal aggression. Dad himself seems to understand as much. In the subsequent scene, he tells Dino to stay away from the settlement house. "Now they're blaming me for the son I got," he screams. "It's my fault, huh?" Dino goads him into a confrontation: "Why don't you smack me? Yeah, just like old times. You've been doing it since I was old enough to stand up!" Dad complies, repeatedly. That night, Dino enters his parents' bedroom and puts a gun to his father's head. Tony tries to stop him, but only a look at his sleeping mother makes Dino reconsider.

At the next therapy session, Dino breaks down and tearfully relives his abused upbringing. On father: "What'd he want to hit me for, the dirty crumb? Even on my birthday." On mother: "I don't remember no one ever kissing me." On them both: "All they ever wanted was me outta there—so I went to reform school." The shrink tells Dino, and presumably the audience, not to blame his parents ("What they did to you, someone else did to them"), but every other detail in the film says otherwise.

In part, stacking the deck against Mom and Dad is a calculated exploitation strategy: even serious "adult" treatments such as *The Young Stranger* tilted their campaigns at teens. But as products of adult screenwriters and directors, these films reveal as much about parental confu-

Family mediators: the "skull doctor" (Brian Keith) ministers to Sal Mineo in
Dino (1957). (Museum of Modern Art Film Stills Archive)

sion as they do about teenage rebellion. Almost always, delinquent and
parent alike must rely on the offices of a kindly social worker to repair
familial damage. (The juvenile officer played by Ed Platt in *Rebel Without a Cause* was the clear model.) Unable to handle things themselves,
1950s families require outside experts: James Whitmore's settlement-
house worker in *Crime in the Streets*, Brian Keith's psychiatrist in *Dino*,
James Gregory's sympathetic cop in *The Young Stranger*, even Jack
Webb's kind-hearted drill instructor in *The D.I.* (1957).

Calling in a social worker would have been unthinkable for an earlier filmic parent. From 1936 to 1946, Judge Hardy of MGM's popular Andy Hardy series effortlessly solved all his son's adolescent crises
with one "man-to-man" talk per picture. Meddlesome priests in the
mold of Bing Crosby's Father O'Malley in *Going My Way* (1944) were
among the few privileged outsiders permitted to inject themselves into
family affairs. Although the mediating agents played by Platt and his ilk
fulfill something of an analogous function by redeeming the families
they minister to, in accord with the postwar era's more secular outlook,

they lack a clerical collar. Also, unlike the priesthood of classical Hollywood, the presence of these professional repairmen signifies the decline of parental competence and control.

The fierce autonomy of teenage life and the inability of parents to penetrate it was a change in familial relations to which mainstream family pictures had trouble adapting. For example, *Andy Hardy Comes Home* (1958), MGM's attempt to update its most successful series, failed miserably at the box office. In what must have seemed at the time an exploitation natural, Mickey Rooney was resurrected and cast as parent to his real-life eight-year-old son. Generously padded with "flashback" film clips from the original series, *Andy Hardy Comes Home* might well have been unearthed from a prewar time capsule, had it not marked itself as a product of the 1950s with the tacit acknowledgment that Andy Hardy as father is less formidable than old Judge Hardy: unlike the judge, the updated model doesn't have an adolescent to contend with. *New York Times* critic Richard Nasan noted the displacement in time: "It recalls the golden days of the motion picture when patrons poured money into the box office to confirm their faith in the happy ending. . . . The main trouble is that the world itself—and the people who go to the movies—have aged more rapidly in their taste for entertainment."

Actually, the mass audience had not matured; it had grown younger and been liberated from the kind of social restraints personified by old Judge Hardy. Despite the peripheral presence of ersatz "teen sensation" Johnny Weissmuller Jr., *Andy Hardy Comes Home* deleted adolescence from the series whose dramatic center it had once been—and thus proclaimed its contemporary irrelevance. The film's end title promised: "To Be Continued." It wasn't.

Where the softie j.d. films speak to causes and offer a cure for juvenile delinquency, the hard-nosed films are mainly concerned with consequences: random violence. The dangerous young punks of the hard-nosed j.d. film are energetic, creepy, and a genuine menace to the polis. Though a psychological explanation may be offered for their derangement, the emphasis is on caging, not curing, these sickies. *Blackboard Jungle*'s Artie West is the immediate model, but West in turn was part of a new criminal type that emerged on screen in the postwar period. These criminals possessed none of the irresistible élan of the early Cagney or Bogart. Incarnated most memorably by Dan Duryea in *Woman in the Window* (1944) and *Scarlet Street* (1945), Richard Widmark in *Kiss of Death* (1948), and Lee Marvin in *The Big Heat* (1953) and *The Wild One* (1954), these were psycho-sociopaths who were truly beyond the pale. They pushed old ladies in wheelchairs down staircases and threw coffee in their girlfriends' faces; they were not tragic heroes but terrifying scum who richly deserved their end-reel fates. The old pros Cagney and Bogart themselves brought a new, twisted edge to the hard cases they played in *White Heat* (1949) and *In a Lonely Place* (1950), respectively.

In *The Wild One*, Lee Marvin's portrayal of the sadistic biker Chino provided the transitional figure that established the association between the young (but still "adult") psycho of the crime melodrama and the juvenile psycho debuted by Vic Morrow in the *Blackboard Jungle*. Like his older brother, the j.d. psycho warrants harsh justice, not understanding; he radiates a wholly different level of disturbance than cuddly Dino. In AA's *Joy Ride* (1958), for example, a demented young car thief is tormented by a former victim (Regis Toomey), who forces the hood at gunpoint to risk his life behind the wheel of a careening auto. (The appearance of Toomey, an icon of common-man decency in many classic Hollywood films, gives the retribution a special resonance.) In Columbia's *No Time to Be Young* (1957), a bloodthirsty punk (Robert Vaughn) kills because he likes to watch people die. Paramount's *The Young Captives* (1959) features "a disturbed young man who gives even less thought to killing than he does to combing his hair."

By the end of the decade, the milder maladjustments of *Dino* and *The Young Stranger* had effectively been overtaken by a reptilian young psycho who, in mainstream films and teenpics alike, became perhaps the era's most familiar screen villain. Clearly, liberal sympathy with the "troubled teen" was wearing thin. Twentieth Century-Fox's *Compulsion* (1959), a powerful treatment of the Leopold-Loeb thrill killing of 1924, was advertised as "a study in youthful behavior": "You know why we did it?" shouted the ad copy. "Because we damn well felt like doing it!" AA submitted *The Cry-Baby Killer* (1958), featuring a very disturbed Jack Nicholson, and released *Crime and Punishment, USA* (1959), an update of the Dostoyevsky classic with George Hamilton in the Raskolnikov role. All this was prelude to Alfred Hitchcock's *Psycho* (1960), in which teen-magazine favorite Tony Perkins, whose screen persona was always a bit on the odd side, changed the bathing habits of a nation. (Besides appearing in his own hard-nosed vehicles, the j.d. psycho occurs frequently as a foil for and temptation to a troubled but more human young hero; in a virtual reprise of his definitive Artie West role, Vic Morrow did exactly this opposite Elvis Presley in *King Creole* [1958].)

If the disease that was juvenile delinquency knew no class bias, Hollywood nonetheless accorded one class preferential treatment. The unredeemable j.d. psycho sprang from the lower orders, the troubled but salvageable youth from the middle class. On screen, few suburban teenagers displayed the insane bloodlust of the urban street punk, and fewer still were held accountable when they did. In Universal's *The Unguarded Moment* (1956), for example, the j.d. psycho at first seems to have penetrated the middle-class veneer. The opening sequence depicts a nighttime street scene, the aftermath of a rape and murder. By way of association, not juxtaposition, the noirish tableau—ambulance, police, reporters, and a shrouded female body—jump-cuts into the serene facade of Ogden Central High School, title credits, and a cheerleading practice supervised by music teacher Lois Conway (Esther Williams). Miss Conway is the typical 1950s career girl, a pretty, bright, and unattached woman who has no business holding down a real job. Inevitably, this threatening anomaly is herself soon threatened by a series of anonymous mash notes. The main suspect is the school's model student and football star, Leonard Bennett (John Saxon, UI's James Dean entry). Leonard assaults Miss Conway in a darkened locker room, breaks into her home, and gets her suspended from the high school by accusing *her* of harassing *him*. As in *Blackboard Jungle*, it is the adult teacher who is the target of the high school students. The boys snicker in the halls, the girls stare and murmur, and the school intercom broadcasts nasty innuendos. Even the principal believes Leonard's impassioned denials, not Miss Conway's unlikely accusations.

Despite everything, Miss Conway thinks Leonard is salvageable. Ignoring the advice of the police lieutenant who is her emerging romantic interest, she refuses to press charges against Leonard. Still wearing the dress he ripped while manhandling her, she tells the police, "That was a high school student in the locker room—a child, just a boy." The lieutenant feels differently: "I'm only eighteen," Leonard whines. "So was Billy the Kid," he snaps.

In the end, Miss Conway's soft-headed psychology wins out over the lieutenant's hard-headed criminology. Leonard is another teenage victim of parental pathology. Raised in a motherless household by a perverse, misogynist father, Leonard has been forced to play out the impotent old man's dreams of physical prowess on the athletic field. As Mr. Bennett, character actor Edward Andrews portrays as demented and vile a patriarch as appears in 1950s cinema. He drums his hatred of women into young Leonard and warns him, "If you knock down what I've spent years building up, I'll break every bone in your body." Unwilling to go where the sexual tension between Leonard and Miss Conway leads, the film turns in its third act to a battle between Mr. Bennett and Miss Conway. Bennett breaks into her home, hides in her closet, and watches her undress. Enraged and aroused, he attacks her. Scared off by the arrival of the lieutenant, he returns to his suburban home to find himself locked out. Climbing up to Leonard's bedroom window, he calls futilely for his absent son to open the window before falling to his death. A coda assures the audience that Leonard, free of his father's influence, has cured his pathology: a photo shows a smiling, well-adjusted army private.

Whatever the diagnosis, virtually all delinquent films revel in their portrayal of juvenile mayhem at the same time that they preach the ultimate squelching of the perpetrators. Like their generic predecessors from the 1930s, they seek to justify their picturesque violence and stylish villains with an end-reel comeuppance by the forces of law and order. Thus, in United Artists' *The Delinquents*, a gang of surly punks spends its time slashing tires, pulling switchblades, robbing filling stations, drinking hard liquor, and kidnapping maidens before a Production Code finale. Throughout the havoc, various oldsters voice transparent protestations of concern over the "problem of juvenile delinquency."

This rhetoric had the same function and level of sincerity as the disclaimers tacked onto *The Public Enemy* and *Scarface*. A common teenpic dodge, the purpose of these pronouncements was to deflect anticipated objections from watchdog parent groups. Columbia pioneered the strategy with a publicity campaign for *The Wild One* that sought to "stress its value in the nationwide fight against juvenile delinquency." "This is a shocking story," promised a brief pretitle preface. "It could never take place in most American towns—but it did in this one. It is a public challenge not to let it happen again." Whereupon Brando and his motorcycle gang roar forward into center screen, buzzing like hornets past the stationary camera fixing the line of sight. Similarly, a paragraph-length crawl, accompanied by a portentous drumbeat, introduced *Blackboard Jungle*:

We, in the United States, are fortunate to have a school system that is a tribute to our communities and to our faith in American youth. Today we are concerned with juvenile delinquency—its causes—and its effects. We are especially concerned when this delinquency boils over into our schools. The scenes and incidents depicted here are fictional. However, we believe that public awareness is a first step toward a remedy for any problem. It is in this spirit and with this faith that
BLACKBOARD JUNGLE
was produced.

After serving this notice, the film cuts immediately to a loud mix of "Rock Around the Clock" and a blackboard-printed credit sequence.

For transparent duplicity, *Teenage Crime Wave* outdid the competition. "Over 25% of the crimes committed in this country are perpetrated by teenagers," warned a notation on the film's advertising one-sheet. "Only an aroused public can put an end to this. We hope this picture will open your eyes." Meanwhile, exhibitors playing *Teenage Crime Wave* were urged to concoct a lobby display of teenage gang weapons and supplement it with stills from the film.

The more controversial the teenpic, the more it tried to present itself as a public service. For United Artists' *Cry Tough* (1959), an unusually sexy j.d. teenpic and one of the few with an old-fashioned environmentalist outlook, the company's publicity encouraged tie-ins with "juvenile aid groups of all kinds as well as civic societies, government agencies, and other organizations fighting juvenile delinquency and gangsterism." Such tactics were especially favored by the brief cycle of "dope" teenpics that arose in the late 1950s after a change in Production Code regulations in 1956 permitted the depiction of narcotics on screen. Although the scale of drug (and alcohol) use among 1950s teenagers never approached 1960s proportions, dope had seeped into enough high schools to cause some stirrings of parental concern and public awareness. To take one notable touchstone: in William Menninger's *How to Be a Successful Teenager* (1954), drugs were simply beyond the bounds of conceivable teenage activity; four years later, for an updated edition titled *Blueprint for Teenage Living* (1958), Menninger felt obliged to include chapters on "Facts about Alcohol" and "Facts about Narcotics," which blended straightforward information ("Benzedrine keeps you awake longer but doesn't help you study better") with motivational theory ("Having friends, being liked and accepted by the group is important to everyone, at every age. But it's especially

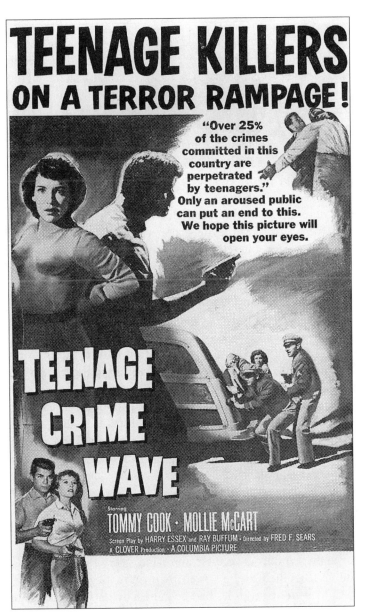

Teenage Crime Wave (1955): the one-sheet called for an "aroused public," while the publicity department suggested exhibitors display zip guns in theater lobbies. (U.S. Library of Congress collection: Courtesy of Columbia Pictures)

important to teenagers."). AIP's *The Cool and the Crazy* (1958) and Albert Zugsmith's *High School Confidential* (1958) both sought the cooperation of high school authorities in their efforts to "expose" dope peddling.

Despite these cynical efforts, j.d. teenpics could be a mixed blessing, as the controversy over *The Delinquents* illustrates. Though released in 1957 amid a glut of j.d. teenpics, *The Delinquents* was produced in 1955 on the heels of *Blackboard Jungle*; film historian Todd McCarthy reports that United Artists grossed nearly $1 million on an investment of $150,000. Opposition to the film was vehement. *National Parent Teacher* almost ran out of pejoratives, branding it "unsavory," "unprepossessing," "unpleasant," "pointless," and "tasteless." Voices from within the industry were equally negative, condemning its "flat-out stressing of teenage excesses on a wholesale scale." A big-city exhibitor assailed it as "at best an inept amateurish job of picture making which will do nothing toward increasing theater attendance, and at worst a nasty little film designed to appeal to nasty minded people." Edward W. Linder, president of the Independent Exhibitors, Inc., of New England and the New England Drive-in Association, sent United Artists a telegram urging the company to withdraw the film from distribution, an unusually serious move from the exhibition end of the business. According to Linder, *The Delinquents* was "harmful to the industry in general and drive-ins in particular."

By "drive-ins in particular" Linder was doubtless referring to a scene in which the gang goes to a drive-in theater to slash automobile tires. *Motion Picture Herald*'s Curtis Mees expressed similar concerns: "The subject of juvenile delinquency is of such serious proportions as to deserve the utmost care and consideration when used as a screen treatment. Trading on this for dollar values without thinking of the potential harm which may be done—harm which can have a very direct effect right in the theaters where such pictures are shown—does the industry a grave injustice."

Like many exhibitors, Linder and Mees were more worried about juvenile violence before the screen than on it. Beginning in the early 1950s, vandalism by juveniles had become a major problem for theater owners. In the big cities, young toughs had been known to fling ushers from balconies. Small-town teenage moviegoers were seldom that demonstrative, but they were often disruptive and occasionally belligerent to theater managers who told them to be quiet, take their feet off seats, or refrain from hurling objects at the screen. In *The Young*

Wild in the seats: troubled teens cause exhibitor headaches in *The Young Stranger* (1957). (Museum of Modern Art Film Stills Archive: Courtesy of Universal Pictures)

Stranger, James MacArthur belts a pushy theater manager for precisely this kind of supervision. Characteristically attending in small groups, teenage boys caused the most trouble, those with dates having other diversions. On occasion, as with *Blackboard Jungle* or an early rock 'n' roll teenpic, actual violence would erupt in a theater: a fight between patrons or an altercation with an usher. Random destruction of property was an expensive and growing problem: trashing lobby displays, slashing seats, and, at drive-ins, speeding off with speakers. According to *Variety,* the young hoodlums caused some exhibitors "more trouble than television":

> Damage runs into thousands of dollars each year. M. Idzal, managing director of the 5,000 seat Fox Theater [in Detroit], states that most of the trouble is caused by teenagers traveling in gangs. . . . "Our problem is not out of control," Idzal said. "We try to screen them out, but it is a difficult job and they frequently get by us. Some sneak in through the exits and cause trouble. They are rough and tough. They descend on the theater in packs, usually on Sunday afternoons. Their ages are from 10 up." . . . Another exib said seat repairs is a never-ending job in his six houses. A crew is kept constantly busy repairing seats slashed by hoodlums. This theaterman stopped

the sale of suckers because youngsters were throwing them through the screens.

Better Theaters, a monthly trade journal published in *Motion Picture Herald*, responded to exhibitor concerns with advice on how to control the "conduct of youngsters, including teenagers—often the worst offenders—while they are members of a motion picture theater audience." Editor George Schutz landed the tactics of one Walter Kessler, a theater manager who supplemented regular usher patrols with "a uniformed county sheriff complete with Sam Browne belt, pistol, etc." The Federation of Film Councils reported that "juvenile deportment on weekends improved with uniformed officers in attendance and when proper dress is required." "Youngsters must be taught to come to the motion picture theater to enjoy the performance for what it is intended to be—and to be bored quietly if the picture turns out to be over their heads," wrote Schutz. Interestingly, although local civic groups worried most about the incitement-to-riot potential of controversial teenpics like *The Delinquents* and *Rock Around the Clock*, many exhibitors agreed with Schutz that the "boring" adult films stimulated greater teen violence. "The youngsters get fidgety and look around for something to do. Then watch out," said one.

Like other controversial teenpic cycles, however, the j.d. films earned profits that outweighed problems. Until his well-mannered brother, the "clean teen," overtook him at the decade's close, the rebellious teenager ruled the teenpic screens, bequeathing an enduring image of the 1950s delinquent as a semiarticulate, switchblade-toting poseur in nascent revolt against an oppressive parent culture. His only real competitors for teenpic turf were the supernatural creatures who were even more alienated than he was.

6

The Horror Teenpics

It used to be that you had a torture scene in a picture and no one seemed to object. Now, they turn on the sound loud and the screams come at you from all sides. Nothing very new about it—we're just working at it harder!

A movie producer, 1955

Teenagers who see those tough juvenile delinquent films can go out and buy themselves a bicycle chain. But no one can go out and make a monster.

Herman Cohen, 1958

or exploitation filmmakers, *The Curse of Frankenstein* was a blessing. Produced in 1956 by Britain's Hammer Films and released Stateside by Warner Bros. in July 1957, the stylish $270,000 horror show earned domestic grosses of nearly $2 million by the end of the year. In the process, *The Curse of Frankenstein* fathered the most prolific and durable of all 1950s exploitation cycles—the horror teenpic. For the next several years, the motion picture industry applied itself to the perfunctory production and imaginative marketing of a disparate collection of immensely profitable teenpic terror that left no film formula unviolated. There was a fright menu for every moviegoing taste: "straight" horror movies (*Horror of Dracula* [1958]), science fiction (SF) horror movies (*The Fly* [1958]), comedic horror movies (*How to Make a*

Monster [1958]), vice horror movies (*Jack the Ripper* [1959]), and even western horror movies (*The Fiend Who Walked the West* [1958]).

Public Domain Monsters

The rock 'n' roll and j.d. teenpics are inseparable from the 1950s front pages, but horror movies, even at their most topical, have a timelessness beyond their historical moment. As an exploitation hook, horror is anomalous, lending tradition to a moviemaking strategy defined by the immediate and ephemeral. The genre has a rich filmic, not to mention literary, history. The German expressionist classics *The Cabinet of Doctor Caligari* (1919) and *Nosferatu* (1922) are its earliest and most honored antecedents. At Universal Pictures in the 1930s, James Whale's *Frankenstein* (1931) and Tod Browning's *Dracula* (1931) advanced the bloodline, and at RKO in the 1940s, the producer-director team of Val Lewton and Jacques Tourneur did credit to the heritage with moody melodramas such as *Cat People* (1942) and *I Walked with a Zombie* (1943). Throughout Hollywood's classical era, filmic fright had a steady and respectable, albeit minor, place in studio production. But after World War II, the horror film proper all but disappeared from the American screen. Perhaps recent history in itself was sufficiently monstrous: memories of the real-life terrors of wartime and the indelible newsreels of the Holocaust made Hollywood attempts at serious fright look amateurish by comparison. Next to Buchenwald, Dachau, and Auschwitz, the once-terrifying trio of movie horror—Frankenstein, Dracula, and the Wolfman—seemed like hale fellows well met, almost laughably harmless. They were soon relegated to straight men for the likes of Abbott and Costello and the Three Stooges. Not even the moppets screamed.

In the early 1950s, the dormant market for filmic fright suddenly awoke. A trio of medium-budget and highly successful George Pal science fiction films (*Destination Moon* [1950], *When Worlds Collide* [1951], and *War of the Worlds* [1953]) and the Arctic horror of RKO's *The Thing* (1951) launched a trend toward alien beings and nuclear mutants that led eventually to the rejuvenation of the humanlike monsters of Gothic tradition.

In terms of taxonomy, where the science fiction creatures leave off and the horror monsters begin is a classification problem best left to the fanzines. Movies like *It Came from Outer Space* (1953) or *The Fly* (1958) quickly muddle any questions of generic purity. There are, however, some commonly acknowledged points of divergence. Generally the more identifiably human the beast, the more horrific. Giant insects, gelatinous blobs, reptilian life-forms, hideous aliens, robots, and atomic hybrids tend to be the province of SF. *Invasion of the Body Snatchers* (1956) is thus considered a horror, not an SF, landmark, because the extraterrestrial pods take human form. In terms of formal narrative, science fiction characteristically concerns an external threat, horror an internal one; SF is communal, horror individual; SF highlights hardware, horror psychology; SF incites wonder, horror fear.

By these standards, science fiction, not horror, was the era's preferred fantasy form. The atomic bomb, particularly the awesome explosion of the hydrogen bomb on November 1, 1952, is the essential background. RKO's low-low-budget *Killers from Space* (1954) offers a representative, if especially schematic, version of this sort of atom-to-alien transference. Its precredit establishing sequence is composed almost entirely of stock newsreel footage documenting the military preparations leading to an atomic bomb test. The title, *Killers from Space*, is superimposed over an aerial view of the earthbound explosion, the letters on screen expanding and exploding outward in pace with the ballooning mushroom cloud. On this level, the killers originate not in space but from ground zero. The anxiety for species as well as individual survival, the fears of what science hath wrought, and the transparent projection of a terrestrial threat onto extraterrestrials underlie virtually all the period's SF movies.

A requisite corollary to the atomic menace was the communist one. Judging from the documentary footage compiled in *The Atomic Cafe* (1982), the era's civil defense films are only slightly more instructive than the typical Hollywood invasion scenario. For modern viewers, *The Thing* or *Invasion of the Body Snatchers* allegorically conjures up McCarthyite paranoia with a vividness that documentaries such as *Point of Order!* (1963) or *Hollywood on Trial* (1976) are lucky to match. As with radioactive behemoths, alien menaces and biological mutants express earthbound threats. At the height of Hollywood's brief foray into HUAC-inspired agitprop, UA's anticommunist SF hallucination *Red Planet Mars* (1952) exposed the generic secret, and later science fiction was no less discreet about the Soviet subsurface. In Universal's *The Deadly Mantis* (1957), as much a manual on American air defense as a meditation on entomological mutations, the threatening creature and communists are well-nigh interchangeable. As the title insect approaches Washington, D.C., officers of the Continental Air Command take to the television airwaves to issue double-edged instructions to some four hundred thousand members of the Civilian Ground Observer Corps. After the commanding general warns that "contrary to rumor and certain newspaper headlines, the so-called deadly mantis is no imaginary danger," a colonel from an advance radar interceptor base deep within the Arctic Circle addresses a montage of vigilant sky watchers:

> We have every reason to believe the mantis is flying south along the Gulf Stream and we believe it will be one of you devoted men and women of the Civilian Ground Observer Corps who will spot it next time it appears. . . . You ground observers are well trained in the identification of aircraft. . . . You spotters should listen for a loud droning sound much like that of a squadron of heavy bombers flying in formation. The Coast Guard and the Navy have been alerted and are standing guard on the eastern seaboard. If the mantis is sighted, the procedure will be the same as though an enemy aircraft has been sighted. Take no chances. Report any unusual flying object.

Less rich hermeneutically but more significant generically was Hollywood's advancing sophistication in special effects technology. Because even the skimpy budgets of early television could match the verisimilitude of a Buck Rogers serial, Hollywood was forced to up the f/x ante. Wider screens, stereophonic sound, and more elaborate models, makeup, matte jobs, and back-screen projection made the big-budget science fiction film an awesome viewing experience. Accompanying the bigger budgets were better scripts and actors, a certain costly realism and professional competence being necessary to attract the over-thirty sophisticates. One result was the emergence of a more serious, adult-oriented science fiction film. Productions such as Twentieth Century-Fox's relentlessly somber *The Day the Earth Stood Still* (1951) and Walt Disney's spectacular $5 million epic *20,000 Leagues Under the Sea* (1954) went after—and caught—a crossover audience of adults, adolescents, and kids. But perhaps by the time of MGM's *Forbidden Planet* (1956), a Freudian extraterrestrial update of *The Tempest* labeled "'Space Patrol' for adults," it was apparent that even successful adult space operas were not cost-efficient investments. Why gamble hundreds of thousands of dollars on special effects if a much smaller investment, a high-concept title, and energetic exploitation of the teen audience was, dollar for dollar, a better investment? A new kind of low-

budget fantasy film, filling the gap left by the death of the studio serials, made do with cheaper sets, inventive publicity, and a not-too-
discerning young audience. Pegged variously as creature features,
space operas, and thriller-chillers, these films constitute a historical
cycle, if not a genre. The trade papers had the best name for them:
"weirdies."

The Weirdies

In the early to mid-1950s, those low-budget motion pictures that
weren't formula westerns or crime melodramas—"oaters" or "mellers"
—were probably weirdies. "Weirdie" was inexact nomenclature for an
offbeat science fiction, fantasy, monster, zombie, or shock film, usually
of marginal financing, fantastic content, and ridiculous title. Con-
strained only by budget and technology, the weirdies knew no bounds
or shame; not since the wild days of the one-reelers had the American
movies given vent to imaginations so unhinged by speculative Darwin-
ism, so unhampered by established conventions. Having better reason
than most to feel a kinship with malformed and hyperthyroidic humans, teenagers were faithful followers of and sympathetic onlookers
to the plight of the hormonally disadvantaged; their own biological
state must have seemed equivalently capricious and uncontrollable.
The sudden swellings and shrinkings of adolescence, the inhabitation
of a body with a mind of its own, beset all sorts of screen creatures, but
the unadorned human frame grew and waned with a distinctly genital
sense of proportion. The hyberbolic proportions of *Cyclops* (1957), *The
Amazing Colossal Man* (1957), and *Attack of the 50 Ft. Woman* (1958) and
the disheartening diminution of *The Incredible Shrinking Man* (1957),
Attack of the Puppet People (1958), and even *tom thumb* (1958) are elastic
expressions of the ebb and flow of pubescent development.

   In one shape or another, sex is the open secret of every weirdie, the
intrinsic perversity, or weirdness, of a ripe desire for sexual congress
mingled with a virginal dread of closure. On screen, a 1950s couple
necking in a parked car is as likely to be interrupted by the Creature
from the Black Lagoon as by a cop with a flashlight. Obviously, too, a
rich vein of psychological dislocation and social estrangement runs
through the weirdies, signaled in readily decipherable shorthand in titles such as *Teenage Zombies* (1957), *Teenage Monster* (1958), and *Teenagers From Outer Space* (1959). A deeper sexual agenda began with

Invaders from Mars (1953), wherein the bodies of family members and friends are taken over by extraterrestrial psychologies. The impenetrability of the opposite sex is the true subtext of *Invasion of the Body Snatchers* and its distaff remake, *I Married a Monster from Outer Space* (1958), films that are less about communism and hidden spies than about marriage and gender dynamics.

Note, for example, how, almost alone among 1950s lovers, the romantic couple in *Invasion of the Body Snatchers* are both divorcees. "I'd hate to wake up one morning and find that you weren't you," says Miles to Becky, setting up the horror of his husbandly discovery that this isn't the woman he married at all: "I never knew fear until I kissed Becky." In the underrated *I Married a Monster from Outer Space*, perennial weirdie heroine Gloria Talbott actually marries a creature of the opposite species, an understandable lapse in discernment given the total separation of male and female spheres and psyche maintained throughout the film.

The weirdies paved the way for, and continued to thrive with, the subsequent cycle of horror teenpics unleashed in the marketplace after *The Curse of Frankenstein*. Beginning in 1954 with its surprise hit *The Creature From the Black Lagoon* (in 3-D), Universal-International spearheaded an industry-wide move to vaguely science-fictional monster-type movies. By mid-1956, UI planned the release, distribution, or production of twenty pictures "in the space or chiller-diller category." As *Variety* reported:

> Hollywood is on a new science fiction and horror kick. . . . These pictures, generally modest budget items, sometimes result in solid payoffs. . . . The main asset of the spacers and the chillers is their susceptibility to exploitation. They're ideally suited for saturation openings accompanied by extensive radio-tv campaigns covering a wide area. In many instances the coin saved in the production is added to the exploitation campaign. Also such pictures make excellent bookings during school holiday periods or when packaged, two science fiction, two horror films, or one of each.

In 1957, the trade journal submitted added evidence of the wisdom of UI's weirdie policy: "A standard practice of the film company has been to produce and release annually several features that broadly fall into the monster-horror-science fiction category. Generally, these pictures are low-budgeters costing $200,000 to $800,000. The releases have been more than satisfactory and have contributed greatly to Universal's coffers."

From 1954 to 1957, UI produced nine weirdies for approximately $4 million: *The Creature From the Black Lagoon* (1954), *Revenge of the Creature From the Black Lagoon* (1955), *This Island Earth* (1955), *Tarantula* (1955), *The Creature Walks Among Us* (1956), *Curucu, Beast of the Amazon* (1956), *The Mole People* (1956), *The Deadly Mantis* (1957), and *The Incredible Shrinking Man* (1957). Overall domestic gross on these nine was $8 million, "indicating a healthy profit during a period of general box office decline." UI's strategy was aped by other companies, the number of low- to medium-budget weirdies growing with awareness of their profitability.

Such fare remained a teenpic staple throughout the 1950s and beyond, but in 1957 there was a discernible shift away from SF-flavored weirdies toward Gothic horror. Ironically, television gave the movement its real impetus. At roughly the same time that *The Curse of Frankenstein* came to life theatrically, the specter haunting Hollywood's present ran headlong into the ghost of its past. In spring 1957, Screen Gems, Columbia Picture's television arm, purchased six hundred features for television syndication from the Universal-International film library, at a reported cost of $20 million. From this, Screen Gems put together a program of "52 of Universal's greatest spine-tingling films," including the original *Frankenstein* (1931), *Dracula* (1931), *The Invisible Man* (1933), and *The Wolf Man* (1941). Exploiting the Halloween tie-in, it offered the "shock theater" package to affiliate stations to show as they wished that October. Dozens of major television markets eagerly signed up, many improvising their own "monster of ceremonies" to host the screenings and provide the proper late-night "terrorvision" atmosphere. (The Code of the National Association of Radio and Television Broadcasters forbade horror shows before 9:30 P.M. because they were bad for children.) The first telecasts of the vintage horror movies earned huge ratings and created a television phenomenon—"the season's biggest sensation," according to *TV Guide*.

On television, the horror movies from Hollywood's vaults were more fun than fright. As "TV-oriented psychologist" Allan Fromme said of video horror, "It won't be pure horror except to children who happen to watch. The screen is too small, the set too much within control, the commercials too frequent to build the mood, the reality of who you are, where you are, is too insistent. . . . All it will do on TV is provide a smile with your milk and cookies at bedtime. After all, you have to be in the right frame of mind to buy the sponsor's product."

But if television had the edge in proximity, a darkened theater offered a more intense fright experience, not to mention the possibility of a scared date lunging for a friendly shoulder. With *The Curse of Frankenstein* a surprise theatrical hit and the Screen Gems package a ratings windfall, commercial moviemakers took heed and acted accordingly. One estimate put the "horribilia" count for 1957 at fifty-two films; the estimate for 1958 was seventy-five. SF technology gave way to spooky psychology as Hammer imports and Stateside imitators resurrected the spirit of the original *Frankenstein* and *Dracula*. No hyperthyroidic insect or bug-eyed alien from Planet X, the Frankenstein monster was "one of us," a recognizably human aberration.

Playing the drama straight and the gore realistic, the Hammer crew treated the monster with the respect due his exalted lineage: a company investigation concluded that "audiences preferred monsters closer to a sympathetic human form than completely 'out of this world.'" James Carreras, head of Britain's Hammer Film Productions, was inundated with offers from American film companies vying to distribute his distinctive *oeuvre* in the United States. An independent company, Hammer produced about six films a year, of which two or three were horror pictures. Carreras believed that an effective horror film demanded talent and top production values; he attributed Hammer's success to the new generation of moviegoers (teenagers) never having been exposed to the genuine item. Carreras had a craftsman's contempt for the accelerated production schedules and careless executions of Stateside exploitation film companies rushing into the horror market, though he personally claimed no particular devotion to the genre. At the height of Hammer's popularity, Carreras remarked, "I'm prepared to make Strauss waltzes tomorrow if they'll make money."

Refusing to sign with any one distributor, Carreras played bidders off against one another on a deal-by-deal basis. Universal acquired *Horror of Dracula* (1958), *The Brides of Dracula* (1960), *The Curse of the Werewolf* (1960, U.S. release June 1961), and *The Phantom of the Opera* (1961, U.S. release September 1962). United Artists, earlier distributors of Hammer's *The Quatermass Xperiment* (1955), also known as *The Creeping Unknown* (U.S. release April 1956), obtained a sequel of sorts, *Enemy from Space* (1957), as well as *The Hound of the Baskervilles* (1959); Columbia's prizes included *The Camp on Blood Island* (1958) and *The Revenge of Frankenstein* (1958); Warner Bros. got *X The Unknown* (1956, U.S. release July 1957); Twentieth Century-Fox secured *The Abom-*

inable Snowman (1957). The Hammer touch was so valued that American studios optioned their horror properties. The English studios refashioned Universal's *The Mummy* (1931) as *The Mummy* (1959) and Paramount's *The Man in Half Moon Street* (1945) as *The Man Who Would Cheat Death* (1959).

A homegrown crop of horror pics was harvested from the ground Hammer had seeded. AIP's *Blood of Dracula* (1957), *I Was a Teenage Werewolf* (1957), and *I Was a Teenage Frankenstein* (1957); United Artists' *The Return of Dracula* (1958); Allied Artists' *Daughter of Dr. Jekyll* (1957) and *Frankenstein-1970* (1958); and Astor's *Frankenstein's Daughter* (1959) rode on the coattails of presold monsters with public domain surnames. Citing *The Curse of Frankenstein* as the "big [box office] surprise" of the year, *Variety* provided a bemused litany of "shocker or exploitation items" that defined 1957's "short-budgeted crop of new features," a broad category that included rock 'n' roll and j.d. pictures but that was dominated by "sci-fi horror shockers": *The Hunchback of Notre Dame, The Invisible Boy, Enemy from Space, Love Slaves of the Amazons, The Monolith Monsters, Attack of the Crab Monsters, Not of This Earth, I Was a Teenage Frankenstein, I Was a Daughter of Dracula, The Amazing Colossal Man, The Viking Women and the Sea Serpent, Nude Invaders, Girl from 2,000,000 A.D.*, and *Reform School Girl.*

The next year the weirdies got weirder but no less profitable. Deftly balancing horror and SF angles in their teenpic double bills, Paramount and Twentieth Century-Fox made huge scores with *The Blob* (1958)/*I Married a Monster from Outer Space* (1958) and *The Fly* (1958)/*Space Master X-7* (1958), respectively. With such pairings, the weirdie bill balanced two related genres, much as other teenpic bills balanced j.d. and rock 'n' roll or male and female interests. Other examples include Columbia's *Earth vs. the Flying Saucers* (1956)/*The Werewolf* (1956); United Artists' *It! The Terror from Beyond Space* (1958)/*The Curse of the Faceless Man* (1958); and AIP's *I Was a Teenage Werewolf* (1957)/*Invasion of the Saucer Men* (1957). AIP offered an alternative combination, *I Was a Teenage Frankenstein* (1957)/*Blood of Dracula* (1957), which paired an adolescent monster (male) with an adolescent vampire (female). At one point the company concocted a novelty program package in which the second feature would be a sequel to the first: *End of the World*, the top half of the double bill, would deal with "events leading up to global finale," followed by *Last Woman on Earth*, featuring an actress from the preceding feature with seven surviving men. According to company head James H. Nicholson, AIP conceived of most of its properties in pairs: "We can put out a package for $400,000, then offer it to a theaterman for the same terms he would receive for one middle-bracket picture . . . and this way he's saved the trouble of going out to get a second feature."

Allied Artists disagreed with AIP's concept of complementary program packages, feeling that "putting two gangster pix together, or two mellers, actually builds both into greater potential than either would have paired with a feature of opposite theme or selected at random." AIP itself employed this tactic with *Machine Gun Kelly* (1958)/*The Bonnie Parker Story* (1958). At the same time, distributors and exhibitors adopted the simplest of all double-bill strategies: playing a popular old film with a current release.

As an exploitation strategy, the double bill had biology and culture on its side. An exhibitor explained its "social function" in teenage dating rituals: "A young couple go out to get away from home. They come to the theater. They don't want to be back two hours later. They may not absolutely want to see two pictures, but it makes them feel good to know they're getting two for the price of one, and it occupies the whole evening for them." In the early 1960s, the Drifters put it another way: "Saturday night at the movies / Who cares what picture you see / When you're dating with your baby / In the back row of the balcony?"

Weirdie filmmakers slyly aided exhibitors by boosting the theatricality of the weirdies within the weirdie itself. Thus *The Amazing Colossal Man* tears apart a Las Vegas drive-in while a necking couple in *Attack of the Puppet People* go to a drive-in to see *The Amazing Colossal Man*. William Castle took weirdie self-reflexivity to its logical conclusion by setting the climax of *The Tingler* (1959) in a silent movie theater where, during a screening of *Tol'able David* (1921), the tingler crawls up the leg of a distracted teenage girl fending off her grab-happy date.

Like other exploitation films, the weirdies strove to kept abreast of current affairs. While the Pentagon panicked over the Russian launch of *Sputnik*, teenpic moviemakers calmly prepared for the heightened box office interest in science fiction films, anticipating "a rush [of] . . . 'space matter'" that "could mean a new cycle, possibly replacing the current run of horror entries." As usual, producers rushed to file exploitable titles with the MPAA Title Registration Bureau. By one reckoning, forty-three science fiction film projects were announced the day after *Sputnik* was launched. Paramount immediately reissued George Pal's *Conquest of Space* (1954), an eerily prophetic tale of space satellites. ("Flash! Paramount has the picture that predicted today's headlines! Play it immediately!" urged the trade ads. "Cash in on history's biggest news!") Within days MGM had crafted a *Sputnik* tie-in for *The Invisible Boy* (1957). ("Not a re-issue! Never in movie annals such an opportunity to capitalize on the headlines!") Warner Bros. moved quickly with *Satellite in the Sky* (1956). (The company's trade ads teased rhetorically: "Has anyone got a picture about the satellite?") Republic came up with an alliterative double bill, *Satan's Satellites* (1958)/*Missile Monsters* (1958); Allied Artists put forth the deceptively titled mystery *Spy in the Sky* (1958); and UA hyped *The Lost Missile* (1958), in which a missile from outer space disintegrates cities until a Nike missile with a modified nuclear warhead intercepts it. All this in addition to Roger Corman's famous "*Sputnik* exploitation" quickie, *War of the Satellites* (1958). "*Sputnik,*" commented an industry wag, "should be in for ten per cent."

American International Pictures

Of all the companies that rode the horror craze to six-figure grosses, none was more successful than James H. Nicholson and Samuel Z. Arkoff's American International Pictures. For over twenty years, AIP gauged the tastes of successive generations of American teenagers, accumulating a filmography that documents the shifting trends, values, and lingo of its audience of the moment. From the beginning the upstart company recognized the value of the teenage audience, but what made AIP unique was its anticipation of the future *supremacy* of that audience. Nicholson and Arkoff decided early on that teenagers made up the only market that could sustain the modern motion picture business. In the 1950s, AIP perfected the exploitation strategies that throughout the next decade it would ride to ever-increasing fortune and legitimacy.

AIP began in 1954 as American Releasing Corporation (ARC), a producing and producer-financing company releasing features via "states rights" distributors (territorial franchises that distributed films on a regional basis). ARC's first releases were three Roger Corman productions: *The Fast and the Furious* (1954), which anticipated the dragpics, and two formula "oaters," *Five Guns West* (1955) and *Apache Woman* (1955). An unmemorable but nonetheless profitable non-Corman "weirdie," *The Beast with 1,000,000 Eyes* (1955), followed. Like other low-budget producer-distributors, ARC soon moved away from producing antiquated "formula" pictures, with narrative roots in the old studio system's B picture, in favor of the new gimmick or exploitation pictures aimed at teenagers. As Arkoff explained, "To compete with television westerns, you have to have color, big stars, and $2,000,000."

In 1956, ARC reorganized as American International Pictures. Though billed as "primarily a distributing outfit," AIP made production arrangements with five independent units (one headed by Nicholson) in order to ensure a regular source of supply. "All these features are being produced on modest budgets with particular attention given to their exploitation and box office possibilities," said Nicholson of his company's premier projects. As to story properties, he explained, "We feel we can create our own [stories] and tailor them to the needs of the current market. We have talked to exhibitors from coast to coast, including circuits and independents, and have outlined our program to them. We have been and will continue to be guided by the advice and opinions of the exhibitor. Good exploitation product for the average theater is badly needed; our program is to fulfill their need." Considering that over eight thousand theaters depended on programmer-type features, AIP had ready customers for its product. "With the market for middle bracket pictures virtually dead," said Arkoff, "the exploitation pictures bridge the gap between the blockbusters."

AIP's program of Katzmanian production soon surpassed that of "Jungle Sam" himself. On a typical AIP project, Nicholson might conjure up the exploitable title, Arkoff oversee general production, and one of the company's youthful stable of on-lease producers craft the actual film to order. As recognition of the teenage market's importance grew, and as AIP's reputation for tapping it widened, the company took care to cultivate a with-it, youngish image. In truth, with the exception of Arkoff and Nicholson, most of the talent was thirtyish at most. "The Young Company with Young Executives Presents Its Young Producers," read a trade industry ad for AIP's Roger Corman, Herman Cohen, Lou Rusoff, Stanley Shpetner, and Burt Topper.

Among this quintet, the company *Wunderkind* was independent producer-director Roger Corman, at age thirty a one-man studio system.

Jettisoning the formula westerns by mutual agreement with AIP, Corman delivered an exhausting series of weirdie teenpics that set in granite the teenpic exploitation style: *The Day the World Ended* (for ARC, 1956), *It Conquered the World* (1956), *She Gods of Shark Reef* (1956), *The Undead* (1956), *The Viking Women and the Sea Serpent* (1957), and *Teenage Caveman* (1958). In his spare time, Corman delivered similar product to AIP's chief rival in teenpic exploitation, Allied Artists: *Not of This Earth* (1957), *Attack of the Crab Monsters* (1957), and *War of the Satellites* (1958), to name a few. Critics may have blanched, but within the industry a track record so profitable could only be exemplary. After the release of *Teenage Doll* (1957), Corman was praised as "one of the industry's most promising newcomers" for "gearing his treatments . . . to that ever burgeoning teenage moviegoing element. He realizes, and rightly so, that such customers are assuming increasing importance in the box office pattern, and that the best story is one readily identifiable with the pre-adult age level."

AIP was always sure to lend its corporate ear to those parts of the industry with the closest connection to the actual (teenage) ticket buyers. Company policy for Nicholson and Arkoff was "strictly and simply a policy of directing their attention to the supplying of the teenager's entertainment demands." In 1957, a revelatory article in *Motion Picture Herald* elaborated:

> The reasoning of Mr. Nicholson, reared on exhibition practices and problems from early boyhood, and Mr. Arkoff, who came to independent production by way of learning the business intimately through serving a goodly number of independents as legal counsel during his years of general practice, is class-room clear. It stems from statistics showing the teenager to be the best picture-goer in the country at this time—the most consistent, the best equipped with leisure time and allowance money, the most gregariously inclined, and to be sure the most romantic—and likely to become gratifyingly more numerous as time goes by.

AIP thus designed its product line for maximum teen appeal and minimum adult offense:

> To provide satisfactory screen material for the teenage audience without estranging their elders or their juniors, and without committing blunders such as have occurred in some of the other media, is the most exacting requirement AIP's policy imposes on its principals. AIP product must appeal to teenagers on a different basis than radio or television product available to them. It must not ever under any conditions seem to have been especially chosen for them, conditioned to their years, or equipped with special mes-

sages. . . . To give the teenagers [the idea] they're being dealt with in a special way, as though they are different in some way than other people . . . is the last thing on earth a teenager wants to be told.

The important words are "seem to have been chosen," for from the start AIP carefully tailored its films to, and marketed them at, teenagers and teenagers alone. Their product often may have been technically slipshod (the special effects were exceedingly unspecial, and microphones tended to poke down from the top of the frame), but their marketing campaigns were always state-of-the-art. "From our modest beginnings," Nicholson later wrote, "we felt that much of the showmanship that has been characterized by the school of thought which advocates 'flying by the seat of the pants' should be supplanted by 'instrumental flight.' Consequently, we instituted a program of intelligently produced exploitation films backed by aggressive, hard-sell policies." In 1958, Arkoff described AIP's creative process: "In most cases we have no more than a title to start with. We think up the title and then kind of pre-test it by springing it on one of our exhibitors. If he likes it—and if it's gory enough, of course—we give it to a writer and tell him to write a script for it, and then we get on to more important things, like the promotion campaign and the publicity." The Nicholson-Arkoff production dictum was simple: "If a property doesn't lend itself to first class exploitation by theater and television trailers, we won't film it."

Arkoff and Nicholson usually made up advertising materials *before* production began. Nicholson recalled an occasion when "we had an artist sketch a horror scene—complete with skulls, etc. 'That's what we want,' we told a writer, 'Now do the script.'" By the mid-1960s, AIP had codified its exploitation strategy into a syllogism its publicity department described as "The Peter Pan Syndrome":

a) a younger child will watch anything an older child will watch;
b) an older child will not watch anything a younger child will watch;
c) a girl will watch anything a boy will watch;
d) a boy will not watch anything a girl will watch; therefore,
e) to catch your greatest audience, you zero in on the 19-year-old male.

AIP zeroed in on that kid with fare that was never as wicked as it promised. Although tame even by the standards of the day, the company always packaged its caution as controversy. As a consequence, it received its share of choice brickbats. J. Edgar Hoover might well have had AIP's 1958 double bill *Machine Gun Kelly/The Bonnie Parker Story* in mind when he castigated the film industry for glorifying violent criminals. Displaying a spiritedness uncommon among Hollywood executives, Arkoff criticized the FBI director for attacking movies while ignoring television. "We're tired of the motion picture industry being used this way. . . . If the FBI is legitimate in its complaint that gangsters are glorified in films, let them go to the homes and do something about the television screen." Observing wryly that the old-fashioned Hoover might not have a television, Arkoff defended AIP's gangster double bill: "We work closely with the MPAA Production Code Administration and observe all the regulations. We certainly don't glorify the criminals in these two pictures and neither title character has been presented heroically."

The most memorable squabble involving AIP occurred at a luncheon the company gave for the Theater Owners Association of America in October 1958. After Arkoff and Nicholson had pitched their product to the assembly, producer Jerry Wald, one of the invited guests, asked to speak. Noting that the Los Angeles Parent-Teacher Association (PTA) had warned children to stay away from AIP's *Hot Rod Gang* and *High School Hellcats*, Wald abruptly launched into an attack on exploitation teenpics. "It's not the type of picture on which we can build the market of the future," he stormed. "While they may make a few dollars today, they will destroy us tomorrow." Nicholson replied, "I'd rather send my children to see these pictures than *God's Little Acre*." After expressing the hope that Wald enjoyed the lunch "which we paid for," Arkoff noted that there were fewer "connotations" in AIP pictures than in *Peyton Place* (1957) or *No Down Payment* (1957), two recent Wald productions. He then uttered the classic line: AIP "monsters do not smoke, drink or lust."

Compared with the original rock 'n' roll and j.d. scandals, AIP's hassles were minor scrapes. One reason the company avoided damaging controversy (as opposed to sought-after, exploitable controversy) was that it consolidated its teenpic hegemony in 1957–59, by which time many of the real teenpic battles were over. Also, as Nicholson's crack about *God's Little Acre* indicated, censors and citizens groups were plenty busy with a rash of Code-crippling product from the increasingly desperate major studios. Perhaps most important, AIP had a knack of defusing any latent licentiousness or casual cruelty with a tongue-in-cheek flair that became the company's trademark. On screen and off, AIP never took itself too seriously and its good humor tended

AIP in adolescence: a relaxed portrait from a 1957 promotional trip reveals that, unlike AIP monsters, Samuel Z. Arkoff (left) and James H. Nicholson (right) drank and smoked. (Quigley Photographic Archive, Georgetown University Library)

to disarm potential critics. "You can get away with a lot in a horror film, let's say, as long as you treat the subject with a comic touch or as a flight of fancy," explained Nicholson. It was difficult to get too righteous about programs with titles like *Attack of the Puppet People* (1958)/ *War of the Colossal Beast* (1958) and *How to Make a Monster* (1958)/ *Teenage Caveman* (1958). The films themselves also held tongue firmly in cheek. Herman Cohen's *How to Make a Monster* concerned a homicidal makeup man who goes on a rampage after his studio switches from horror films to musicals. Typical also was AIP's fourth-anniversary slogan: "Laugh all the way to the bank—book American."

Arkoff and Nicholson were always quick to point out that they maintained a happy working relationship with the Production Code Administration and overseas censorship boards. AIP kept the cleavage of *The Astounding She-Monster* (1958) within prescribed limits; the British censors in turn agreed that because the title creature of *It Conquered the World* was neither human nor animal, it was not entitled to Review Board protection against wanton cruelty and could, therefore, be blowtorched to death. In 1958, AIP noted that its sixteen recent films all had received the PCA seal. The Legion of Decency was mollified as well: with the exception of four B-list films, all had made the organization's A list. Said the ever-guileless Nicholson, "Our stories are pure fantasy with no attempt at realism. Because of this it is difficult to see how anyone could take our pictures so seriously that psychological damage could occur. . . . In our concept of each of our monsters, we strive for unbelievability. Teenagers, who comprise our largest audience, recognize this and laugh at the caricatures we represent, rather than shrink in terror. Adults, more serious-minded perhaps, often miss the point of the joke."

Teenagers seemed to agree a horror teenpic incited more "titters than terror." When the discussion turned to horror pictures at an industry-sponsored forum for high school leaders, one student averred that "instead of shocking audiences, they amused them. They're comedies." As for all that outrageous advertising, AIP freely admitted that its ads were "obviously overdrawn for the deliberate and calculating purpose of bringing people into theaters." For Arkoff and Nicholson, the film business was essentially a carnival business to be dealt with in carnival terms.

I Was a Teenage Werewolf

Nothing typifies AIP product better than the film that brought the company to national prominence, *I Was a Teenage Werewolf* (1957). Riding the crest of the Hammer horror wave and propelled by what was certainly the era's best exploitation title, *I Was a Teenage Werewolf (IWTW)* vaulted AIP into the first ranks of independent film companies. It was a breakthrough film for Arkoff and Nicholson, the spectacular success that would launch their company into nearly fifteen years of unchallenged ascendancy in the teen marketplace. After *IWTW*, AIP set the standards, such as they were, for teenpic exploitation.

Made for approximately $150,000, *IWTW* was released in June 1957 and reportedly caused traffic jams at drive-ins on its way to a $2 million gross. Its unforgettable title telegraphed a powerful dual appeal: part teen problem picture, part horror movie, *IWTW* was a teenpic double bill in one feature. "I had heard that 62% of the movie audience was between fifteen and thirty, and I knew that the movies that were grossing well were horror and rock 'n' roll pictures," explained producer Herman Cohen. "So I decided to combine them with an exploitation title." In 1957, Cohen, like many of his colleagues, realized where the money was. The previous year he had produced a well-made and moderately praised picture with Barbara Stanwyck and Sterling Hayden called *Crime of Passion*. It went nowhere. "So I took ten weeks off from Hollywood, traveled the United States, analyzed what was happening to [the motion picture] industry," Cohen recalled. He spoke with exhibitors, attended shows at four-walls and drive-ins, and discovered for himself just who was going to films. Cohen converted to teenpics.

IWTW owes most of its success to its title, timing, and perfectly executed exploitation campaign. Not to be discounted, however, is a narrative that takes teenage subculture on its own terms. Most teenpics are products of adult minds racing madly to interpret adolescent tastes. By contrast, AIP teenpics seem to be the kind of motion pictures a group of high schoolers let loose with 35mm equipment might come up with, an impression due in equal parts to market savvy, youthful talent, and bargain-basement budgets. With the audience that mattered, the company's unpretentious product generally fared better than the transparently calculating teen attractions of the established studios. Also, as the case in point indicates, AIP's 1950s catalog has proved surprisingly durable in the popular memory. Moreover, though a patent AIP cheapie, *IWTW* has none of the subprofessional look of kindred efforts. In addition to Cohen's seasoned hand in production, the movie boasts the directorial debut of Gene Fowler Jr., who apprenticed as an editor on grand Hollywood films such as *The Ox-Bow Incident* (1943) and *Woman in the Window* (1944). Occasionally, an AIP teenpic did more than graft eighty minutes of screen time onto a high-concept title. The best of them, like *IWTW*, show genuine insight into the inner life of their target audience. In ethnographic terms, they provide not only ritual occasions for subcultural gatherings but ritual representations of subcultural values as well.

The hero of *IWTW* is Tony (Michael Landon), one of Rockdale High School's more troubled students. Tony may look like James Dean, but the introductory sequence, a schoolyard fight, shows he has none of Jim Stark's sense of honor. He fights dirty, throwing sand in his opponent's face and going after him with a shovel. Fowler renders the fight from a taut first-person point of view: whether as participant or observer, the schoolyard showdown is a scene familiar to the target audience. From the sidelines, in an essential detail, students root for Tony's rival. Tony's real trouble is not with adult authority. He has what for a teenager is a far more serious problem: the other teenagers reject him. Unlike Jim Stark or even Artie West, Tony is a pariah.

The film's central scene reveals the depth of Tony's estrangement. Though advised by friendly cops and his worried girlfriend to seek professional help, and despite his own growing suspicion that something is off-kilter, Tony refuses to see a "headshrinker." Not until a youth center party with fellow students does Tony at last realize how sick he really is. After a bongo-playing, life-of-the-party type named Vic sings a painful quasi–rock 'n' roll tune ("Eeny, Meeny, Miney Mo"), the kids start playing practical jokes on one another. Director Fowler bides his time, pacing the sequence for tension and dramatic payoff: a timid girl opens a door and a student falls out with a fake knife in his back; she screams; everybody, including the girl, laughs. Another girl is given a present that explodes in jack-in-the-box fashion; she laughs along with everyone else. Tony himself helps set Vic up for the kicker. Vic opens a door, gets drenched with water from a bucket above, and good-naturedly joins in the common laughter. Finally Tony's turn comes. Vic sneaks up behind him and blows a party horn in his ear. Exploding savagely, Tony belts Vic and shoves his girl away when she tries to intervene. Getting hold of himself, he looks up to see the shocked faces of his peers: at this moment, he decides to see the headshrinker. Tony now wants "to adjust"—but to teenage subculture, not parent culture.

Tony is sent to a maniacal Jungian who wants him to regress through hypnosis to mankind's primitive dawn. Dr. Carver (Whit Bissell) is the basic 1950s scientist, working toward a wacko goal ("to hurl back the human race to its early beginnings") for the betterment of mankind. The patient-doctor byplay bears a studied resemblance to the relationship between a trusting son and a solicitous parent. "I'm the pilot, you're the passenger," the psychiatrist tells the hypnotized teenager.

Tony, of course, regresses right into a werewolf. In this state, too, his aggression is directed at fellow students, not adult authorities like the police or the school principal. Thematically consistent, it also allows the (teenage) audience to empathize with the fright of the (teenage) victims on screen. Fowler skillfully directs the two werewolf attacks. One is a quiet and very effective stalking scene in a forest, the actual

I Was a Teenage Werewolf (1957): peer pressure, not adult advice, pushed Michael Landon into psychotherapy. (Courtesy of American International Pictures)

attack shown entirely by suggestion. The other occurs in Rockdale High's gym as a leotard-clad girl practices gymnastics on a balance beam. To accentuate the identification of audience and victims, Fowler uses an upside-down point-of-view shot when the girl first sees the werewolf. After he kills the pretty gymnast, Tony flees through the halls of Rockdale High, students screaming and pointing after him, a nightmare of adolescent maladjustment.

Tony returns to Dr. Carver's office pleading for help. The doctor, still thrilled at this "perfect case of regression," wants to get Tony's next transformation on film. After reversion to lycanthropic form, Tony kills the doctor's assistant, wrecks the lab equipment, and kills the doctor before police rush in and fill him full of silver. "It's not meant for man to interfere in the ways of God," mutters an onlooker.

An inevitable follow-up, *I Was a Teenage Frankenstein*, sluggishly directed by Herbert L. Strock, was out by Thanksgiving vacation in 1957. It fulfilled Katzmanian expectations by doing about two-thirds the business of the original. As Dr. Frankenstein, Whit Bissell has learned nothing from his experience with a teenage werewolf. Engaged in research "beyond the pale of experimental medicine," he wants to carry "the principle of selective breeding one step higher—to assemble a human being." "The old are dying and dead. The whole trend is towards death," says the mad doctor. "Only in youth is there any hope for the salvation of mankind." No sooner are the words out of his mouth than tires screech outside the laboratory: a group of joyriding teens has obligingly piled up on the highway. Stealthily absconding with a surplus corpse, Dr. Frankenstein returns to his private morgue, bellowing, "In this laboratory there is no death until I declare it so!"

With the help of a squeamish assistant, Dr. Frankenstein sets to work fitting together an assortment of body parts. Reflecting the graphic standards of the previous year's Hammer hits, the operation room scene is markedly grislier than anything in *IWTW*. As the roar of a tiny buzzsaw fills the soundtrack, Dr. Frankenstein removes his patient's bloody limbs, throwing the unusable parts to an alligator slithering about in the basement. As usual, AIP mixes humor in with the gore. During the disassembly-assembly, Frankenstein's weak-willed aide whimpers, "I don't think I have the stomach for this." (The craven assistant has been a stock horror character since the dwarf Fritz in the original *Frankenstein;* his immediate source in teenpic horror is the secondary character in *The Curse of Frankenstein,* who tries to discourage Christopher Lee. Besides comic relief, he functions as an audience surrogate, drawn into and repelled by the evil doings.) When the preliminary work is done, Dr. Frankenstein announces, "Now I have to get two hands and a right leg." Again, fate provides the flesh: an airplane crash kills a high school track team. The doctor goes to the local cemetery and comes up with the hands of a wrestler and a football star's leg.

At last the monster is complete and cognizant, though his face is still wrapped in bandages. With the monster mature, Dr. Frankenstein undergoes something of a transformation himself: he turns into an overbearing 1950s parent. "Speak!" he demands of the hapless creature. "You've got a civil tongue in your head. I know because I sewed it there myself." He gives his creation an electric shock, and when it cries, he marvels that the tear ducts work. "It seems we have a very sensitive teenager on our hands," he taunts. During the monster's early orientation, Dr. Frankenstein upbraids his creation in a truly hissable fashion. He forces it to call him "sir" ("In England, we have a little more respect for the older generation"), teaches him selected Bible quotations ("I will obey you"), and refuses to allow him outside the laboratory ("Don't badger me! You will walk among people when I feel the time is ready!").

The creature escapes for a surreptitious night out and, forgetting Sam Arkoff's antilust injunction, peeps in on a blonde in a nightgown. She screams. Trying to keep her quiet, he inadvertently strangles her. The desperate teenager returns to the lab, where Dr. Frankenstein berates him before offering forgiveness in mock-parental tones ("I was thinking of your welfare entirely.").

Meanwhile, in a weird subplot, Dr. Frankenstein's live-in fiancée is becoming suspicious and unmanageable. She only wants to share in her betrothed's work, though, and on discovering its fruits, she reconciles with the doctor. Breathlessly she sighs, "The monster . . . he's brought us even closer together." The doctor isn't the sentimental type. He maneuvers the monster into killing his bride-to-be and casually throws her remains to the alligator.

Underneath the bandages the monster is hideous scar tissue. As sensitive about his appearance as any teenager, he demands a new face. The doctor drives his teenage Frankenstein to the local lover's lane to search among the necking teenagers for a likely visage. In a clever bit of audience association that became a horror teenpic staple, a youth is ripped from the arms of his screaming sweetheart. His face soon graces the creature's body. "He'll pass for a normal, quite attractive teenager," says the proud doctor.

There's one problem: how to get the passportless creature through immigration for the trip back to England. Dr. Frankenstein decides to disassemble him, put him in boxes, and reassemble the parts on arrival. The monster objects. "I know what's best for you!" shouts the doctor. A fight ensues during which creature/son duels with creator/father until the former throws the latter into the alligator pit, accompanied, presumably, by boisterous cheering from the gallery. When the police burst in, the creature backs into some electrical equipment and gets zapped. "I'll never forget his face after the accident," says the doctor's shivering assistant. A last view of the fright mask fills the screen before the final fade-out focuses on the alligator chomping on a white lab coat.

After *IWTW*, producer Cohen had found his niche; for the next several years, he was AIP's in-house specialist on teenpic horror. By the time he got around to *Konga* (1961), the story of a teenage chimpanzee, the producer realized he was in something of a creative rut. Cohen consoled himself with success, explaining, "It's awfully hard to change when you're making money."

Stiff Competition

The ballyhoo boys in charge of studio publicity were especially delighted with the horror trend. More than any other teenpic cycle, horror thrived on vigorous, wildly imaginative exploitation in its root sense. Welcoming the resurrected *White Zombie* spirit, an ad-pub man said with enthusiasm, "This is something we can really get our teeth into. On these films you can really use your imagination whether it's in the ads or in stunts." Agreed a colleague, "Here, finally, we have a batch of films without any big stars. We can build our ads around the 'horror' angle, the picture itself if you will. We don't have to worry about having the players' names in the same type size as the title of the picture itself, or the position of the star's head in the ad. It's all pure punch, no dilution. It's about time we came back to that."

Exhibitors were of the same mind. Thrilled at the opportunity to attract so ripe a consumer group, they participated enthusiastically in all manner of outlandish publicity schemes. Curtis Mees advised that "horror and science fiction type pictures make particularly attractive programs for late shows or special bookings and, if properly promoted, offer big potentials of increased box office and refreshment stand." Mees's mention of the teenagers' value at the refreshment stand was no afterthought. One exhibitor reported: "When we get a good shocker, the sales go up on popcorn and candy—I guess it saves chewing on their nails." According to a colleague, there was an additional inducement: "My audience—I hate to call them juvenile delinquents, but they throw tomatoes at the screen and carve up the upholstery when they don't like a movie. They seem to calm down a bit when you give them a fairly good thriller. They really seem to be curious about what makes a monster and how it works."

Allied Artists' *Macabre* (1958), directed by the redoubtable William Castle, the most inventive of all 1950s gimmick-meisters, is generally credited with kicking off the horror advertising and exploitation wars, the "stiff competition." Made for $80,000, the film grossed about $1.2 million on the strength of Castle's flair for old-style carnival hustle. Harking back to the glory days of ballyhoo, Castle's colorful scams revived a vintage tradition for Hollywood flim-flam. "I've modeled my career on Barnum," he said. "Exploitation's the big thing in the motion picture business today. Stars and content don't mean much at the box office anymore. The people who go to see pictures because of what's in 'em, they're a minority. Gimmicks, surprise, shock—that's what draws the crowds."

For *Macabre*, Castle drew crowds by offering a $1,000 life insurance policy from Lloyds of London to cover "the death by fright of any member of the audience." The insurance policies, reportedly legitimate, were handed out by uniformed "nurses" stationed in theater lobbies or on street corners. By one estimate, over 10 million "policies" doubling as *Macabre* leaflets were distributed. Castle made exploitation an integral part of the film itself. In a prologue to *Macabre*, a disembodied voice announces: "Ladies and gentlemen, for the next hour and fifteen minutes you'll be shown things so terrifying that the management of this theater is deeply concerned for your welfare. Therefore, we request that each of you assume the responsibility of taking care of your neighbor. If anyone near you becomes uncontrollably frightened, will you please notify the management so that medical attention can be rushed to their aid."

"Of course, it would be an awful thing if somebody actually did die in the theater," Castle said, adding wistfully, "the publicity would be terrific though." In place of the real item, he hired "fright victims" to collapse at selected screenings.

For his next feature, *The House on Haunted Hill* (1958), Castle spent a reported $150,000 on the film and an additional $250,000 on a process (actually a device) called "emergo" in which inflated skeletons danced from the sides of the theater and dangled out over the audience. With earnings of more than $3 million, it was credited with putting the financially troubled Allied Artists in the black. For the now-legendary *The Tingler* (1959), the first LSD film, Castle tried to give the illusion that the title creature was loose in the theater. The screen goes blank as the shadow of the tingler seems to crawl in front of the projector's light and Vincent Price warns: "Ladies and gentlemen, the tingler is loose in this theater and, if you don't scream, it may kill you!" At the same time, in specially outfitted theaters, wired vibrators fitted beneath seats were turned on to give viewers a mild tingling shock. A tireless promoter, Castle made dozens of in-theater appearances around the country to hype his projects personally. He became almost as popular as his films. "I want to tap the entire potential audience—teenagers, children, all devotees of adventure and horror," he announced.

For extravagant exploitation, Castle's only real rival was Joe Levine of Embassy Pictures. Like Castle, Levine was a pioneer in now-standard motion picture marketing practices, such as nationwide saturation booking and spending more on publicity than on distribution rights or production. One of the modern industry's most influential figures, Levine put together scores of distribution and production packages. For years, Embassy Pictures prided itself on not owning so much as a movie camera. Its business was the new Hollywood art form, the "deal." But Levine was also as responsible as anyone for making the foreign art film a viable commercial commodity in America. He imported *Two Women* (1961) and Fellini's *8½* (1963) and backed them up with the kind of well-aimed publicity campaign essential to their survival. Levine went on to score with *The Graduate* (1967). In the mid-1970s, he was one of the few who had either the resources or the ambition to bankroll the multimillion-dollar war epic *A Bridge Too Far* (1977).

Levine came to an early and farsighted appreciation of the possibilities of teen-targeted exploitation. While working as main "exploitation man" for AIP's first really successful dual bill, *Hot Rod Girl* (1956)/*Girls in Prison* (1956), he concluded that the "gimmick film with appeal to teens" would "mushroom" in popularity. "It's just the beginning," he predicted. In the late 1950s, he specialized in picking up foreign weirdies with Stateside exploitation potential, introducing American audiences to Japanese dinosaurs and Italian beefcake. After purchasing American distribution rights at a reasonable price, he would set off a firestorm of impossible-to-avoid pile-driver publicity that made widespread and innovative use of television and radio. He bought the rights to *Godzilla, King of the Monsters* (1954) from Toho Productions for $100,000, made a quick fortune in theaters, and sold it to TV for $50,000. A follow-up "hoho from Toho," *The Mysterians* (1957), fared less well, perhaps because Distributors Corporation of America had scooped him with *Rodan* (1957), which it backed, Levine-like, with $80,000 in publicity, saturation engagements, and a high-powered TV advertising campaign.

Levine next turned to Italy, bringing in *Attila the Hun* (1955, U.S. release 1958) and *Hercules* (1959) for hugely successful Stateside runs.

He reportedly paid $120,000 for U.S. rights to *Hercules*, spent $1.5 million on publicity, and grossed $20 million. Accounting for the appeal of *Hercules*, Levine commented, "It had a lot of sex, and a lot of action, and people loved it. And it had a good title too. I mean, who ever heard of Ben-Hur? But you go in the street and lift up a manhole cover, and ask 'Who was Hercules?' and you'll get the answer."

Again, saturation engagements and TV and radio were used to maximum advantage. The ad copy for *Attila the Hun* pledged "pillaging plundering hordes . . . racing ravishers roaring out of their Asian wastelands to lay waste a pleasure-gorged empire." Levine's audacious formula was to spend roughly 25 percent of the potential gross of a picture on advertising and exploitation. Thus, he reportedly invested $500,000 in *Attila* (which grossed $2 million) before catching the brass ring with *Hercules*.

Not to be outdone on the exploitation front, the competition gave Levine and Castle a run for their blood money. United Artists responded to *Macabre*'s insurance ploy with the claim that *The Return of Dracula* (1958) was so terrifying that they couldn't get insurance, twelve different companies having turned them down. (Unamused, Castle got a restraining order against UA.) Universal stationed "legal" representatives in theater lobbies and encouraged moviegoers to execute their last will and testament before seeing *Horror of Dracula* (1958). The lid of a coffin raises at the opening of AIP's *The Screaming Skull* (1958), and inside is the notice: "This Is Reserved for You." A voice intones: "Ladies and gentlemen, you are about to see a motion picture that may kill you. We guarantee free burial service to anyone who dies of fright." Similarly, UA's *I Bury the Living* (1958) promised a free burial plot for expired viewers. Live bats were released in one theater during a double bill of *House of the Living* (1958)/*The Return of Dracula* (1958).

Recognizing that horror was a boon to numerous spin-off businesses, AIP marketed do-it-yourself kits with *How to Make a Monster* (1958). Novelty companies made fortunes on monster masks and horror accoutrements; monster fanzines multiplied on newsstands; and nearly 200,000 paperback copies of Mary Shelley's 1818 novel *Frankenstein* were sold. Three years later, the "ghoul standard" was still going strong. William Castle's *Homicidal* (1961), a *Psycho* imitation from Columbia, grossed over $3 million. It featured an intermission "Fright Break" during which audience members could "follow the Yellow

Streak to the Coward's Corner and have the admission sneerfully re-funded."

Bad punning was epidemic as exhibitors coined "horrorama shows," "shock around the clock," "screamieres," and "monsterpieces" to pan-der to what was inevitably referred to as the "boy meets ghoul" trade. "We've pumped new blood into the industry," chortled Hammer Pro-ductions. To ballyhoo their Toho import *The H-Man* (1959), Colum-bia constructed a special trailer—the kind on wheels. *Variety* unfurled one of its classic banner headlines: "Don't Kill Thrill Chill Mill."

Not everyone was amused. For *Motion Picture Herald*'s James M. Jer-auld, the ambulances, uniformed nurses, decapitated dummies in water tanks, blood-drenched surgical equipment, coffins in theater lobbies, and horse-drawn hearses carrying signs were a bit much:

> At some point a theater manager has to stop and consider the effect of hor-ror picture advertising and exploitation on his prospective patrons. . . . The-ater men have been competing in efforts to make the advance campaigns gruesome, often without stopping to consider whether they may be keeping patrons away from their theaters. . . . Is that good exploitation? There is no denying that some of these pictures have rolled up important grosses. The teenage appeal seems to be strong, but putting them on Saturday matinees when the children are out in force has stirred criticism.

The debate over advertising highlights the fact that for the first time an exploitation film cycle was living up to the promise of its exploita-tion campaign. The j.d. and teenage vice pictures never matched the violence and sex portrayed on their one-sheets. Amazingly, horror pic-tures delivered the goods. "As gory as the law allows," wrote a trade critic of *Horror of Dracula*, "it is one scare film that will live up to al-most any amount of wild exploitation." Such truth in advertising was unprecedented in teenpic exploitation. The new honesty set off the now-familiar pattern of negative critical response, but this time the in-dustry reacted differently: it went on the offensive. By 1957–58, mo-tion picture companies had already weathered similar protests over the rock and j.d. teenpic cycles. They learned two things: economic con-siderations outweighed social ones, and the social protests were inef-fectual anyway.

For their part, the critics seem to have gone about their task with a tired sense of duty. Arthur Knight commented, "The pictures dropping off the assembly line today are more horrid than horror. The real hor-ror is that these pictures, with their bestialities, their sadism, their lust

Stiff competition: a trade ad for *Horror of Dracula* shows why exhibitors "love that horror." (*Motion Picture Herald*, July 20, 1957)

for blood, and their primitive level of conception and execution should find their greatest acceptance among the young. It is sad enough as a commentary on our youth, but even more so on the standards of the motion picture industry." Martin Quigley Jr. chimed in: "So far as horror is concerned it would seem that a zenith or base has been reached. Ghoulishness is being pursued as a glorious end. Blood in gorgeous color gushes. Sadism is rampant. That's no way to make pictures! No wonder it turns the stomachs of the thousands of [exhibitors] who run the theaters of the world."

In England, where the bright-red bloodfests had originated, *Sight and Sound*'s Derek Hill found ominous political implications in the genre. He pointed to the concentration camp imagery in *The Revenge of Frankenstein* (burning flesh in ovens) and *Blood of the Vampire* (chained humans and lab experiments) and spoke darkly of the "beguiling rumor that Western governments are encouraging the production of these films in an attempt to blunt people's sensibilities sufficiently for them to face the horror of atomic warfare."

Film critics got little support from contemporary psychologists, who had apparently reversed direction since Dr. Fredric Wertham's *Seduction of the Innocent* had led the profession's attack on horror comic books in 1953. Many seemed to feel a midnight movie monsterfest was positively therapeutic. Exploitation filmmakers, accustomed to academic barbs when it came to rock 'n' roll and juvenile delinquency, were in the novel position of dragging out the experts in their defense. Dr. Martin Grotjahn, professor of psychiatry at the University of Southern California School of Medicine, lauded horror films as "self-administered psychiatric therapy for America's adolescents," a healthy way of overcoming childhood anxieties. "Our modern Frankenstein movies," said a colleague, "are no more terrifying to a child than such Biblical stories as the whale devouring Jonah or Daniel in the Lion's den."

Though again the center of a critical storm, the industry displayed little of the timidity that accompanied its previous entries into teenpic controversy. A new confidence is apparent in a matter-of-fact remark from *Motion Picture Herald*: "Horror pictures have reached the stage where psychologists are trying to analyze both the pictures and the patrons, with the result that the exploitation is passing beyond the display of coffins into a new phase." Henceforth, Hollywood would orchestrate public controversy with a new fervor and expertise, not avoid it.

One industry bottom-liner summed it up: "The kids like to see the blood flowing and they're paying to see it. We're trying to make whatever sells tickets. No one is being harmed and the horrified ones are the small, private adult groups who claim to be 'protecting' youngsters."

The critics were forced to agree. *The Revenge of Frankenstein*, said one reviewer, "is gory enough to give adults a squeamish second thought. The kids apparently are impervious." Another reported that *It Conquered the World* contained "a number of fairly gruesome sequences [which] may call down the wrath of groups who oversee kiddie pix fare. But it must be admitted that the packed house of moppets at the show [I] caught loved the gore and continually shrieked avid appreciation."

In literature and in film, horror claimed a history and stature that worked to its social advantage when it became the next subject for teenpic exploitation. As film historian Andrew Dowdy observed, "The teenage monster pictures of which AIP was the architect displaced the anxieties which surfaced openly in *Blackboard Jungle* or *Rebel Without a Cause* into the more acceptable conventions of the horror film." The immediacy of contemporary teenage threats—rock 'n' roll, drag racing, and juvenile delinquency—and the expressions of teenage alienation were, to be sure, sublimated in the horror cycle, but sublimation was distance enough. Next to Artie West and Elvis Presley, Frankenstein and Dracula were reassuringly familiar types with understandable antisocial attitudes. Many 1950s parents must have agreed with Hammer film star Christopher Lee: "A couple of realistic films such as *On the Waterfront* and *Blackboard Jungle* can do more to incite hooliganism than a dozen horror films."

1

The Clean Teenpics

Although she's not king-sized, her fingers are ring-sized / Gidget is the girl for me.

Theme song from *Gidget* (1959)

ccording to Production Code administrator Geoffrey Shurlock, the American motion picture industry owed its international stature to its wholesomeness. In 1956 he informed the Federation of Motion Picture Councils that Hollywood films "occupy 70% of the playing time of the screens of the world" because "the family audience, whether in Santiago or Strasbourg . . . can go en masse to Hollywood movies without being embarrassed. This is very comforting to the conscience of the industry. Happily, it is also comforting to its pocketbook." As in the past, the industry's future lay in purveying good, clean entertainment to the worldwide family of man. "Morality," said Shurlock, "is money in the bank."

Events of the next few years proved his calculus wrong. With a speed that stunned audiences and enraged censors, American movies lapsed into an "immorality" that bruised, bent, and finally broke the Code commandments. Soon what defined mainstream Hollywood production had changed forever. The old mainstream, the mass-audience "family entertainment" enjoyed by all age groups, no longer existed as such. By 1960, independent producer A. C. Lyles's *Raymie* (1960), a heartwarming story of a boy and his fish, stood out as something of a curiosity. Lyles discovered that "what with all the sex and violence going on the screen today, the 'family type' picture—one time the industry's bread and butter kind of product—[was] . . . off-beat." "Family entertainment" now meant "kid stuff," which in turn meant "dubious box office prospect." The same year *Variety* reported, "It is considered sacrilegious to claim unabashedly that a specific entry will appeal to children between the ages of seven and fourteen. . . . Most theatermen are secretly afraid of these entries, especially if they are the type that will not attract adults during the evening hours. . . . The dollars and cents conclusion is that it doesn't pay for a producer to try to make pictures for the family. Adults and the smart-aleck teenagers of today apparently don't want them." Only Walt Disney, with productions such as *The Shaggy Dog* (1959) and *The Absent-Minded Professor* (1961), still regularly struck gold with the old family trade. For the rest of the industry, the vein was played out.

The new mainstream was really adult entertainment, designed, so it was said, for the mature moviegoer bored by conventional and childish television programming. A survey of the then-current box office hits led *Variety* to conclude, "Motion pictures have come to be different . . . there's been nothing like the devastating horror of *Psycho* or the frank discussions of illicit sex in *Strangers When We Meet*. Or, to continue, the rabid evangelist as in *Elmer Gantry*, or a devastating size-up of husbands prone to infidelity in *The Apartment*, or the flippancy about things moral in *Can-Can*." "Fun for the entire family" this wasn't—though lurking in the demographic background was the unspoken certainty that "adult" often meant "teenage." In the ad copy for Warner Bros.' *The Bad Seed* (1956), a wild melodrama attributing preadolescent delinquency to a polluted gene pool, there is a crystalline transparency to the venerable rhetorical ploy: "We believe motion pictures are for everyone. However, the theme of *The Bad Seed* is so special (it has never been attempted on the screen)—its intimate probings so sensational (they will shock some)—this motion picture may not be suitable for younger people without worldly experience."

A few years later, in the exploitation campaign for *The Tall Story* (1959) starring Tony Perkins and Tuesday Weld, the studio dropped all pretense and spoke directly to the concerned party. "Students: if you want to go to college don't let your parents see this picture," teased the ads placed in *Seventeen*, *Teen*, and *Ingenue*. "I've never seen an 'adult type' person ever patronizing one of these adult movies," remarked an astute youngster who called the "adult" label "a great publicity stunt." An industry executive, as confused as anyone about the new cinematic categories, spoke of his studio's upcoming "family pictures" as films with "'adult themes' treated in such a way as to provide entertainment for the entire family."

By relinquishing its place as the chief purveyor of conventional morality, the industry opted for an adversarial stance that meant a seismic shift in the role of movies in American life. A spat between the city fathers of Mt. Sterling, Kentucky, and a recalcitrant theater operator named Anna Ward Olsen exposed the new terms of the relationship. In 1959, the Mt. Sterling Chamber of Commerce, together with four regional parent-teacher organizations and the Jaycees, called on area theater owners "to improve the entertainment standards of the community" by refusing to bring "undesirable movies to their screens, such as pictures dealing with criminal or immoral aspects of teenage life, and seductive films." The civic- or profit-minded theater owner of a previous era would not have been likely to buck so impressive a lineup of local authority. But few exhibitors could any longer afford the luxury of PTA-approved programming. In a response published in the *Mt. Sterling Advocate*, Mrs. Olsen, who operated two theaters and a drive-in, spoke for many of her colleagues when she told the coalition, "Those very pictures you feel should not be shown are about the only real box office attractions left for the exhibitor to buy that will give him a reasonable assurance of a crowded house. . . . You ask for Westerns, Walt Disneys, and family type pictures. We show all these—mostly to an empty house, *for even those who say they want these pictures do not come to see them*" (emphasis added).

In refusing to play to empty houses simply to satisfy the city fathers, Mrs. Olsen recognized one of the new realities facing the motion picture industry: films that *defied* prevailing "community standards," at least as laid down by formerly authoritative groups like the Mt. Sterling coalition and embodied in the Production Code, could be big moneymakers. Conversely, the films most acceptable to the city fathers were often risky box office material.

Exhibitors, many initially only too glad to heed official demands "to improve the entertainment standards of the community," were genuinely shocked at the actual community response to family features. Heralding MGM's ill-fated *Andy Hardy Comes Home* (1958), Curtis Mees predicted:

> It has been a long time since Andy Hardy kept entire families coming back again and again to our theaters as a potent example of the type of picture which builds family trade, and we have the highest hopes—nay,

The death of Andy Hardy, 1958: in belated recognition of just how retrograde a production this was, one ad mat actually tried to sell Mickey Rooney to the "jukebox set." (U.S. Library of Congress collection: Courtesy of Turner Entertainment)

> *expectations*—that the new Andy Hardy series will point the way to continued production of pictures that bear directly upon the problem of family attendance and entertainment. Perhaps the "city slickers" may not go for these pictures so strongly, but this sort of production will mean the salvation of the majority of our small town theaters.

The poignant experience of another small-town exhibitor proved otherwise. Displaying a jaunty literary flair, Charlie Jones of Northwood, Iowa, conjured up the difference between theaters then and theaters now:

When I first saw the trade paper ads on *Andy Hardy*, my mind wandered back to those late 1930s when I was flunkeying around the home town theater, helping to keep the mobs outside from pushing the mobs inside out of their 35-cent seats every time the Hardy pictures came to town. I started to salivate and thoughts began flowing that when the picture hit town I'd be back in business . . . I spent some extra bucks trying to appeal to my age group, hoping they would be interested in sacrificing a night away from their little living room Chautauqua and come out and recapture some of the nostalgic charm of a movie of the type they used to dress up for and leave the house to see.

Sadly, the faith of Charlie Jones in the enduring appeal of Andy Hardy didn't pay off:

Those were some bucks that could just as well have been used to reduce loan interest instead of to buy printer's ink. The "pee-pul" seem either to have become so sophisticated by the intellectual processes of quiz programs, or so convinced by the propaganda that delinquency has taken over both our theater screens and our society, that they can no longer adjust to the simplicities of family life in its idyllic state. If life isn't infested with abnormalities, phobias, and manias, it seems to have lost its appeal on screen.

Like exhibitor Olsen, Jones noticed that although public-spirited adults might on principle demand family entertainment from the local theater, in practice they didn't patronize it. Enumerating the sorry returns on recent family shows such as *The Matchmaker* (1958), *Kathy O'* (1958), and *The Missouri Traveler* (1958), he observed, "We keep citing the Hardys, the Lassies, the Blondies, etc., when we think of the 'good old days' in which they were packing our houses. We keep hollering for a certain type of picture which used to do business, but when we get one in this day and age the results seem to be so poor that it would discourage any producer from putting money into anything but mayhem and horror."

Agreeing with the consensus, yet another small-town exhibitor, James Griffiths of McCarey, Texas, decided to prove the point through an informal poll of the locally troublesome Ministerial Alliance, PTA, and Women's Study Group. He found that the would-be community censors "had not attended any motion picture for several months and were not even familiar with the pictures showing at the theaters." By 1960, Glenn Norris, Twentieth Century-Fox's sales manager, could seriously complain that a distributor peddling traditional family fare had "to go out and [often] knock his head against the wall in order to persuade an exhibitor that by booking and promoting a family film he may well be able to make some good money as well as perform a tremen-dously important public relations job for the entire industry."

No newfound commitment to First Amendment principles inspired this exhibitor rebellion; rather, the pronouncements of once-powerful patriotic and priestly pressure groups had become largely irrelevant to the attendance of moviegoers. The American Legion, the special in-terest group theater owners had feared most in the early 1950s, in-veighed in vain against what it called a "renewed invasion of Soviet-indoctrinated artists" when Hollywood Ten alumnus Dalton Trumbo was hired for *Exodus* (1960) and *Spartacus* (1960) and blacklisted screen-writer Nedric Young for *Inherit the Wind* (1960). Responding in a man-ner that several years before would have been unthinkable, the inde-pendent producers responsible—Otto Preminger, Kirk Douglas, and Stanley Kramer, respectively—told the Legion, politely, to stuff it. None of their films suffered as a result.

The pious fared little better than the political. No longer could the Legion of Decency spell box office curtains for a morally objectionable movie. As Francis Cardinal Spellman discovered when he condemned *Baby Doll* (1956) from the pulpit of St. Patrick's Cathedral, the C rat-ing ("Condemned") might have more box office value than the church's endorsement. The increasingly common B rating (morally objection-able in part for all, the Legion's second poorest film grade) certainly didn't prevent *Peyton Place* (1957) or *A Summer Place* (1959) from be-coming solid hits. (Films rated "B" by the Legion climbed from 14.59 percent of all Hollywood output in 1959 to 24.55 percent in 1960, a rise a spokesman called "astounding." Significantly, 74 of 101 B-rated films in the Legion's bulletin were then being handled by the Majors.) Protestant groups also got more riled as films got more adult. Never as well organized as the Catholics, their attempts to apply leverage were conspicuously unsuccessful. The ministerial protest over *Elmer Gantry* (1960) is noteworthy only because it was so ineffectual.

Although guardians of classical Hollywood's moral universe had not yet become impotent, their influence was certainly flagging. At the 1960 Academy Awards, the popular import *Room at the Top* became the first non-Code-approved film to win top Oscar honors (for Best Ac-tress and Best Screenplay), an event that displayed the Code's super-fluity and validated the industry-wide movement to what was eu-phemistically referred to as greater "frankness" on screen. For the first time, drugs, graphic violence, and the unambiguous depiction of sexual matters (adultery, abortion, impotence, homosexuality, though not as yet nudity) made their way into Code-approved big-budget commercial Hollywood movies. Exhibitors, in turn, showed a feisty new willingness to brave local opposition as long as their cash registers kept ringing. One industry advertising-publicity executive spelled out what many thought but few dared express openly: "All this talk about nice, 'clean' pictures is bunk. We give lip service to it because we're so damn eager to be respectable. Actually, if we completely lived up to the idea, we'd be out of business in a year. The public wants to be shocked. The more talk gets around that films are sexy and exciting, the better for us." Or, as Twentieth Century-Fox president Spyros Skouras blurted out at a meeting of exhibitors, what the public wanted was "blood, guts, and sex."

Despite a reputation for daring, taboo-breaking subject matter (fostered mostly by their own advertising), teenpics played no real part in the decade's important censorship battles. On the contrary, exploitation moviemakers who specialized in teenpics were a conservative and timorous lot, far less willing than the Hollywood establishment to challenge the Production Code. Like Sam Arkoff and James Nicholson at AIP, most sought and obtained the Code seal for their exploits. Arkoff himself was a voice of caution within the industry, criticizing his fellows for an "alarming lack of realistic concern in distribution circles (and almost none in production) over the effect which Hollywood's current crop of films featuring 'adult themes' is having on pro-censorship forces." Singling out as excessive the homosexual-cannibalistic elements of Columbia's *Suddenly Last Summer* (1959), he counseled his colleagues to lie low and not tempt the censor's scissors.

In fairness, the timidity of teenpic producers was probably due to the fact that their films were held to stricter accountability than the fashionably risqué "prestige" projects of the big studios. There was more truth than bitterness in James Nicholson's observation: "If a 20th Century Fox makes *Blue Denim* [1959], and gives it a big and important campaign, there'll be few objections. Had we done the same theme on an exploitation level, there'd have been a big outcry. We understand pretty well what happens and we are guided by it. It's pretty much the same with foreign films. They'll be attacked for something that a Hollywood picture can do with impunity."

Nonetheless, Nicholson and the rest seem to have been quite content to let rival releasing companies pay court costs to establish legal precedent and to have directors like Otto Preminger and Elia Kazan take risks for the sake of greater screen freedom. And, of course, teenpic producers eagerly partook of the new latitude to which they had contributed so little. Only after *The Man with the Golden Arm* (1955) had forced the Code to revise its strictures against screen treatments of narcotics would teenpics such as *The Cool and the Crazy* (1958) and *High School Confidential* (1958) have dared to exploit drug use. Likewise, the j.d. and horror cycles took special advantage of the general relaxation of standards concerning graphic violence. Characteristically, teenpics brought up the rear, settling into territory secured by a more forceful advance guard.

Regardless of how the ground was gained, teenpics thrived in the new surroundings—though not, again, because of any breathtaking explicitness in the films themselves. In the early era of greater screen freedom, they played on possibilities, the lure that they might finally deliver on their advertised come-ons. Given the authentic breakthroughs being made by major producers, the chance that a teenpic might follow suit with a scene of never-before-seen sex or violence was actually within the realm of filmic possibility. After all, what had been cinematically unimaginable only a few years previous had become standard Hollywood fare. Teenpic advertising cleverly fueled the promise that they could confront, and overstep, the (formerly) inviolable lines of screen conduct. That filmmakers could get away with this again and again is less a comment on their acumen as publicists than on an era in motion picture history when so many long-standing barriers were coming down that audiences didn't know what to expect next.

By and large, the strategy worked. The teenage audience, like the broader audience for Hollywood blockbusters or the art-house crowd for foreign films, expressed an unmistakable box office interest in the (real and imagined) explicitness beckoning from the screen. At the same time, however, there was a major reaction against these shocking new changes in American movies. On a mainstream level, this was signaled by the surprise success of 1959, Walt Disney's *The Shaggy Dog*, the year's second most popular film, and by a few other against-the-grain hits, such as Fox's *Dog of Flanders* (1959). In teenpics, too, there was a swing away from the violence-, vice-, and rock 'n' roll–ridden films that had dominated that market since *Blackboard Jungle*. Although the social depredations of wild youth continued to provide fodder for dozens of teenpics, and big-studio productions grew ever more audacious in their assaults on the Production Code, the decade's close saw a concurrent trend toward unabashedly wholesome entertainment that was at once teen-targeted and parent-approved: the clean teenpic.

The Clean Teens

In 1957, Pat Boone's vehicles for Twentieth Century-Fox, *Bernardine* and *April Love*, proved the box office appeal of a clean-cut teen idol in a family picture by nearly matching the grosses accrued by rival record-to-film star Elvis Presley. Boone, whose white bucks, polite manner, and sculpted features made him the "first teen idol even Grandma could love," was the certified "good boy" alternative to Presley, whose own appearances on screen that year in *Loving You* and *Jailhouse Rock* played up a darker, nastier image. Boone's screen popularity seemed to confirm a *Saturday Evening Post* survey conducted in 1957 by Alfred Politz Research, Inc., which described the "typical frequent movie-goer" as a "bright teenager." No delinquent dropout, he or she was a teenager in "high school, who comes from a family that is financially well-off, and perhaps which intends to send him (or her) to college." The review of *Bernardine* in *Motion Picture Herald* highlighted the similarities: "The adolescents in this film come from well-to-do families and their major problems concern whether they will pass their high school exams and who their dates will be for Saturday night. . . . Most teenagers attracted to this film will recognize and identify with such symbols as sneakers and sweaters, cokes and hamburgers, jukeboxes, high school clubs, problems of dating, and the desire to own a car."

Both *Bernardine* and *April Love* attest to the ease with which traditional Hollywood assimilated the clean teen idol. Unlike Presley, who was relegated to a supporting role in a black-and-white western for his first film (*Love Me Tender*) and who was still working in black and white as late as his third and fourth star vehicles (*Jailhouse Rock* and *King Creole*), Boone was from the start accorded the royal treatment cinematically: solid budgets, CinemaScope formats, deluxe color, and a cast of seasoned professionals both in front of and behind the camera (including, significantly, established pop songsmiths Johnny Mercer and Jay Livingston). He presented his handlers with one maddening problem, however. So accommodating in matters commercial, Boone was obstinate in matters of the heart: citing religious scruples, he refused to kiss a woman on screen. Since the efficient exploitation of a clean teen demanded some boy-girl stuff, the scripts to *Bernardine* and *April Love* had to maneuver their way around the roadblock presented by Boone's eccentricity, a limitation making for a strange hollowness in both films. Something is missing at the core.

Bernardine is the more teen-oriented of the pair. One of those dated (even at the time) Hollywood musicals in which characters unaccountably burst into song, the film concerns a clique of high school students who race speedboats for recreation and hunt girls for satisfaction. Because of his aversion to kissing, Boone cedes the romantic initiative to his lovelorn but loser pal Sanford (Richard Sargent), whom he serves as adviser and matchmaker. Hence the drama revolves around the second male lead's klutzy attempts to woo pretty telephone girl Jean (Terry Moore), not around the love life of the featured star. Although Boone occupies most of the screen time and sings all the featured numbers, his relinquishing of the emotional foreground proves a debilitating restriction. For example, he sings his hit song "Love Letters in the Sand" in the boys' clubhouse—absolutely alone—when the musical occasion pleads for a romantic frolic on the beach with a swimsuit-clad beauty.

In accordance with clean-teen class divisions, *Bernardine* portrays the higher income levels of teenage culture. The "gang" here is the after-school Shamrock Yacht Club, a group of preppies whose home lives are strictly upper-crust. The peer culture is ostentatiously well-off (the boys' hobby is speedboat racing), but its internecine relations accentuate generational similarities, not class differences. Boone is first among equals, the natural leader of the pack, smoking, teasing, and buying booze for his mates. The pleasures of the clubhouse are set against the pressures of home life: Boone has a profound rivalry with his older brother (a strikingly harsh and unfunny sibling animosity), and Sanford and his widowed mother have an intense relationship that seems unnaturally close (the boy freaks out when Mom announces her intention to remarry).

But if teen togetherness is a welcome refuge from the family, it is not without its own ugliness. As much as any teenpic of its time, *Bernardine* is ruthlessly honest about the humiliations and forced exclusions inflicted on outsiders by high school cliques. Craving acceptance into the yacht club is the pathetic wimp Kinswood (Hooper Dunbar), a straight-A student of whom one of the guys remarks, "He has that type of shallow mind that's great for exams." The butt of sadistic pranks and

The clean teen clique: Pat Boone shows his nasty side in *Bernardine*. (Museum of Modern Art Film Stills Archive: Courtesy of Twentieth Century-Fox)

the victim of a money scam, Kinswood is treated unmercifully by his peers. On screen as in life, teenage groups often make allowances for the integration of marginal characters (the nerd, the fat boy, the dummy). In *Bernardine*, the outsider is the recipient of the kind of casual cruelty associated with the worst of high school in-crowds. Although a final shot seemingly presents Kinswood as part of the group, no detail in the film accounts for his sudden status promotion from pariah to insider.

Regardless of the lip service paid to the girls, the primacy of boy-boy relationships is a truism of teenage gang pictures, whether of the mean-street or clean-teen variety. Lacking a central female focus, *Bernardine* resorts to a male rift for its peak dramatic moment. Feeling Boone has betrayed him, Sanford impulsively joins the army. In a soliloquy that is both a sop to teenagers and a lecture to parents, Sanford's mother ponders the imaginative gap between herself and "the stranger who's been living with me." She sums up conventional wisdom

on the autonomy of adolescent life: "There's only one thing I'm thinking and that's the foolish notion that I've always cherished that I understood my boy. And all the time he's been living a life so entirely separate from mine that I've never had an inkling of it."

One final marketing note about *Bernardine:* Boone had a lucrative
endorsement deal with Coca-Cola, and the soft drink is shamelessly
plugged throughout the film. The instantly recognizable Coke bottle
pops up everywhere, foregrounded visually and mentioned repeatedly
in dialogue. Perhaps in ironic admission of the blatant pitch, Boone's
mother at one point addresses her thirsty—and conspicuously blemish-
free—son with the remark, "Back on those sweet drinks again? When
your face was clearing up *so* nicely."

Boone's follow-up success, *April Love,* cast a somewhat wider demographic net than *Bernardine,* but it too was very much an efficiently
teen-targeted enterprise. The press book boasts of "eight weeks of
pre-selling on Pat Boone's ABC-TV show," "special Pat Boone endorsement record and interview for radio," and a "sound track album
and single of the title song." The exploitation campaign took a telling
interest in the promotional power of pop music (by now an almost exclusively teenage province) and succeeded brilliantly on all fronts:

> The title song was issued by Dot [Records] on October 1, fully eight weeks
> prior to first play-dates of the CinemaScope hit, to generate national inter-
> est in the film. Dot backed up its release with the greatest campaign in the
> company's history. In order to saturate every corner of the country, extra
> field representatives were hired, double truck ads were inserted in every ma-
> jor music trade publication, and a special juke box campaign was devised to
> assure the inclusion of the record in almost every situation in the country.

Like the same year's *Tammy and the Bachelor, April Love* is set in a rural locale whose landscape is as much psychological as geographical.
Evoking a set of classic American oppositions, the film depicts the rural environs as a pastoral ground for virtue and redemption, a refuge
from the corrupt sophistication of urban life. Nick (Boone, playing
against type as a troubled city youth on probation after a joyride in a
stolen car) works on an old Kentucky home for the summer, his farm
interlude a condition of his parole. The backstory intimates that Nick
got into some "malicious mischief running around with the wrong
crowd," a delinquent lapse attributed to urban temptations and a widowed working mother unable "to ride herd on him in the city." Nick is
placed under the gruff but loving tutelage of his Uncle Jed (Arthur

O'Connell), a man whose philosophy of child rearing owes nothing to Dr. Spock: "Heard a lot of talk you gotta treat kids different nowadays. I don't know what they mean by that. We raised our son the way we was raised—to fear God, to respect his elders, and to mind his manners. And 'til a better way comes along—and I ain't heard of one yet—that's the way it's gonna be with you as long as you're here." Unlike his cousins in the city or suburbia, the down-home patriarch is neither bruising nor weak-willed: he offers his teenage charge the kind of "straight answer" and sturdy guidance Dino and Jim Stark long for.

Taking a different tack from *Bernardine*, *April Love* attempts to make Boone the romantic focus, the object of affection for both the tomboyish Liz Templeton (Shirley Jones) and her older, more ladylike sister, Fran (Dolores Michaels). Again, though, the smooch restriction demands some agility: lovebirds Nick and Liz *talk* about an off-screen kiss and on one occasion are interrupted mere seconds from closure. In compensation, the pair are linked together visually in medium shots and close-ups: in song, on horseback, falling asleep together in the hay. *April Love* makes the occasional concession to contemporary teenage reality—a drag race, some straight-laced swing-based rock 'n' roll—but it is squarely (in both senses) a traditional Hollywood musical: beautifully photographed, well choreographed, and exceptionally performed. Moreover, in the person of Uncle Jed, parent culture gets an able and likable representative. He takes no backtalk from "the boy," and although Boone chafes under his uncle's authority, he never rebels. In *April Love*, one of a handful of 1950s screen hits with intergenerational appeal, both teenagers and adults apparently preferred an imperious patriarch to an impotent one.

Another early demonstration of the profitability of clean teenpics was the success of Universal-International's cornpone *Tammy and the Bachelor* (1957). Starring twenty-five-year-old Debbie Reynolds as a barefoot and blue-jeaned bayou teen, the film expertly played its title character's down-home freshness against the affectations of citified society. In wooing the eligible scion Peter Brent (Leslie Nielsen) and winning over his upper-crust family, the rural savvy of the pigtailed, calico-clad Tammy proves more effective than the haute couture sophistication of her elegant rival, Barbara (Mala Powers). But Tammy's talents are not confined to romance: benefiting immeasurably from Reynolds's spunky portrayal, she emerges as self-reliant, aggressive, resourceful, practical, insightful, and sexually unskittish (assuming city slang, she asks herself, "I'm not a wolf on the make—or am I?"). An independent seventeen-year-old who comes and goes as she pleases, Tammy is one of the few female teenagers permitted to command center stage for the duration of a full-length feature. Apparently, a teenpic product line dominated by male preferences profited by a change of fashion. *Variety* expected *Tammy*'s surprise popularity to induce film companies "to reappraise their story properties": "In an era in which it is believed that only offbeat, hard-hitting themes can achieve b.o. success, *Tammy*, an obviously corny romantic love story in the Cinderella tradition, is emerging as one of the most unusual entries of the summer season." At a cost of a little more than $1 million, the film had grossed in excess of $1.5 million in twelve weeks on the strength of enthusiastic word-of-mouth comment from "the teenage dating set and family groups."

The clean teenpics weren't family entertainment in the old sense: as MGM found out, Andy Hardy really had died. By earlier standards, some of them were downright grimy. *Blue Denim* (1959) concerned teenage pregnancy and an averted abortion; *Going Steady* (1958) dealt with a secret teenage marriage; teenage pregnancy cropped up again in *Because They're Young* (1960); and *Where the Boys Are* (1960) trafficked in premarital sex and what would later be called date rape. Perversely, all these films stressed their basic middle-class decency. To judge from some of their advertising, they were produced solely as cautionary tales for suburban families. In trailers for *Blue Denim*, model mommy Joan Crawford recommended that every concerned parent see the film: "These are no juvenile delinquents," read the ads, "these are nice kids in trouble!" *Going Steady*, a Sam Katzman–Fred F. Sears project, was publicized as a "wholesome fun show the whole family will love," a telling switch in tactics for the team that had virtually invented the exploitation teenpic. Columbia Pictures representative Robert S. Ferguson called *Going Steady* "a sweetheart of a comedy and we know that moviegoing families everywhere will take it to heart." Likewise, producer Joe Pasternak offered assurances that *Where the Boys Are* was the kind of "comedy and entertainment" that "won't cause controversy."

Most clean teenpics treated familial relations only nominally. Their real focus was the self-contained world of the teenager, where adults were sometimes inconvenient but more often peripheral or superfluous. The teenage crisis is typically peer-group puppy love, not parental pressure. In the clean teenpic's baroque phase, AIP's *Beach Party* cycle

(1963–65), parents were banished altogether. As compensation, though, there was little in this portrait of teenage life that would disturb a worried father. Adults were usually absent, but their values were always present. Fulfilling the best hopes of the older generation, the clean teenpics featured an aggressively normal, traditionally good-looking crew of fresh young faces, "good kids" who preferred dates to drugs and crushes to crime. Sweet, sanitized, and sun-drenched, they gave a bright but bowdlerized update to familiar romantic-comedic situations. The filmic world of *Tammy and the Bachelor*, *Senior Prom* (1958), *Summer Love* (1958), *Gidget*, *Where the Boys Are*, and almost anything with Pat Boone or his teen idol ilk is a never-never land, removed from both the social reality of *Dino* and the psychological horrors of *I Was a Teenage Werewolf.* The "kids" are well-behaved middle-class youngsters with few blemishes, facial or otherwise. At a time when good, wholesome middle-class families were proliferating like crabgrass, the market for like-minded movies had been only dormant, not dead.

It may seem odd that the same audience who had lately rebelled with Dean and rocked with Presley should also sigh with Gidget and swoon over Boone. But while moviegoers typically have a definite preference for a certain kind of motion picture—and this preference might be broken down to reveal, say, that women generally like romances and men like action-adventure—avid moviegoers attend all kinds of movies. As the decade's most dedicated class of theater patrons, 1950s teenagers supported the whole range of popular movies. Exhibitors occasionally turned this to their advantage with twin bills that accentuated rivalries—"Boone versus Presley" programs and the like. Voracious in their filmgoing appetites, teenagers could be counted on to support virtually any film format reworked to teenage tastes: the Hollywood musical (*Rock Around the Clock*), the crime melodrama (*Crime in the Streets*), the horror film (*I Was a Teenage Werewolf*), and so on.

Whatever the packaging, most of the early teenpics showcased the underside of teenage life, portraying a reckless, rebellious, and troubled generation beset by problems of inner and/or outer space. Whether imperial and negative or indigenous and affirmative, they accentuated subcultural differences, resistance, and alternatives to parent cultural values. Their appeal, by and large, was to the male half of the target audience. The clean teenpics, by contrast, were light, breezy, romantic, and frankly escapist. They forswore the anguish of the "troubled teen" for the innocence of the "sweet sixteen"; *I Was a Teenage Werewolf* became "I Was a Normal Teenager." They were aimed primarily at the young female trade, which, according to a 1959 survey of teenage girls by *Seventeen* magazine, preferred musicals, romances, and comedies. Sandra Dee, whose string of hits included *The Restless Years* (1958), *The Reluctant Debutante* (1958), *Imitation of Life* (1959), and *Gidget*, was the role model of choice. A 1959 popularity poll that named the seventeen-year-old actress "the Number One Star of Tomorrow" concluded, "Her wide appeal to her own generation as well as adults doubtless stems from the fact that she seems to epitomize that nice 'girl next door.' . . . The image she projects on screen is that of today's teenager beset by problems her own generation can sympathize with and understand. . . . Nearly always these problems involve parental relationships and dating, and Miss Dee solves them by relying on decent instincts and common sense. No juvenile delinquent she."

In fact, "shes" were no juvenile delinquents. One value of the parent culture that teenage subculture fully and faithfully echoed—even exaggerated—was the thoroughgoing subordination and domestication of its female participants. Apart from the occasional reform school girl or hot-rod hellcat, teenage girls were dealt screen roles befitting their sexual status: loyal supporters and civilizing influences to the j.d. hood, ebullient dancers and boy-crazy fans in the rock 'n' roll cycle, endangered innocents in the SF/horror teenpics, and, above all, daintily pretty and enticingly postured sights for male eyes. Teenage boys, as AIP knew, bought most of the tickets.

Of course, from an orthodox feminist perspective, the sexual politics of the teenpic are chillingly retrograde. Though critics have proven adroit at revising, reclaiming, and deconstructing patriarchal Hollywood for matriarchal meaning—discerning liberating impulses in the marked women of a Warner Bros. melodrama from the 1940s, the student nurses of a New World exploitation film from the 1970s, and the stalked cheerleaders of serial-killer films from the 1990s—teenpics from the 1950s have been largely resistant to politically correct rehabilitation. Only occasionally is a teenpic amenable to a reading that may overturn gendered expectations. Consider, for example, Sam Katzman's production *It Came from Beneath the Sea* (1955), which features a strikingly liberated "lady scientist" who fends off male suitors to pursue her career. "You were right about this new breed of woman," the chagrined hero tells his rival in the closing dialogue. Still, taken in sum, teenpics from the 1950s dutifully abide by the gender protocols of their elder genres. In *The Sociology of Youth Culture and Youth Subculture*, Mike Brake sees youth subcultures as elaborate societies for "the celebration of masculinism" in which girls function largely as macho accoutrements. More consistently and egregiously than in parent culture, teenage subculture often relegates the female to a kind of veiled *purdah*, a background figure Brake calls "the invisible girl."

One notable teenpic in which the invisible girl materialized up front was Columbia's *Gidget*, a respectably budgeted (CinemaScope, Eastman Color) romantic comedy granted a high-profile promotion. The title "girl midget" (Sandra Dee) is at the "in-between age," pushing seventeen and not yet interested in the predatory tactics of her boy-crazy friends. Surfer-boy Moondoggie (James Darren) changes her mind, but she seems more enthralled with surfing, a sport the beach boys claim is "too dangerous for girls," than with romance. She resolves to learn to surf and cajoles her affluent parents into buying her a board so she can surf "just like the guys." Gidget waffles between puppy love for an older surf bum (Cliff Robertson) and her preordained dreamboat, Moondoggie. Her tenacity and resourcefulness in learning to surf and her exhilaration at successfully "shooting the curl" are more interesting than the patented boy-girl stuff, but whatever feminist fire simmers within Gidget is effectively doused by Mom ("One of the advantages of being a young lady is it's not up to you, it's up to the young man") and the conventions of narrative closure.

Where the juvenile delinquents and adolescent monsters of other teenpic cycles played to impulses of rebellion and alienation, the clean teenpics offered the prospect of warm, familial acceptance and reconciliation with the parent culture. To later generations tending to value conflict rather than accommodation, the incarnations of the former have always appealed more than the latter: as a cultural icon, Brando in leather beats out Boone in a cardigan. Yet the 1950s film figures indelible for the modern viewer—the neurotics, rebels, and rockers of poster fame—may not have had that preeminent stature for their contemporary audience. Their luster derives from a historical hindsight in which the 1950s rebels without a cause and housewives on the verge of revolt become certified precursors to the 1960s counterculture, hence closer to the sensibilities of the generation that came to write most of the canonical film criticism. The pictures and personalities that showcase an alternative, domesticated image of teenage life in the 1950s tend to be ignored despite the fact that their contemporary appeal rivaled, and sometimes surpassed, the malcontented movies beloved by a subsequent generation.

In 1959, Eugene Gilbert, the dean of youth market research, noted an anomaly in parental attitudes toward teenagers that suggested high school hellcats were not statistically representative. Although the culture still experienced a good deal of worry over the excesses of the younger generation, Gilbert reported, "Paradoxically, many parents find their children too conventional. They wish their daughters would have a few romantic flings before settling down with the boys they were going steady with in junior high school. And they would like—or think they would like—to see their sons dreaming of adventuresome careers rather than steady jobs with dependable pension plans. . . . [Among today's teenagers] conservatism and conformity are clearly on the increase." Gilbert wasn't alone in detecting a secret strain of wholesomeness in the younger generation. Surveying three popular teenage advice books (Pat Boone's 'Twixt Twelve and Twenty, Dick Clark's Your Happiest Years, and Abigail Van Buren's Dear Teenager, all 1959), the New Republic commented, "There is one group of Americans—our adolescents—about whose morals there need be no concern at all. One has only to read one of the current books of guidance, addressed to this class, to see how really virtuous our youth must be."

The music charts got preachier too. Sound advice and churchly accompaniments drowned out suggestive lyrics and raucous backbeats. In 1956, when Frankie Lymon and the Teenagers sang "I'm Not a Juvenile Delinquent," the street-corner celebration of the delivery muted the lecture in the lyrics. Their performance of the tune in Rock Rock Rock! is hilariously ironic, featuring the fourteen-year-old Lymon out front, hands clasped in prayer, eyes heavenward. By 1958, teen singers were playing it straight. The lyrics straightened up and the beat decelerated. To underscore their acceptability, many followed the example of Elvis's 1958 Christmas album, widening their repertoire with hymns and ballads. In Albert Zugsmith's Girls Town (1958), Paul Anka sings "Ave Maria"; in Sing, Boy, Sing! (1958), Tommy Sands croons "Rock of Ages"; and in Go, Johnny, Go! (1959), Julie Campbell addresses her "Heavenly Father." The definitive religious advice song was "The Teen Commandments" (backed with "If You Learn to Pray"), a "code for today's teens." Recorded in 1958 by Paul Anka, George Hamilton IV, and Johnny Nash, the "10-point guide for the rock 'n' roll era" included such couplets as "stop and think / before you drink," "be humble enough to obey / you will be giving orders yourself someday," and "choose a date who would make a good mate."

Such tunes were symptomatic of a creative doldrums in rock 'n' roll, a "treacle period" marking an audible decline in the music's originality, vitality, and volume. Part of the reason for the downturn was the abrupt exit of rock 'n' roll's premier talent. In 1957, Little Richard walked away from "the devil's music" after a Damascus experience reportedly precipitated by *Sputnik*. In March 1958, Elvis Presley was inducted into the army, forfeiting $450,000 in contracted film salaries from MGM and Twentieth Century-Fox for a draftee's monthly wage of $78. The same year, Jerry Lee Lewis became unsalable after marrying his thirteen-year-old cousin. The year 1959 saw Buddy Holly perish in a plane wreck and Chuck Berry indicted under the Mann Act. Finally, the payola scandals of 1959–60 bagged Alan Freed, rock 'n' roll's most enthusiastic proponent and a sharp-eyed nurturer of young talent. A whole pantheon of frenetic musical talent had been rendered inoperative in a remarkably short time.

There was, in fact, a near-universal sense that teenagers had lately straightened up. In 1960, *American Bandstand* host Dick Clark gauged the new teenage zeitgeist: "The thing I've noticed is that the kids are calming down. Their dress is more conservative. We don't let them on the show unless they're reasonably well-dressed—leather jackets are out—but we never have much trouble of this kind. . . . These kids are alright. They wash behind their ears. They don't cut their classes. They wear neckties." The transformation of Elvis Presley from the rebel rocker of 1958 to the beloved entertainer of 1960 is the most commonly cited benchmark. After completing his well-publicized hitch in the army, Presley made his first civilian "comeback" appearance on a TV special hosted by Frank Sinatra. *TV Guide* welcomed his symbolic immersion into the mainstream: "Presley wiggled off to military service in 1958 as a smokey-eyed youth with a history of biting a girl reporter on the hand. ('If you want to get ahead, lady, you got to be different.') . . . He came marching home to Memphis earlier this year [March 1960] shorn of his sideburns and behaving the way a sedate, serious-minded youngster should."

Of course, any single metaphor describing teenage life in the 1950s—whether the generation is called "silent" or "shook-up"—is an oversimplification. If the era's popular teenpics prove anything, it is that 1950s teens were a diversified group with a multitude of (sometimes contradictory) tastes and values. Like subsequent generations, this first teenage subculture had internecine style wars over entertainment and fashion, fought along lines of class, ethnicity, and region. In addition, in teenage terms the difference between the graduating class of 1956 and that of 1960 is a whole generation: the spunky rhythm-and-blues fans of 1956 no longer set the pace for the class of compliant teen-idol worshipers in 1960 (though the age spread for teen-culture participation had already expanded on the high end; by the mid-1960s, there was open admission). The perceived difference in teenage behavior from 1954–58 to 1958–62 is only partly explained by a generational shift or a sudden lurch to the psychological right.

Far more important was the fact that teen-oriented show business had finally come of age. After several years of misjudgments and hit-and-miss experimentation, the major music, television, and motion picture companies had mastered the exploitation of the teenage market. By the end of the decade, executives throughout the entertainment industry acknowledged the importance, if not the primacy, of the teenage market, and—the crucial next step—they now had the expertise to manipulate it with confidence. For Hollywood, this kind of certainty almost compensated for the loss of the old mass audience.

Transmedia Exploitation

The creation and exploitation of the "clean teen idols" offer the best evidence of the entertainment industry's newly acquired sophistication in handling the teen marketplace. These campaigns were well-orchestrated cooperative endeavors in which the motion picture industry acted in concert with—or fed off—the efforts of other teen-dependent media. In one sense, such "transmedia" marketing was nothing new; its history extended back to the grand ballyhoo campaigns waged by turn-of-the-century fast-buck boys for the first generation of show business stars. From the beginning of the Hollywood studio system, the careers of favored contract players had been boosted by press agents and guided by managers. Successive refinements in media manipulation accompanied especially those performers—Al Jolson, Bing Crosby, and Frank Sinatra, for example—who simultaneously dominated recording, broadcasting, and screen entertainment.

By 1945–56, then, when teenagers made their first firm imprint on popular culture, there was a history of transmedia exploitation to draw on. The careers of teenybopper heartthrobs and singing sensations got the saturation treatment, and, like many "overnight" stars, they owed their success (talent aside) to a coordinated attack on the national media. The star-making machinery Colonel Tom Parker built for Elvis Presley set the standard for a well-oiled show business operation. More often, though, the adult professionals who controlled the suddenly teen-oriented film and music industries found the new audience harder to read than hieroglyphics. It was several years before the accumulation of statistical data, the development of cooperative exploitation efforts among the mass media, and a backlog of trial-and-error experience provided these professionals with the confidence and ability to manipulate the teen market systematically and profitably. What distinguished the media campaigns waged on behalf of the teen idols from earlier public relations assaults was a difference more of degree than of kind. Their media hegemony was achieved with greater speed, skill, and certainty.

As the most powerful, publicized, and profitable feature of teen culture, rock 'n' roll music came in for the most intensive manipulation. By 1958, the music industry's initial bewilderment over and suspicion of rock 'n' roll had largely disappeared, and the old business and the young sound were locked in a tight embrace. Schooled in teenage tastes and backed by the latest in mass-marketing sales techniques, a hungry breed of managers, promoters, and hustlers brought new certainty and cynical expertise to the once-unpredictable business of making hit rock 'n' roll singles. In their hands, the "vinyl crap game" that was the record industry became a less risky, more formulaic operation—especially when they played with loaded dice.

The emblematic figure for the new breed of professionals was Dick Clark, the Philadelphia-based disc jockey and television personality who by 1958 had surpassed Alan Freed as the reigning pied piper of teenage music fans. A workaholic of epic dimensions, Clark was involved in every imaginable facet of the music business. At age twenty-nine he made broadcast history by hosting three different ABC-TV shows that gave him daily network exposure: *American Bandstand* (4:00–5:30 P.M., Monday through Friday), *The Dick Clark Show* (7:30–8:00 P.M., Saturday), and *Dick Clark's World of Talent* (10:30–11:00 P.M.,

Sunday). Through the late-afternoon video record hop *American Bandstand*, Clark wielded unmatched influence in the record industry. He reached an estimated 40 million viewers each week, half of whom were teenagers. Securing play for a new record on *American Bandstand* virtually assured momentum on *Billboard*'s charts, and Clark, nicknamed "Mr. Plug" by the trade press, was vigorously courted by eager record promoters.

Unlike Freed, Clark and the hustlers he typified had no commitment to a particular kind of popular music. "I don't set trends," said Clark. "I just find out what they are and exploit them. When you get down to it, I'm mostly a businessman who's *beginning* to learn to be a performer. Like any businessman, the desires of my customers must come first." Entrepreneurs whose specialty happened to be teenage entertainment, Clark and his ilk were most interested in a standardized, reliable, and reproducible product with wide merchandising potential throughout the entertainment field. The clean teen idol answered their needs.

The clean teen idol's immediate big brother was Pat Boone, whose public image and multimedia versatility lit the way for the invasion at the close of the decade. Intelligent, handsome, unfailingly cooperative, and genuinely talented, Boone moved effortlessly from one entertainment arena to another. He had begun his career as a contestant and then a featured performer on Arthur Godfrey's *Talent Scouts* on CBS-TV. By 1955–56, his lovelorn ballads and palatable cover versions of R&B hits (Fats Domino's "Ain't That a Shame" and Little Richard's "Tutti Fruitti") made him one of the few solo artists regularly to challenge Presley's preeminence on the music charts. Boone's subsequent entry into motion pictures built on and contributed to the momentum of his TV and recording careers.

To take an early example: "Love Letters in the Sand," the smash from *Bernardine*, hyped the film, which in turn hyped the hit song. Although Hollywood had long recognized the box office value of popular theme songs (e.g., Bing Crosby's "Swinging on a Star" from *Going My Way* [1944], Doris Day's "Secret Love" from *Calamity Jane* [1953], and Frank Sinatra's title hit from *Young at Heart* [1954]), it had only lately begun coordinating teen-oriented music and teen-targeted movies. Director Richard Brooks's experience acquiring the rights to "Rock Around the Clock" for *Blackboard Jungle* (1955) illustrates the industry's shortsightedness. The director recalled:

Johnny Green, who is a marvelous composer and was running the music department at MGM at the time, said, "This record ['Rock Around the Clock'] is no good." He said, "It was a flash in the pan about three years ago and it lasted about two weeks and the whole craze was gone in two weeks." I said, "I know, but after all, it's not a matter of music doing anything special." I said, "It just belongs in this picture." So he inquired and . . . said, "Well, it's going to cost $5000 for unlimited use of the record." I said, "How much will it cost us to own the record?" He said, "Well, that will cost $7500—that's $2500 more." I said, "Why don't you get the whole thing?" . . . He said "No, that's enough." So we bought it for $5000, unlimited use for *this picture.* They bought the record and six months after the picture opened, it had sold over two million copies. The company would have owned that. They didn't.

With the release of *April Love,* Hollywood's business smarts had improved measurably. As *Motion Picture Herald*'s notice smugly pointed out, "By one of the most smartly arranged coincidences in modern merchandising history, this wholesome little story about a big city boy in the country goes to market simultaneously with the sale of the star's millionth recording of the title song."

By 1959, moviemakers considered theme-song tie-ins, with music-score soundtracks, "the greatest ticket-selling box office adjunct developed during the past few years . . . in the selling of motion pictures to the public." According to songwriter Sammy Cahn, "As far as returns are concerned, the most profitable investment the producer makes is the $10,000 to $12,000 which he pays for a title song. This doesn't even begin to cover what the radio time alone would cost if he had to pay for it every time a recording, plugging his picture, is aired."

For movies and music aimed at the teen audience, the mutual advantages of such tie-ins were more convincingly established by Boone than by Presley. Even at the time, many recognized Presley for what he was—a unique phenomenon. Whereas Presley was a wild card who appeared out of nowhere to incite a pop revolution, Boone was a traditional show business type whose white bucks were firmly planted on familiar ground. Presley was one of a kind; Boone was replicable. The clean teens may have taken their look from Presley, but their image was cast from Boone's model.

The representative figure of late-1950s/early-1960s popular music, the clean teen idol played Trilby to a business-wise Svengali who groomed his or her career to teen market specifications. Carefully packaged and relentlessly promoted, teen idols were the entertainment equivalent of Daniel Boorstin's "pseudo-event," wherein performance is subordinate to presentation. It wasn't how well they played guitar but how well they played the interdependent and increasingly teen-dependent entertainment network. The savvy Svengali attended mainly to product presentation, seeking to coordinate image and visibility among four key media: fan magazines, Top 40 radio, TV, and movies. If the publishing, music, television, or motion picture company had direct initial investment in the idol, cooperation was usually forthcoming, though just as often they participated simply out of a sense of common interest. Fan magazines in particular had lately become almost the exclusive province of teenagers. Greeting the emergence of a new entry called *Stardom* in 1958, freelance columnist Joe Cal Cagno observed, "Fan mags as we knew them in the old days featured the top movie stars and were snapped up by chubby matrons who drooled over the contents whilst ensconced on a downy couch munching bon-bons. . . . Now the fan mags concentrate on young disk talent [because teenagers] demand only the younger artists in print. Ricky Nelson, the Everly Brothers, Frankie Avalon, and, of course, Elvis. Pat Boone draws well, as does Dick Clark and Bobby Darin. The old singers—almost nothing."

The symbiotic relationship between the fanzines and the music industry was only one of the mutually advantageous interconnections among the entertainment media. Much of it, naturally, was frankly institutional, foreshadowing the huge entertainment conglomerates of the next decades. Beginning in the mid-1950s, motion picture studios awoke to the lucrative potential of music soundtrack tie-ins. In April 1958, Columbia's entry into the record business completed "the Hollywood studio platter line-up." United Artists, Twentieth Century-Fox, and Warner Bros. had lately set up their own labels; MGM had long had a record division; in 1956, Paramount bought out Dot Records (Boone's label); Universal was controlled by Decca; and RKO owned the Unique label. The next year *Billboard* noted that "the new film-based companies, which until recently have been fairly inactive chartwise, have begun to make a strong impact on both the best-selling singles and album charts." Significantly, two of the companies had clicked with teen-idol types amenable to multimedia exploitation: Columbia's Colpix label had James Darren singing the title song from *Gidget*, and Warner Bros. Records had Tab Hunter, whose "Young Love" had been a huge hit for Dot Records in early 1957, scoring respectably with "Jealous Love" and "Apple Blossom Time."

Offering maximum exposure on minimum investment, the record industry and television provided the best breeding grounds for aspiring teen idols. Motion pictures, by contrast, seldom "broke" a teen idol. Even a teenpic budget was too substantial to place solely on the shoulders of untested young talent. More important, movies couldn't provide the instant saturation availability young fans demanded of their idol of the moment. Once an idol was established, however, filmmakers of whatever degree of solvency were ready to lend their medium to the hoopla. Thus, whether their "home medium" was recording (Frankie Avalon, Fabian, Bobby Darin, Bobby Rydell, Tommy Sands, Paul Anka, Jimmy Clanton, and Connie Francis), television (Ricky Nelson, Johnny Crawford, Edd "Kookie" Byrnes, Annette Funicello, Paul Peterson, and Shelley Fabares), or movies (James Darren, Tab Hunter, Troy Donahue, or Sandra Dee), the clean teen idols moved with varying degrees of ease through the entire spectrum of teen-oriented entertainment. (Epic Records actually backed a recording career for Tony Perkins.) A beachhead secured in one corner of the teenage entertainment market was the base from which an idol, or more likely his managerial Svengali, could launch a concerted assault on kindred media. The careers of three clean teen idols—Tommy Sands, Edd "Kookie" Byrnes, and Fabian—are illuminating case histories.

On Wednesday, January 30, 1957, a relatively unknown nineteen-year-old singer named Tommy Sands appeared in an *NBC Kraft Television Theater* presentation called "The Singing Idol." This hour-long drama about a young singing sensation and his unscrupulous manager drew shamelessly on *The Jazz Singer* (1927) and the career of Elvis Presley for narrative inspiration. Still, Sands's performance in the title role made him an overnight sensation. On the show he had sung a lachrymose ballad called "Teenage Crush," which was immediately released as a single on Capitol. The next week *Billboard* reported that "the impact of TV is amply demonstrated by the story of 'The Singing Idol.'" Not only had the project immediately been bought as a feature film by Twentieth Century-Fox, but "Teenage Crush," "based on its send-off on the Kraft Show," was expected to sell five hundred thousand copies. The estimate was conservative: "Teenage Crush" ("a timely ballad about the kids who BUY the records," as the trade ads put it) broke into the top ten in three weeks and sold a million copies within eight weeks.

Throughout, Sands was kept in the teenage eye via fanzines and regular appearances on network shows. In keeping with the clean teen idol code written by Boone, his presentation occupied the ground to Presley's right. *Time*'s description was on the mark: "As uncomplicated as most of the songs he sings, Tommy neither drinks nor smokes, lives with his mother in a four-room Hollywood apartment, drives a red Ford convertible and, he says, reads philosophical and religious books 'to find out what makes people tick.' Tommy explains, his brown eyes watering, 'I think all religions are the greatest.'"

Dick Clark defined the clean teen idols as "stars who specialized in being nice young men underneath it all instead of rock 'n' roll stars" and reiterated the widely quoted qualification that, like AIP monsters, "white teen idols didn't smoke, drink, or swear." The most fervent fans of the clean teens were barely pubescent girls for whom the idols functioned as the next step up from stuffed animals: platonic, not carnal; cuddly but never penetrating.

Twentieth Century-Fox highlighted Sands's devout dreamboat image in its 1958 feature film version of "The Singing Idol," *Sing, Boy, Sing!* Under the tag line "the preacher's son who became a rock 'n' roll king," Sands plays a compact Elvis clone named Virgil Walker. The opening scene has preteen Virgil crooning a hymn ("I'm Gonna Walk and Talk with My Lord") before the congregation at his grandfather's hellfire tent-show revival meeting. After a dissolve signals a quick flash-forward, the full-grown Virgil, dressed in white and backed by a huge band, is on stage performing a jerry-built rhythm-and-blues version of the same number. Spaced between several lushly orchestrated quasi-rock 'n' roll numbers, including the title tune and the memorably awful "Soda Pop Pop" ("He's the only one on the street / who makes soda with a beat"), Virgil anguishes over loneliness at the top (he's reduced to hiring a peer-group friend, a nincompoop Okie played by Nick Adams) and Granddad's deathbed admonition to give up the devil's music (like Little Richard, he tearfully promises to become a preacher and sing only for the Lord).

The jaundiced portrait of the teen idol business in *Sing, Boy, Sing!* is instructive. Virgil's manager, given the eponymous name of Mr. Sharkey and a splendidly unsympathetic portrayal by Edmond O'Brien, is a greedy, vicious Svengali who calls every shot for Virgil—personal, professional, and artistic. Mr. Sharkey censors Virgil's mail, withholds the news of Granddad's near-fatal heart attack, negotiates motion picture

Obey, boy, obey: teen idol Tommy Sands takes instructions in *Sing, Boy, Sing!* (1958). (Museum of Modern Art Film Stills Archive: Courtesy of Twentieth Century-Fox)

and merchandising tie-ins, and, significantly, decides what music to record. At a recording session, a producer suggests that Virgil's next album be called "Rock of Ages," with one side of gospel music and one side of rock 'n' roll. The idol is enthusiastic, but the manager vetoes the concept as uncommercial. Allied with Mr. Sharkey is a somewhat more humane public relations man named Arnie (Jerry Paris), who handles the media manipulation with state-of-the-art ingenuity. For Virgil's arrival in New York, Arnie commissions an old man to paint makeshift "Welcome Virgil" signs, coaching him to misspell a few words "so they'll look like kids did 'em." In an implicit acknowledgment of commercial radio payola, he has several compliant disc jockeys announce Virgil's arrival downtown. When a mob of teenagers shows up (with the presupplied signs), Arnie tells the surprised and unknowing Virgil, "That's the kind of demonstration you can't fake."

Less urgent than the churchbiz-versus-showbiz dilemma of Jolson vintage is the question of Virgil's personal autonomy: when will he slip out from under Sharkey's thumb? In the climactic scene, a distraught Virgil runs from his grandfather's funeral after squealing teenyboppers disrupt his rendition of "Rock of Ages." He next attacks a newspaper photographer who sneaks a shot of him praying. Sharkey tries to control the media damage by compelling Virgil to get down on his knees and pose for the press corps. At this he finally erupts, ejects the reporters, and fires Sharkey and Arnie. But Sharkey knows his boy: he assures the press that nobody has been fired, that Virgil is just upset from the recent pressure. After the church-showbiz complication is resolved, it turns out Sharkey is right. In a concluding airport departure scene, a reunited manager, public relations man, flunky friend, and singing idol fly back to the big city and the rock 'n' roll merry-go-round. Despite the hometown girl's last-minute shot at Sharkey ("I'll be around Virgil a lot longer than you"), it is she who stays on the tarmac. For Hollywood filmmakers and teenage audience alike, the idea of a clean teen idol taking control of his own career was beyond imagining.

Twentieth Century-Fox had high hopes for *Sing, Boy, Sing!* The studio's general sales manager, Alex Harrison, announced that "in these days when we are all fighting hard for every box office dollar the market can produce, I firmly believe Tommy Sands in *Sing, Boy, Sing!* is pure gold for theaters everywhere." Accompanied by Ted Wicks, his personal manager, Sands undertook a personal-appearance tour to publicize the film, reportedly meeting with "mob hysteria" in his hometown of Houston. The sweeping transmedia assault and the cynicism of the whole operation was captured in *Motion Picture Herald*'s notice: "The young and recording-tested Tommy Sands would have a go at selling tickets to the boys and girls of his generation. . . . [Twentieth Century-Fox] came up with a film as sure to click with the rock 'n' roll crowd as anything can be sure in these days of topsy-turvy box office. That's the crowd with the ticket money and the mood to spend it."

But *Sing, Boy, Sing!* sank like a stone. The Sands exploitation picture had been released nearly a year to the day after "The Singing Idol" telecast. Although this was speedy by the standards of a major studio, Sands's teenybopper appeal had peaked well before January 1958. In addition, Sands culled his fans from the barely pubescent, predating, pre–driver's license teen set, a group that didn't attend movies in the numbers their older siblings did. Last, and most obvious, Sands fans had already seen the show on television. Even in Houston it closed in two days. "It was a good personal appearance," said the local theater manager, but "our attendance figures showed it was time to pull the film, though our runs usually extend for a week."

Teen idol transmedia exploitation advanced apace in the career of Edd "Kookie" Byrnes. In 1958–59, Byrnes, a costar on Warner Bros.' ABC television series *77 Sunset Strip*, parlayed pseudo–jive talk and a quirky hairstyling backswing into multimedia stardom. Although Byrnes emerged from the show more or less spontaneously as a screen-teen dreamboat, his subsequent exploitation was a tactical masterpiece. Month after month, fanzines kept his features before the high school crowd. Although *77 Sunset Strip* rotated different episodes around its two featured players (Efrem Zimbalist Jr. and Roger Smith), filming simultaneously on separate sound stages, Byrnes's teen idol status demanded his appearance on every show.

Kookie conquered another medium in spring 1959, when George Avakian, A&R man for Warner Bros. records, guided nonsinger Byrnes through a recording session for a novelty pop tune called "Kookie, Kookie (Lend Me Your Comb)," which featured Kookie-talk ("Baby, you're the ginchiest") and Connie Stevens (soon to be a femme screen star herself on Warner Bros.' *Hawaiian Eye;* Stevens did most of the actual singing). In three weeks the song was in the *Billboard* Top 10. Avakian later recalled how, while watching Kookie on *77 Sunset Strip* one evening, the concept came to him: "I was offended that there should be someone who looked like that and talked like that. But in the same instant I was struck by an obvious inspiration—he should make rock 'n' roll records. I was sure the kids would like him, especially a way he had of looking out of the corner of his eye. And—the real clincher for his popularity with kids—parents would loathe him." (Actually, parents found the clean teens fairly innocuous, especially considering the alternatives.)

The inevitable Kookie movie followed, Warner Bros.' *Yellowstone Kelly* (1959), a standard western that also featured Warner Bros. TV contract players Clint Walker *(Cheyenne)* and John Russel *(The Lawman)*. The cagiest filmic exploitation of Kookiemania came from AIP, however. Before hitting it big on *77 Sunset Strip*, Byrnes had done a little movie work, most notably as a Troy Donahue substitute in *Darby's Rangers* (1958). He had also appeared in AIP's *Reform School Girl* (1957), dismissed at the time with the remark that the "pic offers employment to large corps of local young actresses, perhaps its only real justification." Two years later, with Byrnes hotter than a pistol, AIP reissued *Reform School Girl*, gearing promotion and advertising largely to his presence. Again, *Motion Picture Herald* made a comment that applied to Kookiemania in particular and to clean teen idol exploitation in general: "This personable chap seems to be something that the females of the country's teenage set are buying at the moment and who's to argue when such substance is available in current product release."

In Fabian, teen idol presentation achieved a logical fulfillment. Fabian was fabricated by Bob Marcucci, cofounder and operator of Chancellor Records, located conveniently in Philadelphia. The definitive idolmaker, Marcucci didn't so much discover performers as manufacture them. Through native hustle and proximity to *American Bandstand*, he had made the marginally talented Frankie Avalon a teen scream sensation in early 1958. Fabian, though, was to be his purest creation—and the surest proof that the teen market, in skilled hands, could be played like a violin.

There are several different accounts of how Marcucci came across his raw material. The usual version has him stopping in front of a home in South Philadelphia to assist an ambulance driver who is treating a heart attack victim who turns out to be Fabian's father. On meeting the man's son, struck by the fourteen-year-old's features, Marcucci delivers the classic "Hey, kid, how'd you like to be a star?" line, to which Fabian replies, "You crazy?" Marcucci recalled, "Somehow I sense here was a kid who could go. He looks a little bit like both Presley and Ricky Nelson. I figured he was a natural. It's true he couldn't sing. He knew it and I knew it. But I was pretty sure he could be taught something about singing. The only trouble was, he didn't want to give up playing football."

Three frustrated voice teachers later, Fabian still couldn't sing. Fortunately, technology provided an added push to the swing from performance to presentation. Sophisticated refinements in audio recording techniques had lately made vocal abilities optional for aspiring singing idols. Recording engineers had nothing like the digital complexity of modern techno-pop studios, but through comparatively primitive "sweetening" processes (reverb, overdubbing, splicing, and echo) they could make an off-key croak sound passable. Fabian himself frankly reported, "If my voice sounds too weak, they pipe it through an echo chamber to soup it up. If it sounds drab, they speed up the tape to make it sound happier. If I hit a wrong note, they snip it out and replace it by one taken from another part of the tape. And if they think the record needs more jazzing, they emphasize the accompaniment. By the time they get done with the acrobatics, I can hardly recognize my own voice."

In a 1960 article on teen idol vocal skill occasioned by a $400,000 TV special titled *Coke Time*—hosted by Pat Boone, graced with most of the then-current teen faves, and sponsored by the consumer-wise soft drink company—*TV Guide* reported, "It's no secret in the trade that some of these young vocalists would be totally lost without recording tricks devised for them. As a result, when they appear on a live TV-show, they can't be trusted to sing. Instead, one of their recordings is played out of sight of the audience."

Fabian's first singles failed, but in March 1959, after Marcucci executed one of the era's textbook publicity scams, he finally broke into the top ten with "Turn Me Loose." (In a sequence of prominent ads, Marcucci first announced "Fabian Is Coming!" followed the next week by "Who Is Fabian?" and capped with a breathless "Fabian Is Here!") Twentieth Century-Fox, still on the lookout for a new teen screen magnet, quickly signed Fabian to a motion picture deal. Later that year he was introduced in *Hound Dog Man* (1959), directed by Don Siegel and produced by AIP nemesis Jerry Wald. Like most clean teen idol vehicles, the film was pitched as a "family picture." Fox sales manager Alex Harrison again gamely predicted that the film debut of "the Fabulous Fabian" should repeat his company's "historic experience with Elvis Presley in *Love Me Tender* and Pat Boone in *Bernardine*," promising that *Hound Dog Man* "will be in the tradition of the finest entertainments of Movieland, and will come to the screen endowed with an unmistakable set of values, including a story of broad appeal, exciting situations and youthful electric personalities. . . . The entire family audience [will] enjoy this rich entertainment together."

Hound Dog Man is, in fact, one of the more excruciating legacies of the clean teen era. The Presleyan reverberations of the title are a sham; the film has nothing to do with rock 'n' roll. Fabian plays a down-home farm boy in a rustic community where the local color is strictly Hollywood Dogpatch: coon hunts, square dances, cornpone jargon, and rural aphorisms ("Either a man handles the liquor or the liquor handles him"). Woven into the romantic complications are several tunes of abysmal badness (Frankie Avalon gets a composing credit), one of which, the title song, made the Top Ten. Despite energetic teen-targeted ballyhoo (including a "Why I Would Like to Have a Date with Fabian" contest sponsored by *American Bandstand*), financial returns on

Hound Dog Man (1958): transmedia exploitation reaches its logical conclusion with teen idol Fabian. (Museum of Modern Art Film Stills Archive: Courtesy of Twentieth Century-Fox)

the film were disappointing. One Fox executive blamed "tremendous public rejection" of Fabian. Others speculated that *Hound Dog Man* "had banked too heavily on a rock 'n' roller at a time when rock 'n' roll is on the way out" and, more accurately, that "Fabian is really a favorite of the very young kids and not of the ticket-buying teenagers."

Despite the less-than-encouraging returns on teen idol vehicles such as *Sing, Boy, Sing!, Yellowstone Kelly,* and *Hound Dog Man,* Hollywood continued to court teen talent. In 1959, *Billboard* reported, "In an effort to discover another record artist with the box office pull of Elvis Presley or Pat Boone, the major Hollywood film studios are signing up best-selling disk names today as fast as they hit top 10. . . . The interesting aspect of these recent signings is that artists involved are all playing dramatic roles (with their vocalizing strictly secondary to their thesping) whereas in the past most rock 'n' roll warblers were utilized mainly in special music sequences." The emphasis on a clean teen's "dramatic ability" was out of necessity. The original rock 'n' rollers, after all, were electrifying performers: think of Little Richard in *Don't*

Knock the Rock, Presley in *Jailhouse Rock*, or Jerry Lee Lewis in *High School Confidential*. The clean teen idols, their celebrity built on looks and marketing, were always limited, and frequently pitiful, musical talents. Movies *had* to showcase their ersatz thespian talents.

Appropriately, once idolmakers surrendered the pretense that their charges were musical sensations capable of carrying a film, the teen idols did quite well for themselves on screen. Presley, it turned out, was unique after all: throughout the next decade, his variations on the clean teenpic formula proved that he alone could sustain a major (if awful) motion picture at the box office. Burnt when it built entire productions around a young sensation of the moment, Hollywood fared better with the traditional tack of introducing new faces into projects of proven appeal, thereby widening the demographic net. Although as featured players this generation of teen idols seldom rose above AIP-caliber material (at best), as second bananas in major and medium-budget movies they were a cost-efficient bow to the teen market.

Filmmakers employed several different strategies to provide a film with so-called youth insurance. A clean teen might be paired with an older, established star: for instance, Ricky Nelson and Fabian were matched with John Wayne in *Rio Bravo* (1959) and *North to Alaska* (1960), respectively, while Alan Ladd tutored Frankie Avalon in *Guns of the Timberland* (1960). Adult romance was often complemented by clean-teen puppy love, as in *A Summer Place* (1959: Dorothy McGuire and Richard Egan/Sandra Dee and Troy Donahue) *High Time* (1960: Bing Crosby and Nicole Maurey/Fabian and Tuesday Weld), *Come September* (1961: Rock Hudson and Gina Lollobrigida/real-life marrieds Bobby Darin and Sandra Dee), *Portrait in Black* (1960: Anthony Quinn and Lana Turner/Sandra Dee and John Saxon), and, fittingly, the Elvis Presley satire *Bye Bye Birdie* (1963: Dick Van Dyke and Janet Lee/Bobby Rydell and Ann-Margaret). Large-scale action adventures generally made a place for a teenage favorite in the ensemble: Pat Boone in *Journey to the Center of the Earth* (1959), Horst Buchholtz in *The Magnificent Seven* (1960), James Darren in *The Guns of Navarone* (1961), and Frankie Avalon in *The Alamo* (1960) and *Voyage to the Bottom of the Sea* (1960). The strategy of "casting to everyone's taste" reached absurd lengths in the platoon commissioned for Columbia's Korean War film *All the Young Men* (1960), an ensemble that included "Sidney Poitier for international and black [fans], Alan Ladd for old-timers, heavyweight champion Ingemar Johansson for sports fans,

Mort Sahl for eggheads," and James Darren and Glenn Corbett for the teenage audience, "without whom, it seems, the nation's theaters would perish."

When it became apparent that the clean teens might not have major drawing power singly, filmmakers banked on combinations: Tommy Sands, Pat Boone, and Gary Crosby in *Mardi Gras* (1958); Sal Mineo and James Darren in *The Gene Krupa Story* (1959); Sal Mineo, Gary Crosby, and Barry Coe in *A Private's Affair* (1959); Fabian and Tommy Sands in *Love in a Goldfish Bowl* (1961); and Bobby Darin and Pat Boone in *State Fair* (1962). Finally, teenage domination of pop music radio, coupled with their box office importance to filmmakers, shifted Hollywood attention away from LP soundtrack tie-ins (still largely an adult market) to the Top 40 singles charts (a teenage market). Some of the more successful tie-ins include the title songs from *Friendly Persuasion* (1956) and *Anastasia* (1956), both sung by Pat Boone; from *Gidget* (1959), sung by James Darren; from *A Summer Place* (1959), performed by Percy Faith and his Orchestra; from *Where the Boys Are* (1960), sung by Connie Francis; and "Tammy," sung by Debbie Reynolds (on Decca, from Universal's *Tammy and the Bachelor*).

The mechanical efficiency that the entertainment industry—particularly the record business—brought to clean-teen exploitation lent a modicum of security and regulation to a business still fraught with risk and uncertainty. In a few short years, teenagers had become well-defined and well-attended culture consumers. Their entertainment tastes were not only being predicted with a new degree of assurance, they were being dictated. Rock critic Greg Shaw has written that the teen idol era (which he dates from 1959 to 1963, though Sands's January 1957 emergence is an equally good starting point) was a "product of the assumption that the kids were endlessly gullible, utterly tasteless, and dependably aroused by a comely face or a gratuitous mention of 'high school' or 'bobby sox.'" "Pop Music," George Avakian agreed, "is in such a low state that it can't be injured by non-musical performers."

The promulgation of the clean teen idols meant more than contempt, however. At its beginning, rock 'n' roll music had elicited at best only bemused condescension from record executives. "If the public wants Chinese music, we'll give them Chinese music" was radio programmer Todd Schultz's motto. But as the surprise that greeted the great rock 'n' roll explosion of 1954–56 testified, at least then teenagers had the greater say in selecting their musical diet. With the clean teen idols, the record industry increasingly determined the items on the menu. The means used were both fair (exploitation) and foul (payola).

Payola

Billboard defined "payola" as that "under the table device whereby record companies and distributors win plugs and influence disk jockeys," generally through gifts, favors, or cash. Payola had been around ever since Marconi, but in 1959–60, the enormous financial rewards at stake in Top 40 radio programming, the scale of corruption, and the still-controversial arena of activity (rock 'n' roll) inspired an unprecedented surge of government and public scrutiny into record business practices. The fact that the quiz show scandals of 1958–59 had tainted a kindred medium served to intensify suspicions of radio foul play. In addition to independent investigations by three federal agencies (the Federal Trade Commission, the Federal Communications Commission, and the Internal Revenue Service) and state grand juries, the House Legislative Oversight Subcommittee, chaired by Oren Harris (D–Arkansas), undertook "the first exhaustive probe of the entire music industry in the history of America," promising special attention to the more subtle "relationships of the unwholesome payola situation to American teenagers."

The most famous subjects of the payola investigations were Alan Freed and Dick Clark, two men who throughout the 1950s had made very public and profitable livelihoods in the teen marketplace. These former disc jockeys had seen the rock 'n' roll revolution coming and had ridden it to fame, fortune, and interconnected investment opportunities. Their fingers were in everything: songwriting, publishing, record manufacture and distribution, concert promotion, radio and television broadcasting, and motion picture production. During his testimony before the Harris Committee, Clark provided information on thirty-three corporations he had full or partial interest in, submitting a flowchart illustrating the labyrinthine connections among them. In a business in which exposure was so crucial and tie-ins so lucrative, the temptations to play with loaded dice were irresistible. Besides the fairly uncomplicated charges of play-for-pay, each disc jockey was also assumed to have used his influence to promote the songs he had a direct financial stake in. For example, as a credited composer for the Moonglows'/McGuire Sisters' hit "Sincerely" and Chuck Berry's "May-

Always in the middle: avuncular Alan Freed listens to both sides in *Rock Around the Clock* (1956). (Museum of Modern Art Film Stills Archive: Courtesy of Columbia Pictures)

bellene," Freed got royalties when the songs were played on his radio and TV shows. Likewise, Clark was suspected of using *Bandstand* to hype songs and artists he owned a piece of.

The major casualty of the payola scandals was Alan Freed. After refusing "on principle" to sign an ABC oath denying involvement with payola, he was fired from both his nationally syndicated radio show on WABC and his local WNEW-TV show in November 1959. In May 1960, the self-proclaimed "King of Rock 'n' Roll" was permanently dethroned when a New York grand jury named him in two criminal informations for illegally receiving $30,650 from various record companies. Freed eventually pled guilty to some of the charges and received a suspended sentence in 1962. Two years later he was indicted for income tax evasion on the payola he had accepted in 1957–59. Closure came to the bad movie when, on January 20, 1965, Freed, impoverished and forgotten, died of uremia at a Palm Springs hospital.

Freed wasn't a blameless victim of government persecution, but it was hardly accidental that he ended up taking the fall when standard operating procedure within the music business was suddenly rendered immoral. Freed was an outspoken champion of the rhythm and blues–based rock 'n' roll produced on small record labels. The emergence and ultimate dominance of rock 'n' roll in the singles market after 1954 is largely the story of these upstart labels' growth at the expense of the established record companies. In 1950, the independent record companies' share of the market had been minuscule; by 1957, they claimed 70 percent of the year's hit pop singles.

To break the major companies' hammerlock on radio airplay, the smaller labels had to court powerful disc jockeys with more than promotional 45s. Hence there was a logical association between small record labels and payola that led some die-hard critics of rock 'n' roll, unable by this late date to disdain the music as a passing fad, to conclude that the scourge might never have taken hold had not bribed deejays pushed the stuff on their infinitely malleable teenage listeners. In 1959, disc jockey Ed McKenzie explained why "teenage rock 'n' roll junk" had become so popular: "Payola really got started about ten years ago. Until then, the record business was controlled by the big companies like Decca, Columbia, RCA-Victor, and Capitol. When the obscure little record companies started up and began turning out offbeat records by unknown artists they looked for a way to get their product distributed and played. The answer was payola: offering disc jockeys cash to play records they wouldn't ordinarily play."

Ironically, what gave the charge credence was the ample contemporary evidence that teen music tastes were indeed being manipulated on a grand scale. Prior to the clean teen idols, the independence and unpredictability of teenage music fans were a record industry truism, as well as something of a national scandal. During 1954–58, the quality or morality of rock 'n' roll might be questioned, but no one could deny its authenticity as teen-inspired culture. By 1958, the natural hierarchy had reestablished itself. The clean-teen phenomenon was a quite literal product of the parent culture, fabricated from above, peddled down below.

In its blend of classic and clean teen rock 'n' roll sensibilities, *Go, Johnny, Go!* (1959), Alan Freed's last teenpic, highlights the differences and captures the transition between the two eras. Part of the film is the basic Alan Freed rockpic, featuring a top-notch lineup of performing talent that includes Jackie Wilson, Eddie Cochran, Chuck Berry, and "the late" Richie Valens. The rest is a bow to the clean-teen wave and, like *Sing, Boy, Sing!* an unwitting depiction of the underlying artificiality of the whole phenomenon.

Freed plays himself as a Svengali looking for the right boy to mold into a teenage idol whom he will name "Johnny Melody." The raw material is another Johnny, played by the marginal clean teen idol Jimmy Clanton. In flashback, we see Johnny's story. Kicked out of the church choir for playing rock 'n' roll during hymn rehearsals and fired for bopping to the rock 'n' roll concert he's supposed to usher, the ambitious kid approaches Freed to audition for Johnny Melody. Freed tells him to finish high school; the whole idea was just a publicity stunt. Undaunted, Johnny records a teen ballad with the help of his girlfriend, "Julie Melody," and submits it anonymously to Freed. To a background of Freed financial interests, the chaste courtship between Julie and Johnny blooms. They cuddle on a sofa and watch Chuck Berry do his duck walk to "Memphis" on Freed's WNEW-TV show, and they stroll past Freed's concert marquee on Loew's State Theater on Times Square. Inevitably, Freed plays Johnny's record on his WABC-radio "Big Beat" show. Audience response is tremendous; but who is this unknown singer? Freed resolves to play the song once every hour until the mystery teen comes forth.

Meanwhile, a despondent Johnny is unaware of the sensation he's causing. Desperate to get Julie a pin she wants for Christmas, he contemplates robbing a jewelry store. Alerted by Julie, Freed shows up at the store just as Johnny has tossed a brick through the window. Freed hustles the kid into a car. When the cops show up, he pretends to be a rowdy drunk—here, too, he takes the fall. In the final back-to-the-present scene, Johnny is knocking them dead at a Freed concert. The closeout coda is the rockpic cliché: bopping away in the audience is rock 'n' roll's newest convert, Johnny's former choirmaster.

A "second wave" rockpic, *Go, Johnny Go!* treats the music as a cultural given and keeps generational strife at a minimum. The choirmaster who hopes rock 'n' roll is "just a fad" dates himself, not the picture. The normal adults are Julie's parents, who groove with the kids to the Cadillacs and Jackie Wilson during a chaperoned night out at the Krazy Koffee Kup. Most of the talent has its roots in the classic rock 'n' roll era, but the thematic elements are pure clean teen: benevolent parents, juvenile puppy love, showbiz ambition, and the egregious machinations of a teen idolmaker (Freed). Indeed, the unconscious revelation in Freed's self-portrait was a kind of confirmation of the up-coming payola charges. His dominance over different areas of teen en-tertainment (recording, concert promotion, radio, television, and mo-tion pictures) and his unique influence with the teenage audience are repeatedly and explicitly emphasized. In *Go, Johnny, Go!* Freed virtually sets himself up.

Dick Clark was smarter. In both his business affairs and screen pre-sentations, he escaped the entanglements that brought about Freed's downfall. Where Freed associated himself with black rhythm and blues, riotous rock 'n' roll concerts, and motion pictures that explicitly depicted the whole controversial scene, Clark tended toward puppy-love ballads, sock hops, and clean teenpics. The teenpics he plugged on *American Bandstand* had nothing to offend anybody. (He began his relationship with Columbia by giving his personal endorsement to *Gidget* in a series of carefully targeted trailers and radio spots.) Clark's reputation for knowing "better than anyone else what makes good box office for [the] key [teenage] segment of [the] movie audience" secured him a motion picture production deal of his own. His first production was *Because They're Young* (1960), in which he played a helpful, upright, and understanding high school teacher; his involvement in the equally sparkling *Gidget Goes Hawaiian* (1961) apparently fell through, but in the American Medical Association–approved *The Young Doctors* (1961), his guise was again a trustworthy young man.

Because They're Young was fortuitously released during Clark's time of crisis: the payola hearings of 1960. After ABC picked up *American Bandstand* for national syndication in November 1957, Clark became the most powerful deejay in the country. Throughout 1959, he, as much as Freed, was the implicit target of the rumors and charges that resulted in government investigation of the recording industry. Al-though Clark steadfastly maintained no amount of airplay exposure could turn a "stiff" into a "hit," there seemed to be a statistically sig-nificant relationship between frequency of occurrences on *Bandstand*, chart standing, and Clark's investment portfolio. To take the heat off, Clark and ABC mutually crafted an affidavit, signed on November 16, 1959, in which Clark denied any wrongdoing. Clark also complied with ABC's demand to divest himself of any direct involvement in the record business, a sacrifice he later estimated cost him $8 million.

Charges against Clark persisted throughout that winter until, on April 30, 1960, the payola scandals reached a climax when Clark began

Transmedia exploitation: deejay/TV emcee Dick Clark endorses *Gidget* in a special trailer for Columbia, 1959. (Quigley Photographic Archive, Georgetown University Library)

two days of emotional public testimony before the Harris Committee. As usual, Clark was well spoken and well prepared. He came armed with financial disclosure forms, charts illustrating his financial empire, and a Computech survey analyzing his playlists. Certainly, Clark profited from some of the music played on his shows. His own survey found that he had a financial stake in 27 percent of the records played on his show between August 5, 1957, and November 3, 1959. That estimate was probably skewed in Clark's favor because the Computech statisticians counted the *Bandstand* theme song, which Clark held no interest in, 1,322 times. Still, the money had not come in white envelopes but was delivered as salary consideration from one of the many companies he invested in and performed a legitimate service for. The money came to Clark as royalties. Freed, in contrast, was found to be on the payrolls of companies he held no interest in. To some on the committee, the distinction was hairsplitting: Clark's fiercest congressional inquisitor, Steven Derounian (R–New York), told him that he may not have accepted payola but "you got an awful lot of royola."

Clark asserted that "the receipt of royalties, normal business procedures, making of income from interest in which you have ownership, that is not payola."

Despite some rough spots, Clark emerged from the hearings in better shape than he went in. At the conclusion of the testimony, Oren Harris pronounced him "a fine young man." ABC, which had so righteously fired Freed, backed Clark. Perhaps this was because he had acquiesced to their demands and made such an effective appearance before the committee. Or perhaps, as Freed suggested during his own closed-door testimony, it was because Clark's "gross income must be in the neighborhood of $12,000,000 for the network as against $250,000 a year I was grossing."

Although rock historians have interpreted the payola hearings as, in part, an anti–rock 'n' roll witchhunt that fostered the clean-teen treacle of the postclassic, pre-Beatle era, the Harris Committee was less interested in musical styles than in musical manipulation. Most of its ire, therefore, was directed not at R&B-based sounds (the traditional target) but at the clean-teen sound. True, the distinction was lost on chief counsel Robert Lishman, who broke up the gallery when he castigated Clark for not playing Frank Sinatra, Perry Como, Frankie Lane, or Bing Crosby on *American Bandstand*. But if some committee members exhibited an abysmal ignorance of popular music, others proved that even representatives of the Eighty-sixth Congress heard the difference between an authentic rock 'n' roller and a manufactured clean teen.

Fabian and Frankie Avalon were repeatedly criticized by the committee, not because they performed rock 'n' roll but because they performed so badly. Although Clark claimed no financial ties to either singer, he was grilled about them because of the frequent appearances the Philadelphia-bred pair had made on *American Bandstand*. Of Fabian, Congressman Derounian—who had earlier referred to Presley as "an outstanding artist"—inquired, "Why hasn't he sung more frequently in his own flesh instead of getting those hormone treatments on the records? . . . Isn't it true about the engineers jazzing up the records of Fabian?" Walter Rogers (D–Texas) suggested they could settle the matter by having Fabian sing for the committee, but Fabian, alas, was in Hollywood making movies. Congressman William Springer (R–Illinois) mentioned that when he heard Frankie Avalon on *American Bandstand*, the curious thing was that Avalon seemed to be singing off-key. Addressing Dick Clark, Derounian summed up the expert methodology of the idolmaker: "The singer appears on your program physically—and apparently that is your format, you get a big hunk of a young man who has got a lot of cheesecake to him and the kids are thrilled by this on the television program—and then you play his records, but you don't have him sing too often. That is the way you sell records and that is a pretty cute way to do it."

For the congressmen, the transmedia success of the clean teens was prima facie evidence of payola at work, and that September they formally outlawed the practice. But payola was only half the equation: modern exploitation methods remained, and, if anything, in the next few years the Svengalis consolidated their control of teen-oriented entertainment. Not until the Beatles arrived in 1964 would American teenagers again dictate the terms of their culture.

Generation after Generation of Teenpics

It's hard to tell if our problems are with *adult* juveniles or *juvenile* adults. If anyone could successfully answer this question, we would know the showmanship formula that never fails. It's hard to tell where to aim when you may have direct hits in either field, without any intention to make a bull's eye.

Walter Brooks, *Motion Picture Herald*, 1957

American civilization tends to stand in such awe of its teenage segment that it is in danger of becoming a teenage society, with permanently teenage standards of thought, culture, and goals. As a result, American society is growing down rather than up.

Grace and Fred M. Hechinger, *Teenage Tyranny*, 1963

n 1958, Arno H. Johnson, vice president and senior economist for the J. Walter Thompson Company, submitted a forecast of "The Economy of 1958–59" that had powerful implications for the motion picture industry. A front-page headline in *Variety* summed it up: "Film Future: GI Baby Boom." According to Johnson, the thirteen- to twenty-one-year-old market had grown from 19.6 million in 1952 to 22.4 million in 1958; an increase to a formidable 30 million was projected for 1965. Johnson informed moviemakers, "The growth of the 'teen market' is bound to make itself felt in many areas, but nowhere is it of greater significance than in the film field, both in terms of audience potential and as a guide to motion picture content. Not only are these the future homemakers, but they represent the 'restless' element of the population, the people who don't want to stay home and watch TV and who are still immune to any sophisticated disdain of run-of-the-mill screen offerings."

Johnson's film future looked to be a more extreme version of the film present. In 1955, Hollywood had initiated its courtship of the teenage audience with great reluctance; by 1960, it had become a devoted suitor. Delinquent dramas, Dean-agers, *Rock Around the Clock*, adolescent werewolves, and the sanitized spawn of Presley and Boone had, in turn and cumulatively, asserted the singular value of teenage moviegoers. Within a few short years the teenpic, a motion picture targeted at teens even to the exclusion of their elders, had become the most marketable of movie commodities.

When the first waves of the great 1946–57 baby boom came of "teenage age" in the 1960s, the consequences for the motion picture industry bore out Johnson's prediction. In 1968, Jack Valenti, Eric Johnston's successor as MPAA president, announced a Daniel Yankelovich audience research survey that reinforced the findings of earlier studies. According to Yankelovich, teenagers still filled out the lines at box office windows and older folks still stayed home. The sixteen-to-twenty-four age group made up 48 percent of box office admissions; 54 percent of that group were "frequent moviegoers," a number that rose to 78 percent when only the sixteen- to twenty-year-olds were considered. A zealous moviegoing cadre designated as "hard-core frequents" represented 76 percent of the actual paid admissions, a group that was "markedly unrepresentative of the total population." As the report concluded, "Being young and single is the overriding demographic pre-condition for being a frequent and enthusiastic moviegoer."

The Yankelovich survey also pointed up the "fascinating fact that the more 'adult' films have become, the more they appeal to teenagers and the less they appeal to their elders." This was hardly a revelation: the "adult" brand had long been bait for nonadults and a code word for salacious film content. "In the summer of 1960, for four weeks at one resort, there was not a single movie which was not on the objectionable list," lamented Thelma C. Purtell in *The Intelligent Parents' Guide to Teenagers* (1961). "Some were excellent adult fare; none was suitable for thirteen-year-olds." It is doubtful, however, that these summer-placed kids avoided the movies that the adults deemed objectionable.

Nor did adult movies avoid teenagers. Even so undeniably a non-adolescent thriller as Alfred Hitchcock's *Vertigo* (1958) swooned before the teenage moviegoer. After citing statistics that "52% of all theater patrons are under 20," the trade press advertising for *Vertigo* laid out a farsighted teen-targeted exploitation strategy. "Paramount aims a massive barrage at today's major motion picture market—the young customer," declared the ads. "Sindlinger, Politz, and Opinion Research surveys all point out that more than half of all moviegoers are in the younger-than-20 group. Every type of dynamic promotion will be aggressively used to hit hard at this market"—and, almost as an afterthought—"as well as to reach the general adult audience." What the ballyhoo boys called a "gross-building penetration" included "a ticket-selling use of TV," special advertisements in high school and college newspapers, and a "scientifically blue-printed radio promotion" for "the hit song 'Vertigo' to register millions of sales impressions as its recordings start spinning from coast to coast on the turntables of dee-jays most listened to by the under-20 audience."

Likewise, no expensive blockbuster could afford any longer to neglect the teenage market. For the $15 million epic *Ben-Hur* (1959), at the time the costliest movie ever made, MGM established a special Ben-Hur Research Department that surveyed two thousand high schools in forty-seven cities to gauge teenage interest and published an extensive *Ben-Hur Study Guide* to assist educators. In *King of Kings* (1961), even the austere realm of the biblical epic was revamped to youth-oriented sensibility when *Rebel Without a Cause* director Nicholas Ray highlighted blue-eyed dreamboat Jeffrey Hunter in the title role. (Irreverent critics dubbed the film "I Was a Teenage Jesus.")

In short, although the scale of youth's demographic advantage has ebbed and flowed, teenagers have held steady as the prime audience for motion picture patronage in America. Since 1960, teenpics have been an industry staple, if not the dominant production strategy for Hollywood cinema. Once questionable economically and disreputable aesthetically, they have grown in budget, frequency, and even respectability as teenagers have grown in fortune, numbers, and influence.

The Gentrification of the Teenpic

Just as each successive teenage generation is a kind of subculture, creating "symbolic forms" with its own "patterns of meaning," each in turn contributes its own unique permutations to the original, persistent teenpic cycles. In pinpointing the year of release for any given teenpic, the slang, fashion, and music soundtrack of the moment are more accurate than carbon dating. Lifting off with the new decade and a new generation, the teenpic entered a series of postclassical phases retreading, revamping, and reinventing the generic blueprints of the original teenpics of the 1950s.

By the mid-1960s, the founding teenagers of the second half of the 1950s had ceded pride of place to the soon-to-be mythic baby boomers. As teenagers, that permanent demographic bulge—the hump in the census python, the most pampered and populous of all twentieth-century generations—inherited and extended the subcultural province of the American adolescent. The remarkable fact about the youth movement of the 1960s was the movement of "youth" away from a term denoting chronological age or developmental phase and toward an ever more ephemeral experiential realm. As the prerogatives of the teenager expanded, the requirements for entry loosened. The 1960s generation of adolescents admitted to subcultural status millions who could not technically meet the age qualification. Date of birth became a rough but not required criterion for membership; "youth" became concept, not chronology. To keep up with the times, by around the mid-1960s, the term *teenage culture* was supplanted by the more expansive *youth culture*.

Nowhere was this clearer than in the generational gentrification of rock 'n' roll music, which by the late 1960s had assumed the steadier rubric befitting its status as *the* major cultural diversion: rock. On the evidence of films such as *A Hard Day's Night* (1964) and *Charlie Is My Darling* (1965), the early audiences for the Beatles and the Rolling Stones were recognizably adolescent, not at all unlike the composition of the crowds at Alan Freed's 1950s rock 'n' roll shows. By the close of the 1960s, teenagers were no longer rock's exclusive clientele. When the camera pans the crowds in *Gimme Shelter* (1970) and *Woodstock* (1970), the attendees are a good five to ten years older than the house at a "Big Beat" show. The teenage experience of 1964–68 was so seductive and enjoyable, and the consumer economy so compliant, that members extended their tour. Plainly, teenage-like life in America was no longer the exclusive province of teenagers. The advertisers caught the era's shift in a soft drink slogan: a time for those who *think* young.

Throughout the 1960s, Hollywood followed and forged the generation of the moment with variations on the teenpic species of the pre-

ceding decade. The clean teens took up surfing in AIP's pert and popular *Beach Party* series (1963–65). The rock 'n' roll teenpic came of age
as both musical comedy (*A Hard Day's Night*) and documentary (*Woodstock*). Rebellious youth was progressively criminal (*The Wild Angels*,
1966), alienated (*The Graduate*, 1967), and political (*Wild in the Streets*,
1968), qualities that, when put together and played to a rock music
soundtrack, culminated in *Easy Rider* (1969), a teenpic amalgam as influential in its time as *Rock Around the Clock* had been in 1956.

Film historian Peter Biskind conjured the "cultural convulsion that
upended the film industry" during the 1960s as an executive-suite version of the record-smashing scene in the classroom in *Blackboard Jungle*: "Then came, pell-mell, a series of premonitory shocks—the civil
rights movement, the Beatles, the pill, Vietnam, and drugs—that com-
bined to shake the studios badly, and send the demographic wave that
was the baby boom crashing down about them." To be sure, the old
guard was dragged under and drowned, but a new cadre of filmmakers
rode the wave safely, and quite profitably, to shore.

As teenagers became "youth" and subculture became "counterculture," teenpics became "youth-cult films," an open-ended label loosely
defined by Seth Cagin and Philip Dray in their 1960s-oriented *Hollywood Films of the Seventies* as "Hollywood productions specifically designed to address the counterculture." But though the terminology had
changed, the marketing techniques and demographic targeting of the
motion picture industry remained right on course. Indeed, as youth
and the movies fulfilled the J. Walter Thompson Company's predic-
tions, the boundaries between counter (film) culture and mainstream
(film) culture all but evaporated. Box office smashes and critical successes such as *Bonnie and Clyde* (1967), *The Graduate*, and *2001: A Space
Odyssey* (1968) straddled what in the 1950s had been a great divide. In
a manner beyond the ken of bygone industry fathers such as Eric Johnston and Sam Goldwyn, movies had once again become a medium with
crossover appeal—but one now geared unequivocally and unapologet-
ically to the young. If their elders came along to the theaters occasionally, so much the better, but when in need of a reliable audience, no end
of the motion picture business—production, distribution, or exhibition—trusted anyone over thirty. Moviemakers might stumble in reading the capricious youth audience—in the wake of *Blow Up* (1966) and
Easy Rider (1969), MGM's effort to seduce 1960s youth culture with
Zabriskie Point (1970) was on a par with the record industry's campaign

to sell polka music to 1950s rock 'n' rollers—but such blunders are always the result of tactical miscalculation, never of a lack of solicitous concern.

Appropriately, and somewhat ironically, only American International Pictures kept the old categories straight, fragmenting an audience that had become united in a wholly unclassical Hollywood way. AIP's youth-cult hit *Wild in the Streets* crossed the two generational fashions, politics and rock, to become the company's most financially successful picture up to that time. Imagining a not-too-distant future when the voting age is lowered to fourteen and the country is ruled by a messianic rock star, the film takes age obsession to its logical political level in a dystopia where adults over the age of thirty are corralled into concentration camps and immobilized with LSD. Freud quickly gives way to Orwell, however, when the parental pattern of dominance and oppression is reenacted by the young on the yet younger. The final shot frames a resentful preteen who promises, "We're gonna put everyone over ten out of business."

But youth, or at least the fantastic privileges accorded youth in a flush American economy, was more fun to join than to fight. *Easy Rider* is the touchstone. If the teenpic formula for the 1950s offered moviemakers much gain for little risk, *Easy Rider* held out the promise of astronomical gain for infinitesimal risk. Directed by Dennis Hopper, a member of Buzz Gunderson's old gang in *Rebel Without a Cause*, *Easy Rider* resembles nothing so much as an over-the-hill teenpic featuring actors adolescent in attitude only. The film is an amalgam of virtually every teenpic type that thrived in the 1950s: vice, motorcycles, rock 'n' roll, delinquency, and even—in Jack Nicholson's marijuana-induced monologue on the extraterrestrial Venusians—weirdies.

In the 1970s and 1980s, the teenpic continued to provide the model for Hollywood despite the fact that the latest crop of teenagers had lost something of their privileged generational allure. Demographers took to calling the new youth generation "postboomers," the name itself a testament to the tenacious centrality of boomers in American culture: whether in middle age or dotage, the baby-boomer generation remained too numerous and self-involved ever totally to relinquish the cultural spotlight. Writing in 1979, film historian James Monaco lamented that "the main thing new about American movies in the seventies is what's old. The seventies have no culture of their own, no style, unless it's nostalgia." Yet what Monaco bemoaned was not nos-

Thirty-somethings extend their adolescence: Dennis Hopper, Jack Nicholson, and Peter Fonda in *Easy Rider* (1969). (Courtesy of Columbia Pictures)

talgia but crossover. The paeans to 1950s and 1960s pop culture that so dominated film production in the 1970s and 1980s made perfect demographic sense. Teenpics about past teenagers could appeal jointly to the teenage audience of the moment and their nostalgic elder siblings and parents. In addition, then, to the 1950s atmosphere and antics revisited by the likes of *American Graffiti* (1973), *Grease* (1976), and *Dirty Dancing* (1987), the rock 'n' roll personalities featured in the original teenpics became a prime source of major studio product: Alan Freed (*American Hot Wax*, 1978); Fabian (*The Idolmaker*, 1980); Richie Valens (*La Bamba*, 1987); and Chuck Berry (*Hail! Hail! Rock 'n' Roll*, 1987). No wonder the postboomers clung so passionately to the one authentic showcase for the music and fashion of the era, the disco-driven, polyester-clad *Saturday Night Fever* (1977).

Teenpics also served as the inspiration for the two most successful filmmakers in the postclassical era, George Lucas and Steven Spielberg. In the 1950s, Lucas and Spielberg might well have been Sam Katzman and Roger Corman, spirited producers operating ably and profitably on the margins of the industry. In the 1970s and 1980s, they became the ascendant auteurs in Hollywood, moguls on a par with the legends of the studio era. Reared on the teen-oriented fare of the 1950s, their success was as much a comment on the shifting role of movies in American life as on their own estimable talents. Only in a juvenilized industry could their special vision so dominate film culture, with so much of Hollywood following their lead. Material that in the late 1950s would have warranted a five-figure budget and eight-day shooting schedule was now a big-budget, saturation release. The difference between Roger Corman's threadbare *Little Shop of Horrors* (1960) and the lavish Warner Bros. musical *Little Shop of Horrors* (1986) offers an extreme example. More typical was Hollywood's tireless excavation of 1950s weirdies for update, whether as outright remakes—*Invaders from Mars* (1953)/*Invaders from Mars* (1986), *Invasion of the Body Snatchers* (1956)/*Invasion of the Body Snatchers* (1978), *The Thing from Another World* (1951)/*The Thing* (1982), *The Fly* (1958)/*The Fly* (1986), and *The Blob* (1958)/*The Blob* (1988)—or as partial adaptations—*It! The Terror from Beyond Space* (1958)/*Alien* (1979) and *The Incredible Shrinking Man* (1957)/*The Incredible Shrinking Woman* (1981).

Contemplating the remakes and retreads, smug boomer critics, now crankily approaching middle age, tended to sneer at the generations of teenagers born after the Kennedy assassination and Watergate as more predictable and compliant, more derivative and dependent in their tastes and subcultural affinities, than their own exalted generation of the 1960s. If this was so, part of the reason was that the entertainment industry ran a more ruthlessly efficient machine for teenage exploitation, a fusillade of transmedia synergy fixing Hollywood's most desirable film audience dead center in its crosshairs. Increasingly, the distinctions between media zones—cassettes and CDs, television, films, and teen-type magazines—were impossible to discern. In 1981, the advent of MTV consummated the on-again, off-again flirtation of rock music and television, supplying core programming composed of record company commercials doubling as motion picture trailers for films that incorporated video techniques and rock music soundtracks. With the blockbuster success of the MTV-marketed *Flashdance* (1983), the distinctions between music, music video, television, and motion picture made up a Marshall McLuhan house of mirrors—or, to mix metaphors, a perpetual-motion exploitation machine, pulsating steadily and spiraling wildly through the space of American culture.

Among the compensations of the new teenpic commerce was the quality of the talent working in the genre, ambitious filmmakers who

The Fly (1958) / *The Fly* (1986): with bigger budgets, prestige directors, and saturation exploitation, the 1950s teenpic goes mainstream. (Courtesy of Twentieth Century-Fox)

saw not a quick payday for disposable trash but a rich canvas for auteurist invention. At some point in the mid-1970s, the throwaway creativity of the 1950s was supplanted by a more self-conscious artistry.
The inheritor of a cinematic tradition, the postclassical teenpic operated under the burden of history and the anxiety of influence, two pressures that eroded its original off-the-cuff élan and, against all expectations, raised the teenpic brow from low to high, or at least to middle.
Roger Corman's New World Pictures thus became not so much the
1970s answer to AIP as the 1970s ancestor to AIP, a company that built
on earlier strategies, co-opted predecessor narratives, and revamped
old genres. New World's *Rock 'n' Roll High School* (1979), for example,
is a slick catalog of teenpic influences, cheerfully appropriating and de-
molishing the conventions of the 1950s prototypes.

More carefully marketed and calculatingly created than their predecessors, postclassical teenpics tend to function knowingly on multiple
levels. *Fast Times at Ridgemont High* (1982) and *Risky Business* (1983) are
teenpic-like in their target audience and content, but their consciousness is emphatically adult, the artistry in their double vision unmistakable. Just as John Ford, Howard Hawks, and Anthony Mann had
brought repute to a western genre traditionally held in ill esteem, a
growing number of talented filmmakers invested the postclassical teenpic with a shrewd sense of craft and complexity. Like rock 'n' roll, the
teenpic genre underwent serious gentrification—though art-house afi-
cionados besotted by the most turgid Anglophilic soaper from Mer-
chant-Ivory are still apt to disdain the likes of *Heaven Help Us* (1985),
Matinee (1993), and *Dick* (1999).

A film genre that in the 1950s began in rebellion and resentment
and helped fashion an autonomous subculture, the teenpic confronted
another vexation in its postclassical mode. Up against a parent culture
that was ever more accommodating and appeasing, ever less authoritative and overbearing (not to mention present), the teenage rebel faced
a problem *The Wild One* (1954) never anticipated. The adult villains in
teenpics such as *Risky Business* and *Ferris Bueller's Day Off* (1986) are
overdrawn caricatures, no real threat; they're played for laughs. Since
the 1960s, the most fascinating trend in teenpics has been their palpable desire for parental control and authority, not their adolescent rebellion and autonomy.

A huge crossover hit, *Breaking Away* (1979) was typical: a teen-
oriented family film with a 1950s-style dad. In the postclassical teen-

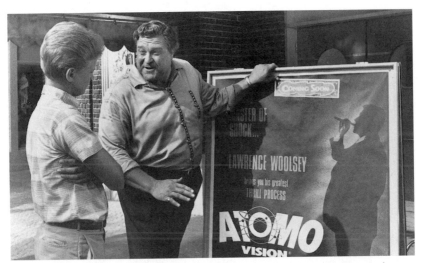

The anxiety of influence: John Goodman plays a William Castle–like exploitation filmmaker in Joe Dante's gentrified teenpic *Matinee* (1993). (Courtesy of Universal Pictures)

pic, parents are more likely to be condemned for being self-centered, weak, and uncertain than for being overbearing, intrusive, or present. If Jim Stark's scream was "You're tearing me apart!" the cry of his descendants is "You're leaving me alone!" In a culture of loose rules and relative morality, the teenage rebel lost his best foil. "What d'ya got?" sneers motorcycle-riding misfit Marlon Brando in *The Wild One* when asked the object of his rebellion. For the modern teenager, the question may not be rhetorical. Since the 1960s, the teenpic hero has more often been a Weird or Wimpy One, more liable to flash watery eyes than snarling lips. He is a hapless kid seeking direction, not a tough rebel fleeing restriction. The postboomer teenagers prefer the instruction, discipline, and obedience of *Star Wars* (1977) and *The Karate Kid* (1984) to the deranged delinquent chaos of *Class of 1984* (1982) and *Bad Boys* (1984). Tellingly, the two emblematic teenpic rabble-rousers in the postclassic era, the JFK-era *National Lampoon's Animal House* (1978) and the Eisenhower-era *Porky's* (1981), are both set in the remote teenage past, when school authority was a vital opponent worthy of attack.

One teen-targeted film format did get wilder and weirder in its postclassical mode. With the "axploitation" cycle of the late 1970s and early 1980s, horror, that teenpic perennial, reached hysterical heights and forensic depths undreamed of by William Castle. Perhaps the dearth of deserving parental opponents in the real world explained the astonishing proliferation of horror films, the dominant teen-oriented form since the 1970s. From *Halloween* (1977) and *Friday the 13th* (1978) through their myriad sequels and progeny, the teenage massacres are almost always the handiwork of fellow adolescent, not parental, monsters. Traditionally, horror was thought to originate in the psychological repressions of the nuclear family. In the postclassical teenpic, the kids seem more wary of one another.

The Teenpic in the Age of AIDS

In the signature scene from Paul Brickman's *Risky Business* (1983), Tom Cruise performs a ballet of unbridled liberation. Clad in his undies, with bass on lowest registers and volume on highest, he lip-synchs and plays air guitar to the gutbucket strains of Bob Seeger's "That Old Time Rock 'n' Roll." Then he calls up a prostitute, has hot sex on the staircase, and transforms his stately home into a thriving, rollicking bordello for his high school friends. Needless to say, the folks are not home.

Jump-cut to *Home Alone* (1990), where the antics of eleven-year-old Macaulay Culkin are a kind of prepubescent version of Cruise's moves in *Risky Business*. Like Cruise, he dances alone in his upper-crust residence, outwits criminal intruders, and masters his personal fears. But where Cruise defaces the home, Culkin defends it; where Cruise revels in his freedom, Culkin craves security; and where Cruise wants to lose his virginity, Culkin wants his Mommy.

The age differential between the two adorable housesitters marked time with a grim historical passage. Soon after the blithe, orgiastic days of *Risky Business*, sex became just that: AIDS, the horror nascent in real-life sex, reshaped the moral landscape of the teenpic genre.

Incubating in the gay community and among intravenous drug users since the late 1970s, acquired immune deficiency syndrome (AIDS) exploded as a national (that is, nonhomosexual) health menace in 1984–85 and sent out shock waves until the end of the century. A spate of stark statistics and famous obituaries forced America to confront the most publicized and dreaded plague since the Salk and Sabine vaccines defeated the polio epidemic in the 1950s. The death of Rock Hudson

The folks are not home: Tom Cruise performs a ballet of liberation in *Risky Business* (1983). (Museum of Modern Art Film Stills Archive: Courtesy of Warner Bros.)

The downsizing of the teen protagonist: Macaulay Culkin gets the girl—Mom (Catherine O'Hara)—in *Home Alone* (1991). (Courtesy of Twentieth Century-Fox)

in 1985, an icon of masculinity since the 1950s; the convalescence of teenager Ryan White and his death in 1990, a sympathetic symbol of the omnipresence of risk and social ostracism for the nongay majority; and the announcement of the HIV-positive status of beloved sports star Magic Johnson in 1991 gave faces to numbers charting the exponential spread of infection and the appalling mortality rates. In countless news reports, talk shows, and movies of the week, television broached the heretofore forbidden details of sexual congress, airing language and images unimaginable not only to the 1950s but to network standards and practices of just months earlier. From the Office of the Surgeon General, in the stern warnings of public service announcements, and on the blackboards of high school sex education classes, a consensus message was boldfaced throughout American culture: "unprotected" sex meant death. Not all the bulletins bothered with the qualifier.

Against that diagnosis, the recreational adolescent fornication celebrated and spied through peepholes in *Animal House, Porky's, Private School* (1983), and *Revenge of the Nerds* (1984) suddenly seemed less a joyous rite of passage than a jump into the fire. To eliminate sexually transmitted audience discomfort, Hollywood's teen-targeted films covered up the nudity and closed down the sex play. In a scenario set in high school, teenage sex became the extracurricular activity that dared not speak its name.

Of course, even in the age of AIDS, the content of teenpics remained varied and multivalent enough to confirm just about any label tagged on the always carped-about younger generation: teenagers as soulless nihilists (*River's Edge* [1986], *Heathers* [1989], *Kids* [1999]), slack-jawed sloths (*Slacker* [1991], *Clerks* [1994], *Suburbia* [1996]), or ironic romantics (*Say Anything* [1989], *Reality Bites* [1994], *10 Things I Hate About You* [1999]). Yet to scan the box office hits and gauge the median temperature of the teenpics produced in the shadow of AIDS is to observe two dominant and culturally resonant trends: the chronological downsizing and sexual neutering of the American adolescent.

In the wake of AIDS, the favorite ingenue in teen-targeted films was often not a teenager at all but a preteen youngster. Wes Craven's *The People Under the Stairs* (1991) showcased a young boy who is vulgarly but revealingly described as "too old for tit, too young for pussy." That time frame set the beginning and outer limits of the new youth hero. In film after film, teenagers were crowded out by their younger siblings: *Stand by Me* (1986), *Child's Play* (1988), *Honey, I Shrunk the Kids* (1989), *Little Man Tate* (1991), *The Addams Family* (1991), *The Profes-*

sional (1995), and *The Sixth Sense* (1999). Often the kidcentric entries—*Home Alone* (1990), *Terminator 2* (1991), *Jurassic Park* (1993), *Toy Story* (1995), *Lost World: The Jurassic Park* (1997), the first post-AIDS edition of the *Star Wars* series, *The Phantom Menace* (1999), and *Harry Potter and the Sorcerer's Stone* (2001)—were the top box office hits of their respective years. The incredible shrinking protagonist reached extremes in Amy Heckerling's *Look Who's Talking* series (1989/1990/1994), films whose featured players could not yet walk upright.

When not chronologically downsized, the young were sexually neutered. The hormonally crazed teenagers who once cluttered the camps of the axploitation films and animal comedies went the way of hot rods and hippies. Compared to any previous cycle of teenpics, and especially the explicit gross-outs and sexcapades of a few years earlier, the teenpics in the age of AIDS were noteworthy not for promiscuity and licentiousness but chastity and temperance. Multihyphenate teen specialist John Hughes caught the wave early on, making a virtual franchise of PG-13-rated and G-sensibility teenpic fare such as *Pretty in Pink* (1985), *Ferris Bueller's Day Off* (1986), and *Some Kind of Wonderful* (1987); but everywhere, the once-required content of teenpics—coupling, nudity, voyeurism, and the desperate surrender of virginity—was censored with a Production Code–like ferocity. Sex proliferated on cable television and the Internet, but on the motion picture screen, AIDS-chastened teenagers almost always preferred cuddling to copulation.

To appreciate the gulf in sensibility, compare the cruel comedy and sexual shenanigans of *National Lampoon's Animal House* (1978) and *Porky's* (1981) to the loopy humor and chaste decorum of the enormously popular *Wayne's World* (1992/1994) and *Bill and Ted* (1989/1993) series. Buttoned-down and other-directed, the 1990s teenpics rejected the orgiastic excess and revelry in rebellion that typified their predecessors. Oppressive adults and violent peers were banished or peripheral, and, in a socially significant burst of wish fulfillment, one of the quainter conceits held that, absent, inattentive, or neurotic boomer parents notwithstanding, the kids are *(mutatis mutandis)* well adjusted and mature, everything Mom and Dad aren't. In *Don't Tell Mom the Babysitter's Dead* (1991), adolescents liberated from adult authority turn into—responsible adults.

Of course, the repressed always returns. If explicit sex play was airbrushed from teen-targeted comedy and romantic melodrama, the smothered urges and subliminal fears of adolescence erupted with a vengeance in the more congenial regions of the horror genre. Rivaling the exploitation brilliance of *I Was a Teenage Werewolf* both in the marquee value of its first-person title and the cultural-historical resonance of its plotline, the finger-pointing *I Know What You Did Last Summer* (1997) depicted the backfire from a casual holiday fling: contrary to expectations, the summertime transgression committed by randy, joyriding teenagers was murder, not sex, but the dormant residue still surfaces with lethal consequences. Drenched in a venereal horror, a flood of vampire films and blood-infected chillers—*The Lost Boys* (1987), *Bram Stoker's Dracula* (1992), *Innocent Blood* (1992), and *Interview with the Vampire* (1994)—served as transparent allegories for the omnipresent fear of fluids. Driving a stake through the heart of a vampire was a less threatening form of physical contact than other types of penetration.

Three Victorian narratives, spaced throughout the 1990s, unspool as apt indexes of the adolescent withdrawal from sexual congress. Cultural bellwethers all, each preferred to look backward to a romanticized past instead of forward into an anxiety-ridden future.

A fated meeting of mind and material, Stephen Spielberg's *Hook* (1991) was a lavish update of the Peter Pan story. Before matriculating into adulthood with *Schindler's List* (1993) and *Saving Private Ryan* (1998), Spielberg expressed his boyish exuberance in child's-eye views of celestial spectacles: luminous visions that glow in the distance and reflect light back on a shimmering, spellbound face, a mirror image of the spectator in the motion picture theater. Anglo-American culture's favorite tale of arrested development seemed a perfect match for an auteur whose motto had long been a petulant "I won't grow up!"

Written in 1904 by J. M. Barrie, *Peter Pan* was one of the two great Victorian excursions into a fabulous Never Neverland, Lewis Carroll's *Alice in Wonderland* being the other. Of the pair, *Peter Pan* is the lightweight entry, having none of the through-the-looking-glass horror and subversive undertow of Alice's dreamworld. Where Alice emerges from the rabbit hole older and wiser, Peter ducks back down, forever young and dumb. Barrie's tale is a little boy's dream of not growing up and facing adulthood—namely, sexuality, girls, and all that other icky stuff.

Most Americans know the fairy tale not from bedtime readings or stage productions but from Walt Disney's animated classic *Peter Pan* (1953) and ritualistic television broadcasts of the Broadway play, with an elfin female cross-dressing in the title role. In whatever medium, the attraction of Peter Pandom is the utter freedom from adult authority and grown-up responsibility. In Never Neverland, the repressive harness of the omnipotent Victorian parent no longer reins in the frisky child. A Freudian game of connect-the-dots exposes the transparent symbolism of the handily castrated father figure, Captain Hook.

Whether in Victorian England or Cold War America, the lot of the bourgeois child was obedience and confinement, a regulated existence overseen by almighty adults. In 1990s America, where "parent" was as often a verb as a noun, child rearers practiced arcane nurturing skills while sharing "quality time." Single-parent homes, pandemic divorce rates, and day-care upbringing made the venerable Victorian nuclear unit less an overbearing presence than a nostalgic memory.

In keeping with modern family affairs, the hook for *Hook* reversed the child-parent trajectory. The point of identification—the point of the original story—shifted from the children's yearning for liberation and self-assertion to the adult's movement toward child rearing and self-sacrifice. *Hook* isn't about a boy who won't grow up but about a father who won't pay attention. The original Wendy, Michael, and John wanted Mom and Dad to let up a little: hence the lure of flight with Peter. Their yuppie-spawned descendants Maggie and Jack want their Dad to attend school plays and cheer playground exploits. He (and they) has to be dragged kicking and screaming into Never Neverland. Spielberg reworked a classic escapist fantasy for children into an ode to parental involvement.

Hook was emblematic of the child's play of the 1990s: an adult-themed movie that catered to the children, a children's story that was mainly about parenthood, a youth-oriented film that exiled sexuality from its landscape and teenagers from the screen. Above all, its fidelity to the father-headed nuclear unit was truly Victorian. No wonder all the eye-popping spectacle of Never Neverland never, but never, matched the storybook appeal of the magical family moments, and Maggie and Jack feel no temptation to stay behind. In an age of Victorian rigidity, the free-for-all atmosphere of all-boy gangs and pirate ships was the stuff of wild daydreams; no longer. The real never-never land had become the cozy, upper-class extended family, presided over by a warmly authoritative patriarch. In his revision of *Peter Pan*, Spielberg lent an imperative tag line to Hollywood cinema in the 1990s: clap if you believe in fathers.

A quaint English backstory also informed Amy Heckerling's gentrified clean teenpic *Clueless* (1995). Bracketed by the trademark teenpic elements—the catchphrase kicker ("As if!"); the transient teen slang (favorite phrases: "going postal," as in "to lose mental balance, like a disgruntled postal worker," and the adverbial "way," as in "way harsh" or "way existential"); and the wall-to-wall rock soundtrack (the bubblegum pop sounds of "Supermodel" and "Kids in America")—it hadn't a mean bone or rebellious instinct in its body. Heckerling drew for inspiration on *Emma* by Jane Austen, the early nineteenth-century author who also served as a leitmotif in another paean to rich kids, Whit Stillman's *Metropolitan* (1990), and as the source of a popular cycle of "clothes and furniture" films, *Sense and Sensibility* (1995), *Emma* (1996), and *Mansfield Park* (1999). Like the condom, the corset offered a protective shield against sexual contact.

Clueless starred the baby-fat siren Alicia Silverstone as Cher, a blonde and beautiful California princess with a flare for accessorizing and social commentary. With her equally muddled friend, the fashion adventuress Dionne (their bond is solidified by the fact that both girls are named after popular singers from the 1970s who appear in infomercials), Cher devotes herself to the urgent curriculum of the American school system, namely, popularity. Seemingly an airhead for life, she becomes inflated with sense and sensibility when her college-age stepbrother accuses her of shallowness and selfishness. Resolving not to be "a ditz with a credit card," she turns to busybody altruism—playing cupid to her ugly-duckling teachers, taking under her wing a clodhopper transfer student in desperate need of a makeover, and moving into social action and charity work by coordinating the Pismo Beach Disaster Relief Fund. Occupying a privileged realm unknown to the minimum-wage, "Would you like fries with that?" stratum, the Beverly Hills kids are nonetheless free of ethnic animosity and homophobia. This being Southern California, however, the class distinctions of regional geography are too embedded to reform. "Every place in LA takes twenty minutes," her father warns when Cher ventures into the badlands of— the Valley.

Cher showers her daffy perspective on the beyond-satire rituals of the loco locals: talismanic amulets (cell phones, platform shoes, hair extensions), body rituals (chin jobs, rhinoplasty, liposuction), and the unabashed consumerism that coats the SoCal lifestyle like sunblock. For all the reputed illiteracy and ineloquence of the teenpic genre, almost all the humor in *Clueless* is verbal, a nonstop patter of quotable epigrams, asides, and ironic byplay. Heckerling's eye for teen gesture is sharp (the girls all do mean lip curls), and her ear is attuned to the

A Jane Austen adolescence: Alicia Silverstone and the clean-teen crew from *Clueless* (1995). (Museum of Modern Art Film Stills Archive: Courtesy of Paramount Pictures)

proper backbeat undercurrents (the "complaint rock" of college versus the faux hip-hop of high school).

As in Victorian novels and slasher films, the heroine of *Clueless* is a virgin. "You see how long it takes me to decide on a pair of shoes," Cher explains, "and they only go on my feet." Though a marijuana cigarette is passed around and some sex talk exchanged, the ethos recalls an earnest film on dating etiquette from the 1950s: smoking is not cool, drugs are even uncooler, and good grooming is a definite plus. When, after failing her driver's test, Cher is described harshly as "a virgin who can't drive," it is the latter designation that cuts more deeply.

Capping the decade, the most gargantuan of all Victorian narratives sailed into motion picture history as the highest-grossing film of the twentieth century: the zeitgeist leviathan that was James Cameron's *Titanic* (1997). Set in 1912 and thus technically Edwardian in lineage, the romance blended state-of-the-art special effects with retrograde courtship rituals. Transporting teenagers back to a time before AIDS, before feminism, before radar, *Titanic* steered a steady course toward a set of archaic gender dynamics. A poor but beautiful princess must marry a dark prince for his money, but her true love, from the lower orders, holds her heart tight. Notes are passed, assignations arranged, dances danced, and passionate love is consummated before disaster upends their idyll. The old-fashioned buoyancy of the breathless romance, not the sinking of the luxury liner, kept the ungainly vessel afloat.

Though a phenomenon as mammoth as *Titanic* is by definition a crossover attraction, the film owed its hyperbolic success to repeat viewings from battalions of moonstruck teenage girls, who boarded the vessel again and again, often in packs, to enjoy the vicarious rush of courtship in an age of sexual convention—when young love could be recklessly consummated in the backseat of an automobile; when un-protected sex with an attractive young stranger meant a night to re-member, not a death sentence. *Titanic* was a true salvage operation: the glimpses of arty nudity and soft-focused coupling can't conceal the affinity for a bygone age of corseted fashions and rigid manners.

2001 and Beyond: Projected Teenpic Odysseys

As the motion picture industry slouched toward its second full century, the health of teen-targeted cinema was as vibrant as at any time in Hol-lywood history. Besides the teen-magnet *Titanic*, the two sleeper block-busters of the lucrative summer of 1999 neatly paired off the twin im-pulses of the postclassical teenpic in the age of AIDS: *The Sixth Sense*, a brilliant supernatural thriller that showcased a young boy whose pre-pubescent precocity surpassed even that of Macaulay Culkin, and *The Blair Witch Project*, a camcorder-age horror film that managed to send off two boys and a girl to sleep in the woods without once mentioning sex. Even *American Beauty* (1999), the most critically esteemed film of the year, was careful to devote as much screen time to its dysfunctional teenage couple as its dysfunctional married couple.

Tragically, the bewitching projects and titanic cataclysms of Holly-wood soon paled beside the video record of a real life horror show. With a sickening suddenness, the serene odyssey into the next century veered into a second date which will live in infamy. However the shockwaves from September 11, 2001, radiate through American cul-ture, the emergency call on 9-11 will mold generations neither as com-placent about national security nor as confident about linear progress as their immediate predecessors. As ever, the fallout on Hollywood cin-ema will be as multifarious and mysterious as previous seismic jolts to the national psyche, but one suspects that the allure of computer-gen-erated carnage and apocalyptic narratives that fueled the teen-targeted blockbusters of what so instantly became a bygone era may be put on extended hiatus. When the disintegration of urban architecture and the collision of passenger vessels into icy edifices unfold as lethal scenarios no longer beyond imagination, the likes of *Independence Day* (1996) and *Titanic* seem culturally redundant. Perhaps somewhere a Gen-X descendant of F. Scott Fitzgerald is already penning an elegy for the halcyon 1990s entitled "Echoes of the Jive Age."

Even so, the three provisions that have long mediated the relationship between Hollywood and American adolescence seem likely to shape future negotiations, with the caveat—always wise, lately rueful—that the forces of history have a way of shattering the most ironclad of contracts.

First, since the 1950s, teenagers have been the demographic target of choice for the American film industry. With television usurping motion pictures as the dominant mass medium, with the collapse of the classical studio system and the desertion of its great intergenerational audience, Hollywood found its salvation in the young, always the most loyal and gregarious of moviegoers. Down through the decades—from *Blackboard Jungle* (1955), *Wild in the Streets* (1968), *Saturday Night Fever* (1977), *Ferris Bueller's Day Off* (1986), and *Clueless* (1996) to *Bring It On* (2001)—Hollywood's teen-targeted material has mainly meant teen protagonists coping with teen dilemmas in a teen milieu. The *sine qua non* is a certain verisimilitude in the stylistic expressions and cultural rites of the moment, notably the inside-dope details of vernacular, fashion, and music. In holding up a mirror to teenage culture—even a cracked or distorted one—Hollywood lends a recognition, validation, and celebration to successive subcultures defined not by race, class, or ethnicity but by age.

Second, where psychologists, demographers, and parents sketch the limits of childhood and adolescence by stages of biological growth or psychological development, the motion industry is firmly and confidentially chronological. At the ticket window as at the motor vehicle registration office, adolescence is purely a matter of birthdate. Hollywood sets its boundaries in the well-known rating systems of the Motion Picture Association of America: G, PG, PG-13, R, NC-17, and X. The PG-13 rating ("may be unsuitable for younger children") was devised in 1984 after children, or rather their parents, complained of the bloodletting in Stephen Spielberg's *Indiana Jones and the Temple of Doom*, notably a sequence in which a human sacrifice has his heart ripped out during a pagan ceremony. In 1990, after a controversy over Philip Kaufman's *Henry and June*, the label of NC-17 ("no children under seventeen") was designed so sexually explicit but ostensibly highbrow art-house product might circumvent the porno onus and advertising restrictions of an X rating. (In practice, the multiplex mall contracts that forbid the screening of X-rated material also prohibit NC-17 films.) Regardless of how academic disciplines and census takers set the age limits, in the precise calculus of official Hollywood, humans under thirteen are children; humans between the ages of thirteen and seventeen are adolescents; and humans over seventeen are adults.

Of course, at mall level the enforcement system is a farce, and much of the ostensibly R-rated parent- or guardian-accompanied viewing is an unsupervised activity for most children and adolescents. No exhibitor with twenty-four screens, six ushers, and one central entrance-way can enforce a restricted attendance policy. In marketing if not in rating terms, the motion picture industry assumes as much. A good example of Hollywood's calculated duplicity is the R-rated *Terminator 2* (1991), whose twelve-year-old protagonist was the point of identification for targeted spectators nominally too young to purchase their own tickets.

Replaying the alarms over horror comic books and juvenile delinquency in the 1950s, Washington politicians periodically wake up to Hollywood's seductions of the American teenager, or at least the electoral advantages of investigating the same, usually in the wake of some horrid eruption of teenage violence allegedly instigated by baleful media influence. In September 2000, after the Federal Trade Commission issued a shocking report revealing that R-rated films are actually marketed to pre-seventeen-year-olds, the Senate Commerce Committee berated a chagrined lineup of studio executives about violence in film. The salons were righteous, the moguls were humble, and the hypocrisy was suitable for audiences of all ages. No one mentioned that any twelve-year-old who can't sneak into an R-rated film must be an underachiever for his age group.

Third, the cultural meaning of teenpics is as varied and complex as adolescent psychology itself. In film as in life, adolescence is always going to be a period of conflicting trends and mutually exclusive values, a phase balancing and bouncing back and forth between impulses for freedom and security, between rebellion and reconciliation, between cross-sex fertilization and same-sex bonding. But despite the persistent and dueling dualities of the genre, Hollywood's teenpics since the 1950s and 1960s have reflected a distinct movement away from leather-jacketed alienation and countercultural rebellion toward well-scrubbed conformity and sexual restraint. The adolescent racket that begin in 1955 with *Blackboard Jungle* and *Rebel Without a Cause* and that pumped up the volume in the 1960s with *Wild in the Streets* and *Easy Rider* modulated its melody in the late 1970s. Since then, the young have been more likely to obey their elders than to defy them. From *Star Wars* to *The Matrix* (1999), aimless youths seek out nurturing mentors who drill them in the spiritual and athletic ways of the world. With an almost religious devotion, they recite the father figure's words of wisdom and follow like good sons in his footsteps. During the 1950s and 1960s, when parent culture was at its strongest and most authoritative, the teenpics catered to rebellion against Mom and Dad and liberation from the confines of the home. In an age where parent culture is vacillating, disjointed, or absent, the teenpics commemorate filial duty and stoke the home fires. The urge for parental (read: paternal) authority is far more likely to fuel a teen-targeted box office hit than is the urge for rebellion. The lightning bolts of 9-11 seem likely to cement the trend toward stern discipline and father-son bonding in the teenpic.

To say that the return of the patriarch and the palpable yearning for discipline and authority are the striking qualities of teenpics since the 1960s is not to proclaim the death of adolescent rebellion in film. As the fear of AIDS slackened in the late 1990s, a dormant testosterone gushed forth in a minirevival of the "bone-headed" gross-out comedy of the early 1980s. Yet whether in the slapstick-laden *There's Something About Mary* (1998), the cartoonish *American Pie* (1999), or the animated *South Park: Longer, Bigger & Uncut* (1999), the fluids wallowed in were more often excremental than sexual, the playful spirit more an emotional regression to potty training than sexual experimentation. Quite simply, profligacy is no longer what teenpics are usually about, and when teenagers do run wild, their rebellion is of a diminished capacity. The hissable enemies are bullies and prom queens, not teachers and assistant principals.

Typically, the person-to-person linkups teenagers seem most emotionally invested in involve new communications technologies, not sexual partners. Just as hot rods and rock 'n' roll obsessed the original teenagers, two screens—the television and the computer—focused the attention and filtered the perspective of the *fin de siècle* teenager.

The television-trained vision of teenagers in the age of cable finds an eyeline match in the frenzied style and videocentric content of Hollywood cinema. As if afflicted with a moving-image variant of attention deficit disorder, the modern teenpic buzzes with fast-paced editing and swirling camera movements. Baby boomers reared under the limited horizons of three-network hegemony seldom appreciate the gulf in small-screen aesthetics between the 1960s and the age of cable. Expert channel surfers through the narrowcast menu, children of cable evince an intimate facility with televisual aesthetics. Their rapid eye movements outpace the speed of their remote-control clickers.

No wonder video-generated landscapes appear in such heavy rotation on the teenpic dial. The terminally dim dudes in *Bill and Ted's Excellent Adventure* are living in their own camcorder heavy-metal fantasy (that turns out to be true), and the metalheads Wayne and Garth in *Wayne's World* host their own cable-access television show. In *Beavis and Butthead Do America* (1996), the main activity of yet another dim pair of nonsexual teens—in this case actual, not metaphorical, cartoons—is to watch rock videos. Hence the seamless matching of screen selves and real selves in teen-targeted Hollywood cinema, an attraction to the motion picture image at once fetishistic and narcissistic. Previous generations wanted to possess the image; cable-bred babies want to be the image, to blend into the world projected on screen.

Fulfilling the fantasy while cautioning against it, teenpic horror is also permeated with videocentricity. When not plunging stakes into vampires, the genre dotes on monsters born of video and serial killers carrying camcorders. Creatures generated from television screens and homicidal auteurs obsessed with videotaping the act of mass murder zap in and out of video-screen life and real-screen life in a manner that doesn't so much break down borders as deny them. The one-step-removed vantage of the screens within screens has made irony the preferred stance of the horror teenpic, notably in Wes Craven's hugely successful *Scream* (1997) franchise. Only aging senators, out of the loop and not in on the joke, were appalled when snippets from the film were played at congressional hearings in 1999.

Surpassing even video as a teenpic trope is the computer. As Hollywood cinema came to rely more and more on digital technologies and computer graphic imaging, the aesthetics and narratives of the films followed suit. Teenagers, the most Internet savvy of all moviegoers, bring their computer skills to the motion picture screen, which in turn presumes their expertise and caters to their obsessions.

Since the prophetic *Wargames* (1983), an emblematic hero of the teenpic has been a hacker surfing the Net, a social nerd turned cyberspace ace with mouse and keyboard. In *The Matrix*, the most elaborate cinematic treatise on computerized metaphysics, the loner/hacker Neo (Keanu Reeves) is born again as a cyberspace Christ figure who comes to save the world from the illusion that is the world: not the word made flesh but the flesh made digital. The felt experience of reality is, in reality, a computer software program, an elaborate worldwide web of hallucination. Meanwhile, the corporeal form resides in coffin-like capsules to serve as a source of electrical energy for artificially intelligent arachnids. The programmers of *The Matrix* knew that for many teenagers, the connections to cyberspace are more intense, more rewarding, and more real than the gnawing frustrations of high school reality.

The intensity of the cyberspace matrix accessed at the keyboard has beset the motion picture industry with familiar trepidations about the latest living-room competition. Just as television menaced Hollywood in the 1950s, the audiovisual banquet provided via the computer looms to detract from theatrical screen time. As in the 1950s, however, the new media revolution that threatens Hollywood with annihilation seems more likely to succumb to assimilation. "In a decade of spiraling production budgets, studio failures, labor woes, and the chaotic reign of multinationals, one of the few constants in the film biz has been rising box office," *Variety* reported in 2000. And as long as theatrical exhibition remains the preferred outlet for motion pictures—and despite the attractions of high-definition television and home deliveries via the fiberoptic superhighway, it seems likely to remain so—the outgoing American adolescent will continue to be Hollywood's most reliable audience, and teenpics the most viable film form.

Reliable and viable, however, do not equal predictable. Since the 1950s, moviemakers setting their sights on the teen market have been armed for exploitation with a mounting accumulation of expertise to fortify their most decisive weapon: control of the means of production. In 1953, in a famous essay attacking postwar mass culture, the critic Dwight Macdonald spoke for a generation of disgruntled adults when he condemned the methods of the larcenous "Lords of Kitsch" who served up degenerate dreck to the unwashed teenage multitudes. "It is very different," sniffed Macdonald, "to *satisfy* popular tastes, as Robert Burns' poetry does, and to *exploit* them, as Hollywood does." To Macdonald and like-minded critics, "technicians hired by businessmen" impose their wares from above, in imperialistic fashion, onto a dully receptive adolescent populace—and, to be sure, the young natives regularly fall prey to the best-laid plans of the worst-grade exploiters.

But although the entrapment of the teenage audience may be routine, it is never quite systematic. "Teen movies have suddenly gone colder than the corpses in a slasher pic," *Variety* fretted, lamenting a teenpic bust in 2001 against a teenpic boom in 1999. "There was a time not so long ago when making movies for young audiences seemed a license to mint $8 bills, so instinctive was teens' rush for the box office, [but] the Clearasil set of 2001 seems to be rejecting teen films in all genres—horror, comedies, and romances alike." Despite the considerable conning and cashing in, teenagers retain a subcultural solidarity that makes them elusive marks for Hollywood's gamesters, a cultural impenetrability that beats back intrusions from sociologists, psychologists, market researchers, and parents. Generation after generation, that autonomy has been the American teenager's best defense against exploitation, from Hollywood and elsewhere.

Notes

Chapter 1: American Movies as a Less-than-Mass Medium

Page 1 **"Like all great arts . . .":** Terry Ramsaye, *A Million and One Nights: A History of the Motion Picture, I* (New York: Simon and Schuster, 1926): xi.

Page 1 **"Films have to be . . .":** "U.S. Nation of Teenagers," *Variety*, June 19, 1957: 50.

Page 2 **"art for the millions . . .":** Will H. Hays, *Annual Report on the Motion Picture Industry* (New York: Motion Picture Producers and Distributors of America, 1933): 11.

Page 2 **moviegoing *was* a familial:** Like everything else in film studies, the composition of classical Hollywood's audience is a matter of controversy. Throughout the 1930s and 1940s, the motion picture industry surely overstated the frequency of family moviegoing and underplayed the rate of juvenile attendance. "There has been misrepresentation by motion picture organizations of the amount of child attendance," Edgar Dale charged in *Children's Attendance at Motion Pictures* (1935), one of the twelve studies supported by the Payne Fund. Summing up his findings, the author argued: "Data have been presented in this report to show that children and youth the country over are regular patrons of motion picture theaters. Further evidence has been presented to show that they contribute a proportion of the total audience that is far greater than we have commonly been led to believe." Significantly, however, Dale concludes from this that "the effect of motion pictures is, therefore, *universal*" (emphasis added). That is, movies affect the young *in equal measure* to other groups. Not until the 1950s did it become unmistakably clear that the movies were *disproportionately* a juvenile medium. Edgar Dale, *Children's Attendance at the Motion Pictures* (New York: Macmillan, 1935): 9, 73.

Page 3 **". . . a great picture and adequate exploitation":** Jack Alicoate, *The 1933 Film Daily Year Book of Motion Pictures* (New York: Wid's Films and Film Folk, 1933): 101. (Hereafter references to annual editions of *The Film Daily Year Book of Motion Pictures* will cite only the appropriate year and page number.)

Page 4 **basic meaning of "exploitation":** Ibid.: 674.

Page 4 **promotional perennial, the contest:** Ibid.: 675.

Page 4   **The birds performed well:** Adolph Zukor with Dale Kramer, *The Public Is Never Wrong: The Autobiography of Adolph Zukor* (New York: G. P. Putnam's Sons, 1953): 203.

Page 4   **Universal's Carl Laemmle:** Carl Laemmle, "The Business of Motion Pictures," in Tino Balio, ed., *The American Film Industry* (Madison: University of Wisconsin Press, 1976): 158.

Page 5   **"After we stopped . . .":** Kevin Brownlow, *The Parade's Gone By . . .* (Berkeley: University of California Press, 1968): 481.

Page 6   **The wise moviemaker "exploited":** On the relationship between the early movies and their audiences, see Lary May, *Screening Out the Past: The Birth of Mass Culture and the Motion Picture Industry* (Chicago: University of Chicago Press, 1980), and Richard Koszarski, *An Evening's Entertainment: The Age of the Silent Feature Picture, 1915–1928* (Berkeley: University of California Press, 1994).

Page 6   **"exploitation pictures" as "films . . .":** Whitney Williams, "'Exploitation Pictures' Paid Off Big for Majors, Also Indie Producers," *Variety*, January 9, 1946: 36.

Page 6   **As examples of exploitation pictures:** Ibid. In its litany of 1945 exploitation pictures, *Variety* did, however, include two Monogram titles that anticipate the disreputable low-budget exploitation fare of the next decade: *Allotment Wives* and *Black Market Babies*.

Page 7   **"ad-pub" departments:** Samuel D. Berns, "Timing Provides the Opportunity for 'Exploitation Naturals,'" *Motion Picture Herald*, May 26, 1956: 33.

Page 7   **Movies of this ilk:** In an interview with the author on April 20, 1983, producer Roger Corman said he remembered the phrase "exploitation film" becoming standard around the time he began his moviemaking career in 1954. It seems to have acquired an additional meaning in the early 1960s, being used to describe sex or nudie films, the kind of fare that was also called "sexploitation" or, later, simply "porn." For example, in 1963, Frank Ferrer averred in *Film Comment* that "the film industry defines an exploitation film in this way: a low-budget film that deals with sex, rape, murder, corruption, drug addiction, perversion, and any other distorted emotion that will attract huge audiences capable of paying a dollar and fifty cents per seat to over two thousand theater owners who deal in this kind of tripe." The next year, in an interview in the same journal, nudie producer Barry Mahon testified: "We use the term 'exploitation' to describe the sexual-attraction type film, as distinct from the 'nudie' which typically has the females posing as models with no sexual overtones involved. . . . Both . . . are referred to commonly as exploitation pictures because the advertising generally oversells what you see when you get inside." See Frank Ferrer, "Exploitation Films," *Film Comment* 6 (Fall 1963): 31; Gordon Hitchens, "The Truth, the Whole Truth, and Nothing but the Truth about Exploitation Films," *Film Comment* 2 (Spring 1964): 1.

Page 7   **Typically, the lapse:** As network censorship has relaxed and the speed of television production has accelerated, the made-for-TV movie has largely supplanted the theatrical movie's headline-grabbing function.

Page 7 **"... a *Sputnik* picture ..."**: Ed Naha, *The Films of Roger Corman: Brilliance on a Budget* (New York: Arco Publishing, 1982): 128. Corman's recollection may be faulty. *Variety* "previewed" *War of the Satellites* on May 8, 1958, some seven months after *Sputnik*. *Motion Picture Herald* gives its release date as April 6, 1958.

Page 8 **Throughout the 1950s:** "Atomic Submarine," *Variety*, August 13, 1958: 1.

Page 8 **pilot Francis Gary Powers:** "Briefs," *Wall Street Journal*, May 19, 1960, p. 1, col. 5.

Page 8 **Castro wanted Marlon Brando:** "Castro Biopic via Jerry Wald," *Variety*, April 29, 1959: 1.

Page 8 **Sam Katzman, a founding father:** "Batista Busteroo," *Variety*, January 21, 1959: 1.

Page 8 **Within an hour:** "Timely," *Motion Picture Herald*, January 21, 1956: 9.

Page 9 **"so-called exploitation picture":** Hy Hollinger, "Teenage Biz vs. Repair Bills," *Variety*, December 19, 1956: 20.

Page 10 **scholarship grounded in genre:** See especially the two collections edited by Barry Grant: *Film Genre: Theory and Criticism* (Metuchen, N.J.: Scarecrow Press, 1977) and *Film Genre Reader* (Austin: University of Texas Press, 1986). For a bibliography of film studies on genre, see Larry N. Landrum, "Recent Work in Genre," *Journal of Popular Film and Television* 13, no. 3 (Fall 1985): 151–58.

Page 10 **Genre criticism aptly begins:** John G. Cawelti, "The Question of Popular Genres," *Journal of Popular Film and Television* 13, no. 2 (Summer 1985): 55.

Page 11 **a definition instructive in its looseness:** Thomas Schatz, *Hollywood Genres: Formulas, Filmmaking, and the Studio System* (New York: Random House, 1981): 6.

Chapter 2: A Commercial History

Page 14 **motion picture industry was dominated:** Tino Balio, *Grand Design: Hollywood as a Modern Business Enterprise, 1930–1939* (Berkeley: University of California Press, 1993), and Thomas Schatz, *Boom and Bust: Hollywood in the 1940s* (Berkeley: University of California Press, 1997), the fifth and sixth volumes of Charles Harpole's History of the American Cinema series, are the essential, comprehensive studies of the business of moviemaking during this period. By the mid-1950s, with RKO an economic basket case and Universal coming on strong, membership in the Big Five and the Little Three had become somewhat fluid. In some lists of the Big Eight, Republic Pictures replaces United Artists, though the latter was not a studio proper but an outfit specializing in financing and distribution.

Page 15 **period of oligarchic control:** The authoritative work on the subject is David Bordwell, Janet Staiger, and Kristin Thompson, *The Classical Hollywood Cinema: Film Style and Mode of Production to 1960* (New York: Columbia University Press, 1985).

Page 15   **"that gilded hussy . . .":** "Then Came the Dawn," *Business Week*, February 8, 1933: 12.

Page 15   **weekly attendance plummeted:** *The 1940 Film Daily Year Book of Motion Pictures*: 43. *The 1960 Film Daily Year Book of Motion Pictures*: 105, revises the 1930 weekly attendance estimate downward to 90 million. Movie attendance and box office figures should always be read skeptically. Statistical information from the 1930s especially tends toward inflation or uncertainty. *The 1933 Motion Picture Almanac*, for example, "estimates" the 1932 weekly attendance at between 55 and 70 million. Although the more recent data are generally considered more accurate, the era's own statistical reports better conjure up the industry's contemporary sense of itself.

Page 15   **The close of 1932:** *The 1933 Film Daily Year Book of Motion Pictures*: 3.

Page 15   **Several theater chains went bankrupt:** "Then Came the Dawn": 12.

Page 15   **By mid-decade:** See Andrew Bergman, *We're in the Money: Depression America and Its Films* (New York: Harper Row, 1972).

Page 15   **attendance rebounded to 70 million:** *The 1940 Film Daily Year Book of Motion Pictures*: 43.

Page 15   **The renewed patronage:** Garth Jowett, *Film: The Democratic Art* (Boston: Little, Brown, 1976): 260–61.

Page 16   **By 1945, weekly:** *The 1946 Film Daily Year Book of Motion Pictures*: 49. See also the charts reprinted in Jowett, *Film*: 472, 483.

Page 16   **This flood of black ink:** "Hollywood Wows Wall Street," *Business Week*, May 11, 1946: 60.

Page 16   **Reflecting a widespread optimism:** Terry Ramsaye, ed., *1945–46 International Motion Picture Almanac* (New York: Quigley Publishing, 1945): vi.

Page 16   **In one stroke Congress:** "Tax Cut Prime Profit-Booster," *Variety*, December 18, 1946: 3, 70.

Page 16   **The Paramount Decree:** Michael Conant, *Antitrust in the Motion Picture Industry: Economic and Legal Analysis* (Berkeley: University of California Press, 1960): 107–53.

Page 17   **other developments contributed to the desperation:** Gladwin Hill, "Big Hollywood Studios Grapple with Changes," *New York Times*, July 28, 1957: sec. 4, 6.

Page 17   **Hollywood-the-place was dispensable:** Gene Arneel, "Footloose Foreign Fancies," *Variety*, June 29, 1955: 3, 16.

Page 18   **hailed an "independent revolution":** Max E. Youngstein, "The Independent's Progress," *Saturday Review*, December 20, 1958: 13.

Page 18   **something of a misnomer:** See "When You Say 'Indie' Use Quotes," *Variety*, April 17, 1954: 3, 18.

Page 19   **some of the most exhaustively documented chapters:** See John Cogley, *Report on Blacklisting I: The Movies* (New York: Fund for the Republic, 1956); Larry Ceplair and Steven Englund, *The Inquisition in Hollywood: Politics and the Film Community* (New York: Anchor Press/Doubleday, 1980): 254–397; and Patrick McGilligan and Paul Buhle, *Tender Comrades: A Backstory of the Hollywood Blacklist* (New York: St. Martin's Press, 1997).

Page 19 **"the present atmosphere"**: Robert Warshow, *The Immediate Experience: Movies, Comics, Theater, and Other Aspects of Popular Culture* (New York: Doubleday, 1962): 196.

Page 19 **"the end of intellectual content . . ."**: Charles Higham, *Hollywood at Sunset* (New York: Saturday Review Press, 1972): 64–65.

Page 19 **Of all the plagues:** Charles Aaronson, ed., *The 1960 International Television Almanac* (New York: Quigley Publishing, 1959): 9A, 14A.

Page 20 **"ulcerous problems":** *The 1957 Film Daily Year Book of Motion Pictures*: 65.

Page 20 ***Television Age* coolly submitted:** "Movie Fan?" *Television Age*, August 11, 1958: 41.

Page 20 **"the electronic monster halitosised . . ."**: Charlie Jones, "Merchant-Exhibitor Collaboration for Better Times for Both on Main Street," *Motion Picture Herald*, October 11, 1958: 29.

Page 20 **The nature of television:** See Frederic Stuart, *The Effects of Television on the Motion Picture and Radio Industries* (New York: Arno Press, 1976): 22–101.

Page 20 **". . . make 'em provocative":** Gene Arneel, "Pix' Big and Bold Bid for Gold," *Variety*, August 8, 1956: 3.

Page 21 **Fred Waller's Cinerama:** *The 1953 Film Daily Year Book of Motion Pictures*: 57.

Page 22 **(The retooling costs for Todd-AO . . .):** "Todd-AO Out-Costs Cinerama," *Variety*, August 10, 1955: 7. The figure is probably inflated.

Page 22 **"This is the year":** *The 1953 Film Daily Year Book of Motion Pictures*: 55.

Page 22 **In the end, only CinemaScope:** "CinemaScope—36,197 Installations Later," *Motion Picture Herald*, September 15, 1956: 20.

Page 23 **By the end of the decade:** For explanations of widescreen technology, see James L. Limbacher, *Four Aspects of the Film* (New York: Brussel and Brussel, 1968), and John Belton, *Widescreen Cinema* (Cambridge, Mass.: Harvard University Press, 1992).

Page 24 **foreign markets surpassed domestic business:** "How Hollywood Hopes to Hit the Comeback Road," *Newsweek*, January 12, 1953: 66–67.

Page 24 **The first casualty:** "B's Buzzing Out of Business?" *Variety*, March 26, 1952: 3, 13.

Page 25 **"a menace to the industry":** "End of 'B' Films," *Newsweek*, June 23, 1952: 74.

Page 25 **still operated double features:** Fred Hift, "'Right Now Is the Dream-Come-True Time for Indie Film Producers,' Sez Albert Lewin," *Variety*, March 10, 1954: 3.

Page 26 **In Philadelphia, attendance dropped:** Ruth A. Inglis, *Freedom of the Movies: A Report on Self-Regulation from the Commission on Freedom of the Press* (Chicago: University of Chicago Press, 1947): 124. See also Gregory Black, *Hollywood Censored: Morality Codes, Catholics, and the Movies* (Cambridge: Cambridge University Press, 1994), and Frank Walsh, *Sin and Censorship: The Catholic Church and the Motion Picture Industry* (New Haven, Conn.: Yale University Press, 1996).

Page 26   **it was a convenient arrangement:** See Jack Vizzard, *See No Evil: Life inside a Hollywood Censor* (New York: Simon and Schuster, 1970): 62–64.

Page 26   **the "art house" played:** W. Ward Marsh, "Let's Keep Garbage out of Art Theatres," *Motion Picture Herald*, September 6, 1958: 16; "Juvenile Conduct in Theaters Occupies Federation of Film Councils Meeting," *Motion Picture Herald*, April 26, 1958: 22.

Page 26   **Lending dignity:** Murray Schumach, *The Face on the Cutting Room Floor: The Story of Movie and Television Censorship* (New York: William Morrow and Company, 1964): 52–79, 90–92.

Page 27   **Ironically, television supported:** "TV Liberal, Screen Strict," *Variety*, April 27, 1955: 7.

Page 27   **"TV's *Dragnet* . . .":** Mike Connolly, "Rambling Reporter," *Hollywood Reporter*, January 16, 1952: 2.

Page 27   **By the mid-1950s:** Abel Green, "What Was, What Is, and Will Be," *Variety*, January 9, 1957: 58.

Page 27   **"The companies are now producing . . .":** "Upcoming Pic 'The Library' to Sneer at Book Burners' Fear of Ideas," *Variety*, July 6, 1955: 1.

Page 27   **Eric Johnston revealed:** "Old Movie Taboos Eased in New Code for Film Industry," *New York Times*, December 12, 1956: 51.

Page 28   **In 1956, Fox's Spyros P. Skouras:** Fred Hift, "Adjustment to TV Is Biggest Issue," *Variety*, January 9, 1957: 66.

Page 28   **Fox's Darryl F. Zanuck:** "Zanuck: Zip, Zig, and Zag," *Variety*, April 13, 1955: 3.

Page 28   **". . . gives away its entertainment free":** Fred Hift, "Exhibs Plead: Don't T(V)KO Us," *Variety*, April 6, 1955: 54.

Page 28   **"How can the theaters . . .":** Ibid.: 1, 54.

Page 28   **"wide open and hungry":** "Increased Flow of 'B' Films No Cure for Biz Say 'A' Distrib," *Variety*, August 15, 1956: 7.

Page 29   **". . . we'll show them":** "Crashing Film Gravy Train," *Variety*, March 30, 1955: 3, 20.

Page 29   **Indeed, to ensure:** They avoided antitrust action from the Justice Department by having no preemptive monopoly on booking the features they helped produce.

Page 29   **an appreciable market:** "Nicholson Finds Playdates Easier," *Variety*, March 30, 1955: 3, 20.

Page 29   **"We don't get the same . . .":** "Birth of an Action-Pic Nation," *Variety*, October 17, 1956: 1.

Page 29   **"How could I convince . . .":** Charles Platt, "Gore Lord," *Heavy Metal* (June 1984): 5–6.

Page 29   **(To increase potential play dates . . .):** "Hurts Budget Producers When Bulk of Films Go Unchallenged," *Variety*, October 14, 1959: 5.

Page 29   **Their total cost:** "Today's 'B' Returns $450,000," *Variety*, August 8, 1956: 5.

Page 30   **at $100,000 apiece:** "Increased Flow of 'B' Indie Films No Cure for Biz": 8.

Page 30   **Moviemakers kept costs:** "Birth of an Action-Pic Nation": 1, 78.

Page 30 **"While Columbia has dropped . . .":** "'Gimmick' Sub for 'Formula,'" *Variety*, June 1, 1955: 4, 22.

Page 30 **"the smaller stations":** Ibid.: 4.

Page 31 **"In recent months exhibitors . . .":** Hy Hollinger, "Teenage Biz vs. Repair Bills," *Variety*, December 19, 1956: 1, 20.

Page 31 **". . . These kids are today's customers":** "Birth of an Action-Pic Nation": 3.

Chapter 3: The Teenage Marketplace

Page 32 **"The trouble with teenagers . . .":** Karin Walsh, "What Is the Press Doing to Teenagers?" *National Parent-Teacher* (September 1956): 4.

Page 32 **"These days, merchants . . .":** Dwight Macdonald, "A Caste, a Culture, a Market—I," *New Yorker*, November 22, 1958: 70.

Page 32 **"the period bounded . . .":** Emma Virginia Fish, *The Boy-Girl Adolescent Period* (New York: Arthur H. Crist, 1911): vii.

Page 33 **F. Scott Fitzgerald's:** F. Scott Fitzgerald, *This Side of Paradise* (New York: Charles Scribner's Sons, 1920; reprint 1970): 59.

Page 33 **Juvenile court judge:** Ben B. Lindsey and Wainwright Evans, *The Revolt of Modern Youth* (New York: Boni and Liveright, 1925): 25.

Page 33 **"enough fire behind . . .":** Frederick Lewis Allen, *Only Yesterday: An Informal History of America in the 1920s* (New York: Harper & Row, 1931; reprint, 1964): 76. For a fuller discussion of 1920s youth subculture, see Paula Fass, *The Damned and the Beautiful: American Youth in the 1920s* (New York: Oxford University Press, 1977).

Page 33 **"The high school . . .":** Robert S. Lynd and Helen Merrell Lynd, *Middletown: A Study in Modern American Culture* (New York: Harcourt, Brace, and World, 1929): 211, 218.

Page 34 **"We believe that . . .":** A. B. Hollingshead, *Elmstown's Youth* (New York: John Wiley, 1949): 441.

Page 34 **"The U.S. is the only . . .":** Harold Wentworth and Stuart Berg Flexner, eds., *Dictionary of American Slang*, 2d ed. (New York: Thomas Y. Crowell, 1975): 538–39. Historian William Manchester dates the term's introduction into the language proper with a 1945 article in the *New York Times Magazine*, "A 'Teen-Age Bill of Rights,'" by Elliot E. Cohen, January 7, 1945: 16–17, 54. See William Manchester, *The Glory and the Dream: A Narrative History of America, 1932–1972* (New York: Bantam Books, 1975): 420. Spelling, by contrast, remains a matter of some uncertainty. To avoid confusion, "teenager" (without quotes) will be used throughout the book.

Page 34 **"a new American caste":** Macdonald, "A Caste, a Culture, a Market": 57.

Page 34 **"Even *before* the baby boom . . .":** Louise B. Russell, *The Baby Boom Generation and the Economy* (Washington, D.C.: Brookings Institution, 1982): 7.

Page 35 **"movement toward [income] equalization":** Robert M. Solow, "Income Inequality since the War," in Robert E. Freeman, ed., *Postwar Economic Trends in the United States* (New York: Harper and Brothers, 1960): 93–138;

Harold G. Vatter, *The U.S. Economy in the 1950s: An Economic History* (New York: W. W. Norton, 1963): 226. Note that Solow sees the main movement toward equalization occurring during the war and continuing, steadily if less dramatically, throughout the 1950s.

Page 35   **"the steady rise . . ."**: Vatter, *U.S. Economy in the 1950s*: 48.

Page 36   **Even in the family:** Dorothy W. Baruch, *How to Live with Your Teenager* (New York: McGraw-Hill, 1953); Paul Landis, *Understanding Teenagers* (New York: Appleton-Century-Crofts, 1955).

Page 36   **the "teenage problem":** Landis, *Understanding Teenagers*: 4.

Page 37   **The term *counterculture*:** J. Milton Yinger, "Contraculture and Subcultures," in David O. Arnold, ed., *The Sociology of Subcultures* (Berkeley: Glendessary Press, 1970): 126.

Page 38   **"it is the fully human adolescent . . .":** Edgar Z. Friedenberg, *The Vanishing Adolescent* (New York: Dell, 1959): 18.

Page 38   **standard Marxist variation:** See, for example, Mike Brake, *The Sociology of Youth Culture and Youth Subculture: Sex, Drugs, and Rock 'n' Roll* (London: Routledge and Kegan Paul, 1980); Dick Hebdige, *Subculture: The Meaning of Style* (New York: Methuen, 1979); and much of the youth culture research done at the University of Birmingham Centre for Contemporary Cultural Studies.

Page 39   **"an historically transmitted pattern . . .":** Clifford Geertz, *The Interpretation of Cultures: Selected Essays* (New York: Basic Books, 1973): 89.

Page 40   **"teenage criminals carving out . . .":** J. Edgar Hoover, "The Twin Enemies of Freedom: Crime and Communism," *Vital Speeches of the Day*, December 1, 1956: 105; Russel MacGuire, "In Mercury's Opinion," *American Mercury* (July 1955): 85.

Page 40   **notorious Joseph Schwartz:** "These Brutal Young," *Newsweek*, March 25, 1957: 36, 39.

Page 40   **"the shook-up generation":** Harrison E. Salisbury, *The Shook-Up Generation* (New York: Harper and Brothers, 1958). For a comprehensive cultural history of official reactions to juvenile delinquency, see James Gilbert, *A Cycle of Outrage: America's Reaction to the Juvenile Delinquent in the 1950s* (New York: Oxford University Press, 1986).

Page 40   **"a vast, determined band . . .":** Richard Gehman, "That Nine Billion Dollars in Hot Little Hands," *Cosmopolitan* (November 1957): 72.

Page 41   **"one where our young people . . .":** G. Stanley Hall, *Adolescence: Its Psychology and Its Relations to Physiology, Anthropology, Sociology, Sex, Crime, and Religion*, vol. 1 (New York: D. Appleton and Company, 1904): xvi-xvii.

Page 41   **"the dreamy teenage market":** "The Dreamy Teen-Age Market: 'It's Neat to Spend,'" *Newsweek*, September 16, 1957: 94; Philip R. Cateora, *An Analysis of the Teenage Market* (Austin: Texas Bureau of Business Research, 1963): 19.

Page 41   **"The American teenagers . . .":** "A New $10-Billion Power: The U.S. Teen-Age Consumer," *Life*, August 31, 1959: 78.

Page 41   **"largely discretionary":** Cateora, *Analysis of the Teenage Market*: 104.

Page 41   **". . . But they share . . .":** Louis Kraar, "Teenage Consumers," *Wall Street Journal*, December 6, 1956: 11.

Page 42   **"to sell a product to . . ."**: "Catching the Customers at a Critical Age," *Business Week*, October 26, 1957: 88.

Page 42   **More insidious were:** "Teenage Consumers": 1.

Page 42   **In 1955, Chevrolet:** "Catching the Customers": 85.

Page 42   **Fitzgerald had noticed:** F. Scott Fitzgerald, *The Crack-Up* (New York: Charles Scribner's Sons, 1931; reprint, 1945): 13.

Page 42   **Of the $10 billion:** "New $10-Billion Power": 78.

Page 44   **"No abstract categories . . ."**: Gary Kramer, "On the Beat," *Billboard*, February 16, 1957: 27.

Page 44   **"the typical management attitude . . ."**: Gary Kramer, "R&R a Teen-Age Must," *Billboard*, November 10, 1956: 21.

Page 44   **"The ostrich act . . ."**: "Fall Blood, Sweat, and Tears Outlook for Brill Building," *Billboard*, September 15, 1956: 15.

Page 44   **Mitch Miller lectured:** "Turning the Tables," *Time*, March 24, 1958: 61.

Page 44   **"If rock 'n' roll . . ."**: Quoted in Steve Chapple and Reebee Garofalo, *Rock 'n' Roll Is Here to Pay: The History and Politics of the Music Industry* (Chicago: Nelson-Hall, 1977; reprint, 1980): 47.

Page 45   **"to wean the teenagers . . ."**: "Polka Rhythm Push Aimed at Teen-Agers," *Billboard*, July 7, 1956: 19.

Page 45   **"Most of our volume . . ."**: Berm Ollman, "Polkas Fade from Mil'kee Juke Boxes," *Billboard*, December 29, 1956: 1.

Page 45   **In 1956, "more money . . ."**: Gary Kramer, "Record Firm Rule of Thumb Slips from Fickle Public Pulse," *Billboard*, December 22, 1956: 1, 22.

Page 45   **"Should an artist . . ."**: "Don't Lose That Kid," *Billboard*, March 17, 1956: 18.

Page 46   **bought Elvis Presley's contract:** Colin Escott and Martin Hawkins, *Sun Records: A Brief History of the Legendary Record Label* (New York: Quick Fox, 1980): 9–11.

Page 46   **(RCA, in a promotion . . .):** June Bundy, "Phonograph Firms' Fall Ballyhoo Points Up Accent on Youth," *Billboard*, September 8, 1956: 1, 24.

Page 46   **Presley alone:** "Teenage Consumers," *Consumer Reports* (March 1957): 140.

Page 46   **". . . magazines for young people"**: Charles H. Brown, "Self-Portrait: The Teen Type Magazine," *Annals of the American Academy of Political and Social Science* 338 (November 1961): 14.

Page 47   **The conventional teen-targeted magazines:** For a content analysis of teen magazines, see Kirk Monteverde, *Teen Magazine: Communication of Values* (Communication Research Center, CRC Report Series 70; Boston: Boston University, March 1975). Monteverde's thesis that teen magazines "project traditional values" seems reasonable enough, but what remains new and noteworthy is that to be persuasive, those values have to be justified in teenage, not adult, terms.

Page 47   **"Because Teen-Agers . . ."**: Edith Heal, *The Teen-Age Manual: A Guide to Popularity and Success* (New York: Simon and Schuster, 1948): copyright page and 142.

Page 47 **In a helpful chapter:** William C. Menninger et al., *How to Be a Successful Teenager* (New York: Sterling Publishing, 1954): 96–97.

Page 48 **raucous new talent:** See "Nets Find R&R No Butt for Jokes," *Billboard*, April 28, 1956: 20.

Page 48 **"How can I restrict it . . .":** Joel Friedman, "Music on Networks Gets Scissors, Sex Is Not Here to Stay," *Billboard*, June 9, 1956: 1, 18; "Censor Can't Dig 'Sally,'" *Billboard*, March 17, 1956: 18.

Page 48 **The preferred teen-targeted:** "Of, by, and for the 'Teens,'" *TV Guide*, January 31–February 6, 1959: 6–7.

Page 48 **"furrow-browed teenagers":** "Tall, That's All," *Time*, April 14, 1958: 64.

Page 49 **"Hollywood . . . is regarded . . .":** Hy Hollinger, "H'Wood's 'Age of the Teens,'" *Variety*, August 22, 1956: 3.

Page 49 **"In the 'good old days' . . .":** Martin Quigley Jr., "Who Goes to the Movies . . . and Who Doesn't," *Motion Picture Herald*, August 10, 1957: 21.

Page 49 **"No wholly satisfactory method . . .":** Howard T. Lewis, *The Motion Picture Industry* (New York: D. Van Nostrand, 1933): 94.

Page 50 **stunningly haphazard way:** See Bruce A. Austin, *The Film Audience: An International Bibliography of Research* (Metuchen, N.J.: Scarecrow Press, 1983): xx–xxv.

Page 50 **In January 1946:** See "Fact Finders, Price Aide Named by MPAA," *Variety*, January 30, 1946: 5. This department, devoted to statistical data and fact-finding, should not be confused with the academy's, later the MPAA's, Motion Picture Research Council, whose research is devoted mainly to technical developments.

Page 50 **"from the standpoint of statistical knowledge . . .":** Robert W. Chambers, "Need for Statistical Research," *Annals of the American Academy of Political and Social Science* 254 (November 1947): 169.

Page 50 **"In an overwhelming number . . .":** Paul F. Lazarsfeld, "Audience Research in the Movie Field," *Annals of the American Academy of Political and Social Science* 254 (November 1947): 162–63, 167.

Page 50 **stoutly ignored the warning:** Leo A. Handel, *Hollywood Looks at Its Audience* (Urbana: University of Illinois Press, 1950).

Page 50 **"You can show . . .":** "More Data about Audience Tastes? Great! But How Does East Get Studios to Act on Findings?" *Variety*, March 23, 1956: 5, 16.

Page 50 **"Hollywood officials hire you . . .":** "The Fans—They Like and Dislike," *Newsweek*, August 4, 1958: 69.

Page 51 **"You can prove almost anything . . .":** Walter Brooks, "You Can Prove Almost Anything by the Statisticians," *Motion Picture Herald*, January 7, 1956: 37.

Page 51 **"mass of coded index cards . . .":** "Film Fans Fact Factory," *Variety*, May 2, 1956: 5, 17.

Page 51 **Not until mid-1957:** "MPAA Releases Results of Survey of Public Opinion," *Motion Picture Herald*, January 25, 1958: 10.

Page 51 **"Making a picture purely . . .":** "Check Public Film Likes, Sirk Urges," *Motion Picture Herald*, June 7, 1958: 21.

Page 52   **"The need for pictures . . ."**: John D. Ivers, "Aim at Youth and Reduce Violence, Panelists Insist," *Motion Picture Herald*, September 8, 1956: 12.

Page 52   **"the most important single area . . ."**: Martin Quigley Jr., "You Must Be Served," *Motion Picture Herald*, June 23, 1956: 7.

Page 52   **"The juvenile market . . ."**: "Pix Static and Boom Economy," *Variety*, April 24, 1957: 16; Hy Hollinger, "'Lost Audience': Grass vs. Class," *Variety*, December 5, 1956: 86.

Page 52   **"I believe in making . . ."**: "Avoids Gats and Gams," *Variety*, January 4, 1958: 1.

Page 53   **"it would be futile . . ."**: Martin Quigley Jr., "For the Young Audience," *Motion Picture Herald*, September 15, 1956: 7.

Page 53   **"what we need today . . ."**: James W. Morrison, "Teenage Incentive," *Motion Picture Herald*, January 5, 1957: 8.

Page 53   **"We know . . ."**: "More Data": 5.

Chapter 4: Rock 'n' Roll Teenpics

Page 54   **"Catering to the teenagers' taste . . ."**: James Fenlon Finley, "TV for Me, if Teens Rule Screens," *Catholic World* 184 (February 1957): 380–81.

Page 54   **"For those producers . . ."**: Albert E. Sindlinger, "Market Research in Motion Picture Merchandising," *Motion Picture Herald*, September 13, 1958: 15.

Page 55   **more than 350 action films:** From the Columbia Pictures Corporation "biography" of Sam Katzman (undated, unsigned) on file in the Georgetown University Library. Used by permission.

Page 55   **prolific Middle Eastern phase:** *The 1954 Film Daily Year Book of Motion Pictures*: 473.

Page 55   **"His chief concern . . ."**: Columbia Pictures Corporation, "Biography: Sam Katzman": 2.

Page 56   **Or, as he bragged:** "Meet Jungle Sam," *Life*, March 23, 1953: 82.

Page 56   **As early as 1946:** *The 1946 Film Daily Year Book of Motion Pictures*: 178.

Page 56   **". . . the same old glands":** "Jungle Sam," *Time*, December 1, 1952: 62.

Page 57   **(A 1956 survey . . .):** "Attendance," *Motion Picture Herald*, March 17, 1956: 9.

Page 58   **an extra $1 million:** Hy Hollinger, "Controversial Pic Backfire," *Variety*, September 14, 1956: 5.

Page 60   **"the Marseillaise . . .":** Lillian Roxon, *Rock Encyclopedia* (New York: Grosset and Dunlap, 1969): 216.

Page 62   **The bureau determined priority rights:** *The 1947 Film Daily Year Book of Motion Pictures*: 820; see also "Test of Title Registry," *Variety*, May 2, 1956: 4.

Page 62   **"high-concept" title:** Richard Meyers submits the following definition of a high-concept exploitation strategy: "high concept is defined as gleaning an entire film's story from one sentence. For instance, *Werewolf in a Girl's Dormitory* (a 1963 Italian film directed by Richard Benson). After that title, actually making the movie is fairly redundant." Richard Meyers, *For One Week Only: The World of Exploitation Films* (Piscataway, N.J.: New Century Publishers, 1983): 25.

Page 62   **Articulating another exploitation commandment:** "Jungle Sam": 62.

Page 62   ***Billboard* spoke for the consensus:** Joel Friedman, "'Rock' Seen Surefire with Teen Brigade," *Billboard*, April 7, 1956: 17, 22.

Page 63   **". . . the sweater-levi crowd.":** "Rock Around the Clock," *Variety*, March 21, 1956: 6.

Page 63   **worldwide grosses of $2.4 million:** "109 Top Money-Making Films of 1956," *Variety*, January 2, 1957: 4.

Page 63   **The racism lurking:** Segregationist Wants Ban on 'Rock and Roll,'" *New York Times*, March 30, 1956: 39.

Page 64   **the Freudian temper:** "Rock-and-Roll Called 'Communicable Disease,'" *New York Times*, March 28, 1956: 33.

Page 64   **To the Massachusetts Public Health:** "Denies R&R V.D. Cause; Alan Freed Sez It's Just 'Adult Entertainment,'" *Variety*, January 15, 1958: 2, 22.

Page 64   **". . . juvenile violence and mayhem":** "Rock 'n' Roll B.O. 'Dynamite,'" *Variety*, April 11, 1956: 1.

Page 64   **". . . the youthful rioters":** "New 'Rock' Explosion of Hot Youth; Branch Mgr. Discounts Morals TNT," *Variety*, May 2, 1956: 1.

Page 64   **police were reportedly so jumpy:** June Bundy, "Freed Replies to R&R Press Slurs," *Billboard*, April 28, 1956: 22.

Page 64   **In England, police arrested:** Thomas P. Ronan, "Rock 'n' Roll Riots," *New York Times*, September 23, 1956: sec. 4, 4.

Page 64   **banning in Belgium:** "Rioters Rock 'n' Roll in Oslo," *New York Times*, September 24, 1956: 3; "Belgian Town Bans U.S. Film," *New York Times*, December 17, 1956: 36.

Page 65   **"It's doing fantastic business":** Thomas P. Ronan, "British Rattled by Rock 'n' Roll," *New York Times*, September 12, 1956: 40.

Page 65   **to conclude his pitch:** "Selling Approach," *Motion Picture Herald*, June 2, 1956: 43.

Page 66   **(marginally) more complicated:** Nik Cohn, *Rock from the Beginning* (New York: Stein and Day, 1969): 17.

Page 72   **"never before . . .":** Joel Friedman, "Spinning Wax Sells Musical Movies Now-adays," *Billboard*, November 10, 1956: 20.

Page 72   **the multiple tie-in:** "Store-Film Tie-in Ups Disc Sales," *Billboard*, January 5, 1957: 18.

Page 73   **Finally, he promised:** June Bundy, "Freed Replies to R&R Press Slurs," *Billboard*, April 28, 1956: 19, 22.

Page 73   **Straddling the generations:** Not incidentally, the end-reel accommodation provides the filmmakers with a good defense against charges of agitating the natives. Freed himself was brought down at least in part by violence that occurred during one of his "Big Beat" shows at the Boston Arena. In May 1958, in a real-life Shake, Rattle, and Rock! scenario, he was indicted for inciting the audience. By the time he was found innocent, the 1959–60 payola scandals were destroying his career. See "The Pied Piper Muted" in *Variety*, May 14, 1958: 2; and the "Payola" section in chapter 7 of this book.

Page 74   **modified colonial metaphor:** Edgar Z. Friedenberg, *Coming of Age in America: Growth and Acquiescence* (New York: Random House, 1963; reprint, 1965): 7–9.

Page 76   **The film's imperial depiction:** For a more sympathetic view of Tashlin's rock 'n' roll vision, see Ed Sikov, *Laughing Hysterically: American Screen Comedy in the 1950s* (New York: Columbia University Press, 1994): 207–31.

Page 77   **"The intrusion of the dopey plot":** David Ehrenstein and Bill Reed, *Rock on Film* (New York: Delilah Books, 1982): 17, 32.

Page 77   **". . . ideal drive-in fare . . .":** Richard Thompson, "Sam Katzman: Jungle Sam or, the Return of Poetic Justice, I'd Say," in Todd McCarthy and Charles Flynn, *Kings of the B's: Working within the Hollywood System* (New York: E. P. Dutton, 1975): 74.

Page 79   **encouragement to the group:** See also Gina Marchetti, "Subcultural Studies and the Film Audience: Rethinking the Film Viewing Context," in Bruce A. Austin, ed., *Current Research in Film: Audiences, Economics, and Law*, vol. 11 (Norwood, N.J.: Ablex Publishing, 1986): 62–79.

Page 79   **"The teenagers seen here":** *"Teenage Rebel," Motion Picture Herald*, October 27, 1956: 121.

Page 79   **". . . one number from another":** *"Rock Around the Clock," National Parent-Teacher Magazine* (May 1956): 49.

Page 79   **"It'll make adults squirm . . .":** *"Rock, Pretty Baby," Variety*, November 11, 1956: 21.

Page 79   **". . . the Battle of the Bulge":** *"Don't Knock the Rock," New York Times*, February 23, 1957: 13.

Page 80   **". . . search for something new":** "$5,600,000 Estimate for Katzman's 12–16 Columbia Pix up to $6,200,00," *Variety*, March 6, 1957: 5.

Page 80   **"to base future production":** Ibid.

Page 80   **". . . giving way to calypso music":** "Warning: Calypso Next New Beat; R.I.P. for R 'n' Roll?" *Variety*, December 12, 1956: 1, 79; see also "The Calypso Craze," *Newsweek*, February 25, 1957: 72.

Page 80   **first crack at such names:** "Calypso Films to Flood Market?" *Variety*, March 13, 1957: 1.

Page 81   **". . . some say already dead":** *"Calypso Heat Wave," Variety*, June 5, 1957: 6.

Page 81   **By the time:** *"Bop Girl Goes Calypso," Variety*, July 17, 1957: 6.

Page 81   **the deluge began:** "Presley Sets House Record," *Motion Picture Herald*, December 1, 1956: 42.

Page 81   **In release for less:** "109 Top Money Making Films of 1956," *Variety*, January 2, 1957: 4.

Page 82   **At the close of 1957:** "Top Grossers of 1957," *Variety*, January 8, 1958: 30.

Chapter 5: Dangerous Youth

Page 83   **"Somehow we must get at the causes . . .":** Estes Kefauver, from the foreword to Dale Kramer and Madeline Karr, *Teen-age Gangs* (New York: Henry Holt and Company, 1953): vii–viii.

Page 83   **"The Right to Professional Help . . .":** Elliot E. Cohen, "A 'Teen-Age Bill of Rights,'" *New York Times Magazine*, January 7, 1945: 54.

Page 84 **"the first American teenager":** Released almost twenty years to the day after Dean's death, Ray Connolly's *James Dean, the First American Teenager* (1975) is a respectful but never sycophantic collection of film clips and interviews with Dean's comrades. Quoting Dean, Dennis Hopper offers a fine insight into the young actor's unique attraction on screen: "I've got Marlon Brando in one hand screaming 'Screw You!' and Montgomery Clift in the other saying, 'Help Me.'"

Page 87 **"Scarcely a city . . .":** "The 'Drag Race' Mania," *Newsweek*, July 23, 1956: 27.

Page 87 **"You're just giving the kids . . .":** Ibid.

Page 87 **"Drag racing started out . . .":** "The Drag Racing Rage," *Life*, April 29, 1957: 131.

Page 88 **". . . of bitter interest to your public":** "Selling Approach," *Motion Picture Herald*, September 15, 1956: 37.

Page 90 **"well-knit programmer[s] . . .":** "*Hot Rod Girl*," *Variety*, September 5, 1956: 6.

Page 90 **"stacked with juve appeal":** "*Hot Rod Rumble*," *Variety*, May 15, 1957: 22; "*Dragstrip Girl*," *Variety*, May 1, 1957: 7.

Page 91 **Surveys had found:** "Teens Tend to Double Bills," *Motion Picture Herald*, February 4, 1956: 18.

Page 91 **In popular double features:** "*Diary of a High School Bride*," *Variety*, August 12, 1959: 18.

Page 91 **Variety concluded the obvious:** "Frantic Fifties: Audience War," *Variety*, December 30, 1959: 55.

Page 92 **"the drive-in is the answer . . .":** Frank J. Taylor, "Big Boom in Outdoor Movies," *Saturday Evening Post*, September 15, 1956: 101.

Page 92 **Throughout the 1950s, concession-stand profits:** Stanley Penn, "Drive-ins Gain; Promise First Upturn in Movie Attendance since 1948," *Wall Street Journal*, October 1, 1959: 1.

Page 92 **One drive-in operator explained:** Ibid.: 9.

Page 93 **recouped at the concession stand:** "Bid for Teens," *Business Week*, May 14, 1955: 114.

Page 93 **exploitation overload:** See the "Smorgasbord" chapter in Mark Thomas McGee and R. J. Robertson, *The J. D. Films: Juvenile Delinquency in the Movies* (Jefferson, N.C.: McFarland, 1982): 40–96.

Page 94 **"While in most cities . . .":** Emma Virginia Fish, *The Boy-Girl Adolescent Period* (New York: Arthur H. Crist, 1911): 70–71.

Page 94 **"The content of current . . .":** Henry James Forman, *Our Movie Made Children* (New York: Macmillan, 1933): viii.

Page 94 **"motion pictures may create attitudes . . .":** Herbert Blumer and Philip M. Hauser, *Movies, Delinquency, and Crime* (New York: Macmillan, 1933): 198.

Pages 94–95 **"possible deleterious effect . . .":** U.S. Congress, *Motion Pictures and Juvenile Delinquency: A Part of the Investigation of Juvenile Delinquency in the United States*, 84th Congress, 2d session (Washington, D.C.: U.S. Government Printing Office, 1956): 1.

Page 95 **"The subcommittee realizes . . .":** Ibid.: 2, 3.

Page 95 **"If crime and violence assume . . .":** Ibid.: 7.

Page 95 **"While the committee recognizes . . .":** Ibid.: 46–47.

Page 95 **Johnston from time to time:** "On Gang Films," *Motion Picture Herald,* May 3, 1958: 9.

Page 96 **"Do you remember . . .":** Bosley Crowther, "Crime in the Streets," *New York Times,* May 24, 1956: 27.

Page 97 **"In the face of . . .":** "Hoover Again Aims Fire at Crime Films," *Motion Picture Herald,* May 10, 1958: 20.

Page 97 **"scripters poring over gangland history . . .":** "Thugs Still in Screen Fashion," *Variety,* November 4, 1959: 3.

Page 100 **"For almost every case . . .":** "Their Children's Keepers," *Wall Street Journal,* May 10, 1957: 8.

Page 100 **the j.d. films improvised two answers:** See also Peter Biskind, *Seeing Is Believing: How Hollywood Taught Us to Stop Worrying and Love the Fifties* (New York: Pantheon Books, 1983): 197–227.

Page 101 **". . . self-destructive, antisocial drive":** Reginald Rose, *Six Television Plays* (New York: Simon and Schuster, 1956): 251.

Page 106 **"It recalls the golden days . . .":** Richard Nasan, "*Andy Hardy Comes Home,*" *New York Times,* December 24, 1958.

Page 107 **"a disturbed young man . . .":** "The Young Captives," *Motion Picture Herald,* February 7, 1957: 149.

Page 110 **"juvenile aid groups . . .":** "UA Product Digest, Winter/Spring 1959": 13, published in *Motion Picture Herald,* January 31, 1959.

Page 110 **an updated edition titled *Blueprint*:** William C. Menninger et al., *Blueprint for Teenage Living* (New York: Sterling Publishing, 1958): 166, 169.

Page 112 **an investment of $150,000:** Todd McCarthy, "The Delinquents (Robert Altman)," in Todd McCarthy and Charles Flynn, *Kings of the B's: Working within the Hollywood System* (New York: E. P. Dutton, 1975): 217.

Page 112 **pejoratives, branding it:** Louise L. Bucklin, "*The Delinquents,*" *National Parent-Teacher* (March 1957): 38.

Page 112 **Voices from within:** "*The Delinquents,*" *Motion Picture Herald,* March 2, 1957: 282.

Page 112 **A big-city exhibitor assailed it:** Eugene F. Ling, "On 'Delinquents,'" *Motion Picture Herald,* March 9, 1957: 6.

Page 112 **According to Linder:** "Delinquents," *Motion Picture Herald,* February 16, 1957: 9.

Page 112 **"The subject of juvenile delinquency . . .":** Curtis Mees, "People and Pictures," *Motion Picture Herald,* September 6, 1958: 30.

Page 113 **"Damage runs into thousands . . .":** "Pompadour Gang with Long Hairdos Most Troublesome of Detroit Vandals," *Variety,* November 25, 1953: 19.

Page 114 **control the "conduct . . .":** George Schutz, "Behavior Control for Young Patrons," *Better Theaters,* in *Motion Picture Herald,* February 9, 1957: 9.

Page 114 **"a uniformed county sheriff . . .":** Ibid.

Page 114 **"juvenile deportment . . .":** "Juvenile Conduct in Theater Occupies Federation of Film Councils Meeting," *Motion Picture Herald,* April 26, 1958: 22.

Page 114 **"Youngsters must be taught . . .":** Schutz, "Behavior Control": 9.

Page 114 **"The youngsters get fidgety . . .":** "Pompadour Gang": 19.

Chapter 6: The Horror Teenpics

Page 115 **". . . working at it harder":** "Horror-in Sound," *Variety*, June 22, 1955: 3.

Page 115 **". . . make a monster":** "Lovers of Frankenstein: Are Horror Films Such Good Business?" *The Economist*, December 6, 1958: 869.

Page 117 **The anxiety for species:** Such, at least, is the critical consensus. At the time, not everyone was buying. *Film Quarterly's* Richard Hodgens was an articulate dissenting voice: "It may be argued that all the atomic monsters of sf films are symbols, and I suppose that they are, but they are inept, inapt, or both. . . . A twelve-ton, woman-eating cockroach does not say anything about the bomb simply because it too is radioactive, or crawls out of a test site, and the filmmakers have simply attempted to make their monster more frightening by associating it with something serious." Richard Hodgens, "A Brief Tragical History of the Science Fiction Film," *Film Quarterly* 13 (Winter 1959): 37.

Page 120 **"Hollywood is on a new science fiction . . .":** "Zombie Pix Upbeat and Durable," *Variety*, May 9, 1956: 11.

Page 120 **"A standard practice . . .":** "Universal's 'Weirdies' Ain't Crazy: $8,500,000 since '54 a Lot of Clams," *Variety*, April 3, 1957: 3.

Page 121 **"indicating a healthy profit . . .":** Ibid.

Page 121 **"the season's biggest sensation":** "I Remember Monster," *TV Guide*, December 14–20, 1957: 5–7.

Page 121 **"It won't be pure horror . . .":** Bob Bernstein, "Horror Era Looms on Video Front; Opinion Divided," *Billboard*, December 9, 1957: 1, 4.

Page 122 **the "horribilia" count:** "Monstrous for Money," *Newsweek*, July 14, 1958: 84.

Page 122 **"audiences preferred monsters . . .":** Allen Ayles, Robert Adkinson, and Nicholas Fry, eds., *The House of Horror: The Story of Hammer Films* (London: Lorrimer Publishing, 1973): 29.

Page 122 **"I'm prepared to make Strauss waltzes . . .":** "Horror Remains a Money Commodity; and James Carreras Oughta Know," *Variety*, May 28, 1958: 7.

Page 122 **Refusing to sign:** Ayles et al., *House of Horror*: 32–34.

Page 123 **A homegrown crop:** Abel Green, "Show Biz: Pain in the Brain," *Variety*, January 8, 1958: 50.

Page 123 **concocted a novelty program package:** "AIP Offers Package: Dual Bill, One Story," *Motion Picture Herald*, December 6, 1958: 10.

Page 124 **"We can put out a package . . .":** "Don't Kill Thrill Chill Mill," *Variety*, March 26, 1958: 5.

Page 124 **"putting two gangster pix . . .":** Jim Powers, "Allied Artists' Revised Dual Credo: Make Both Features Like-Themed," *Variety*, November 12, 1958: 15.

Page 124 **"A young couple . . .":** "Despite Shortage, Double Bills Flourish," *Variety*, February 4, 1959: 14.

Page 124 **"a rush [of] . . . 'space matter'"**: "U.S. Showbiz Angles on Soviet Satellite: Gags, New Space Cadet Spree," *Variety*, October 9, 1957: 1; "H'Wood in Sputnik Spurt; Register Satellite Titles in New Space Pic Cycle," *Variety*, October 9, 1957: 2.

Page 125 **American International Pictures:** For well-informed and appreciative histories of AIP, see Mark T. McGee, *Fast and Furious: A History of American International Pictures* (Jefferson, N.C.: McFarland, 1984), and Robert L. Ottoson, *American International Pictures: A Filmography* (New York: Garland Publishing, 1985).

Page 126 **"To compete with television westerns . . ."**: "Don't Kill Thrill Chill Mill": 5.

Page 126 **ensure a regular source of supply:** "Nicholson-Arkoff Partner," *Variety*, April 4, 1956: 4.

Page 126 **"All these features . . ."**: "American International Is Formed to Produce," *Motion Picture Herald*, March 31, 1956: 22.

Page 126 **"We feel we can create . . ."**: "Five Units to Produce for New Firm," *Motion Picture Herald*, April 7, 1956: 30.

Page 126 **"the exploitation pictures bridge the gap . . ."**: "Don't Kill Thrill Chill Mill": 5. In 1958, Roger Corman submitted one stunningly simple solution to the nabe's chronic product shortage: he proposed that the first-class neighborhood theaters simply declare themselves "first-run" to break the bottleneck caused by downtown theaters tying up current blockbusters with long engagements. To Corman, it made obvious sense to have first-run theaters in suburbs because, after all, that was where the prime theatergoing audience lived. See "Indie Producer Theory on Breaking Downtown Bottlenecks: Let Class Nabes 'Declare Selves' First Run," *Variety*, April 16, 1958: 22.

Page 127 **Corman was praised:** *"Teenage Doll," Motion Picture Herald*, December 7, 1957: 633–34.

Page 127 **"The reasoning of Mr. Nicholson . . ."**: William R. Weaver, "AIP Heads Set Sight on Teenage Patron," *Motion Picture Herald*, May 25, 1957: 20.

Page 128 **"From our modest beginnings":** James H. Nicholson, "Industry Applauds Motion Picture Herald's New Editorial Policy," *Motion Picture Herald*, August 23, 1958: 7.

Page 128 **described AIP's creative process:** Richard Gehman, "The Hollywood Horrors," *Cosmopolitan* (November 1958): 40.

Page 128 **The Nicholson-Arkoff production:** "AIP Launches Big Push for 'Sign of the Gladiator,'" *Motion Picture Herald*, October 3, 1959: 27.

Page 128 **" . . . 'Now do the script'"**: "Birth of an Action-Pic Nation," *Variety*, October 17, 1956: 22.

Page 128 **"The Peter Pan Syndrome":** Robin Bean and David Austen, "U.S.A. Confidential," *Films and Filming* 215 (November 1968): 21–22.

Page 129 **"We work closely . . ."**: "Why Keep Whipping Theater Screens?" *Variety*, April 2, 1958: 3, 18.

Page 129 **AIP "monsters do not smoke . . ."**: "Wald Slams Exploitation Films, Told 'Peyton Place' Pretty Lurid," *Variety*, October 29, 1958: 7.

Page 130 **"You can get away with a lot . . ."**: "Lurid Titles, Harmless Tales," *Variety*, October 14, 1959: 5.

Page 130   **Arkoff and Nicholson were always:** Hy Hollinger, "Is Carny Come-on Necessary?" *Variety*, November 5, 1958: 15.

Page 131   **"Our stories are pure fantasy . . .":** Irving Rubine "Boys Meet Ghouls, Make Money," *New York Times*, March 16, 1958: sec. 2, 7.

Page 131   **Teenagers seemed to agree:** "Youth Wants to Know about the Movies!" *Motion Picture Herald*, October 11, 1958: 21.

Page 131   **carnival terms:** Hollinger, "Is Carny Come-on Necessary?": 15.

Page 131   **telegraphed a powerful dual appeal:** The title also spawned countless send-ups. One of the best was Ernie Kovacs's suggested sequel "I Was a Teenage Supreme Court Justice." Years later the youth-oriented biblical epic *King of Kings* (1961) was dubbed "I Was a Teenage Jesus."

Page 131   **"I had heard that 62% . . .":** "Shock around the Clock," *Time*, September 9, 1957: 110.

Page 132   **"So I took ten weeks . . .":** Herman Cohen, "On Being a Teenage Werewolf," *Films and Filming* 6 (September 1960): 15.

Page 137   **"It's awfully hard . . .":** "'Clean Horror Harms No Kids'—Herman Cohen," *Variety*, February 10, 1960: 21.

Page 137   **"Here, finally, we have . . .":** "Gotta Ballyhoo Horror Films or They Drop Dead," *Variety*, July 30, 1958: 4.

Page 137   **Curtis Mees advised:** Curtis Mees, "Promoting Business-Drive-in Style," *Motion Picture Herald*, April 12, 1958: 36.

Page 137   **"My audience . . .":** "Monstrous for Money," *Newsweek*, July 14, 1958: 14.

Pages 137–138   **"I've modeled my career . . .":** John Kobler, "Master of Movie Horror," *Saturday Evening Post*, March 19, 1960: 97. Years later, with a flare for multiple layers of exploitation that the original might have admired, director Joe Dante cast John Goodman as a thinly disguised version of William Castle in *Matinee* (1993), a self-reflexive comedy-horror film built around a horror film premiere set during the real-life horror of the Cuban Missile Crisis in 1962.

Page 138   **"the death by fright . . .":** "Stiff Competitors," *Time*, August 4, 1958: 66.

Page 138   **The insurance policies:** "Mad, Mad Doctors 'n' Stunts," *Variety*, July 23, 1958: 7.

Page 138   **"the publicity would be terrific though":** Kobler, "Master of Movie Horror": 97.

Page 139   **"I want to tap . . .":** "Queer for Fear," *Time*, August 3, 1959: 58.

Page 139   **"gimmick film with appeal . . .":** Guy Livingstone, "All-Action Stuff Frank Teenage Appeal, Lifting the Down East 'Small Towns' B.O.," *Variety*, October 24, 1965: 5.

Page 140   **grossed $20 million:** See Katherine Hamill, "The Supercolossal—Well, Pretty Good World of Joe Levine," *Fortune* (March 1964): 131.

Page 140   **"It had a lot of sex . . .":** "A Simple Guy," *Newsweek*, February 22, 1960: 100.

Page 140   **brass ring with *Hercules*:** "Levine Plans Second Mighty Campaign for 'Hercules,'" *Motion Picture Herald*, September 13, 1958: 11. Interestingly, like William Castle, though to far less advantage, Joseph E. Levine inspired a motion picture surrogate, the crude Hollywood producer played by Jack Palance in Jean-Luc Godard's *Contempt* (1963), which Levine produced.

Page 140 **Universal stationed "legal" representatives:** "Mad, Mad Doctors 'n' Stunts": 7.

Pages 140–141 **"follow the Yellow Streak . . .":** "Blood Pudding," *Time*, September 1, 1961: 50.

Page 141 **Bad punning was epidemic:** "Gold from Ghouls," *Time*, April 6, 1959: 47; "Don't Kill Thrill Chill Mill": 5.

Page 141 **hearses carrying signs:** "Horror Promotions," *Motion Picture Herald*, May 31, 1958: 845.

Page 141 **"As gory as the law allows":** "Horror of Dracula," *Motion Picture Herald*, May 10, 1958: 825.

Page 141 **"The pictures dropping off . . .":** Arthur Knight, "Tired Blood," *Saturday Review*, October 18, 1958: 57–58.

Page 143 **"So far as horror . . .":** "What Price Horror?" *Motion Picture Herald*, November 8, 1958: 5.

Page 143 **In England:** Derek Hill, "The Face of Horror," *Sight and Sound* 28 (Winter 1958–59): 7

Page 143 **dragging out the experts:** "Quotes Psychiatrist: 'Horror' Aids Kids to Shed Their Primitive Fears," *Variety*, June 4, 1958: 19.

Page 143 **"Horror pictures have reached . . .":** "Psychology Breaks into Horror Acts," *Motion Picture Herald*, September 6, 1958: 966.

Page 144 **"The kids like to see . . .":** Gene Arnell, "M: For Macabre and Mazuma," *Variety*, June 18, 1958: 7.

Page 144 **"is gory enough . . .":** "The Revenge of Frankenstein," *Variety*, June 18, 1958: 6.

Page 144 **"a number of fairly gruesome . . .":** "It Conquered the World," *Variety*, September 9, 1956: 6.

Page 144 **"The teenage monster pictures . . .":** Andrew Dowdy, *"Movies Are Better than Ever": Widescreen Memories of the Fifties* (New York: William Morrow and Company, 1973): 153.

Page 144 **"A couple of realistic films . . .":** Hill, "Face of Horror": 10.

Chapter 7: The Clean Teenpics

Page 145 **"Morality":** "New Wages of Sin: Remorse," *Variety*, April 25, 1956: 7, 22.

Pages 145–146 **"what with all the sex . . .":** Gene Arneel, "New 'Offbeat': Go Wholesome," *Variety*, July 27, 1960: 7.

Page 146 **"It is considered sacrilegious . . .":** "Secret Fear of 'Family' Films," *Variety*, February 24, 1960: 3; Gene Arneel, "Who Really Wants 'Family' Pictures?" *Variety*, February 10, 1960: 5.

Page 146 **"Motion pictures have come . . .":** Gene Arneel, "Pix Peppier as TV Plods," *Variety*, September 14, 1960: 3, 20.

Page 146 **"I've never seen an 'adult type' . . .":** "Kids Debunk 'Adults,'" *Variety*, June 15, 1960: 3.

Page 147   **upcoming "family pictures":** "Kids, Adults, and Congressmen," *Variety*, January 27, 1960: 19.

Page 147   **"Those very pictures . . .":** "More about 'What the Public Wants,'" *Motion Picture Herald*, May 9, 1959: 19b.

Page 147   **". . . a long time since Andy Hardy . . .":** Curtis Mees, "People and Pictures," *Motion Picture Herald*, September 6, 1958: 30.

Page 149   **"When I first saw the trade paper . . .":** Charlie Jones, "What the Public Wants . . . or Does It?" *Motion Picture Herald*, May 2, 1959: 14.

Page 149   **"We keep citing the Hardys . . .":** Ibid.

Page 149   **censors "had not attended . . .":** "PTA Bum-Raps Pix," *Variety*, July 6, 1960: 17.

Page 149   **"to go out and [often] knock . . .":** Vincent Canby, "Exhibs Truly 'Family' Men?" *Variety*, November 2, 1960: 5.

Page 150   **Responding in a manner:** "American Legion Hurls 'Red' Charge at Films," *Motion Picture Herald*, February 13, 1960: 7.

Page 150   **Significantly, 74 of 101 B-rated:** "Catholic Legion 'Alarmed' by Slide in Pic Standards," *Variety*, November 23, 1960: 1; "Do Adults Want 'Adult' Films?" *Variety*, October 19, 1960: 61.

Page 150   **The ministerial protest:** The decline of Legion influence after *Baby Doll* is relative to the tremendous sway it formerly held. Until the mid-1960s, Hollywood producers still reckoned it a force not to be antagonized needlessly. For example, it wasn't until 1961 that another Code-approved film, Albert Zugsmith's *The Private Lives of Adam and Eve*, received a "C" rating. Zugsmith and his distributor, Universal, were worried enough to withdraw 150 prints then in circulation for some judicious editing.

Page 151   **"All this talk about nice . . .":** "'What's Wrong with Sexy Pictures?' Exec Opines 'B.O. Needs Excitement,'" *Variety*, September 2, 1959: 3.

Page 151   **Or, as Twentieth Century-Fox president:** "Skouras Bluntly Instructs Canadians: Public Wants 'Blood, Guts, and Sex,'" *Variety*, June 8, 1960: 3.

Page 151   **Singling out as excessive:** "Biz Blind 'n' Deaf to Clamoring," *Variety*, December 16, 1959: 3.

Page 151   **"If a 20th Century Fox . . .":** "Lurid Titles, Harmless Tales," *Variety*, October 14, 1959: 5.

Page 153   **"typical frequent moviegoer":** "Politz Research Study Uncovers the 'Typical Frequent Movie Goer' as Bright Teen-Ager," *Motion Picture Herald*, November 23, 1957: 15.

Page 153   **"The adolescents in this film . . .":** "*Bernardine*," *Motion Picture Herald*, June 29, 1957: 433.

Page 158   **". . . *Tammy*, an obviously corny . . .":** "What Makes 'Tammy' Run?" *Variety*, September 18, 1957: 4.

Page 158   **"the teenage dating set . . .":** Ibid.

Page 158   ***Going Steady* "a sweetheart . . .":** "Letters to the Herald," *Motion Picture Herald*, February 15, 1958: 6.

Page 158   **"won't cause controversy":** "Pasternak Sees His 'Where Boys Are' First Big Budget Pic Sans Names," *Variety*, October 26, 1960: 7.

Page 160   **1959 survey of teenage girls:** "Teenage Movie-Going Habits," *Motion Picture Herald*, May 16, 1959: 6.

Page 160   **"Her wide appeal . . ."**: Richard Gertner, "The Nation's Exhibitors Select the Stars of Tomorrow," *Motion Picture Herald*, October 10, 1959: 20–21, 25.

Page 161   **"the invisible girl"**: Mike Brake, *The Sociology of Youth Culture and Youth Subculture: Sex and Drugs and Rock 'n' Roll* (London: Routledge and Kegan Paul, 1980): 137–54.

Page 162   **"Paradoxically, many parents . . ."**: Eugene Gilbert, "Why Today's Teen-agers Seem So Different," *Harper's* (November 1959): 79.

Page 162   **"There is one group of Americans . . ."**: Janet Winn, "Oracles for Teenagers," *New Republic*, December 28, 1959: 19.

Page 162   **By 1958, teen singers:** "Am-Par Puts Teen Code on Wax," *Billboard*, November 3, 1958: 3.

Page 163   **Dick Clark gauged:** "Guilty Only of Success," *TV Guide*, September 10–16, 1960: 10–11.

Page 163   **"Presley wiggled off . . ."**: Alan Levy, "Elvis Comes Marching Home," *TV Guide*, May 7–13, 1960: 11.

Page 165   **the "vinyl crap game"**: R. Serge Denisoff, *Solid Gold: The Pop Record Industry* (New Brunswick, N.J.: Transaction Books, 1975): 92–94.

Page 166   **Clark wielded unmatched influence:** "Whatever It Is . . . He's Got It," *TV Guide*, October 4–10, 1958: 12.

Page 166   **"I don't set trends"**: Bill Davidson, "The Strange World of Dick Clark," *Redbook* (March 1960): 111.

Page 167   **"Johnny Green, who is a marvelous composer . . ."**: Bernard R. Kantor, Irwin R. Blacker, and Anne Kramer, eds., *Directors at Work: Interviews with American Filmmakers* (New York: Funk and Wagnalls, 1976): 35–36.

Page 167   **". . . smartly arranged coincidences . . ."**: *"April Love," Motion Picture Herald*, November 23, 1957: 617.

Page 167   **"As far as returns . . ."**: Samuel D. Berns, "Picture Music a Big Selling Aid in the Promotion of Films," *Motion Picture Herald*, February 14, 1959: 10B.

Pages 167–168   **performance is subordinate to presentation:** Daniel Boorstin, *The Image: A Guide to Pseudo-Events in America* (New York: Atheneum, 1961; reprint, 1972): 11–12.

Page 168   **"Fan mags as we knew them . . ."**: Ren Grevatt, "On the Beat," *Billboard*, December 22, 1958: 10.

Page 168   **"the Hollywood studio platter line-up."**: "H'Wood in Disk 100% as Col Sets July Bow," *Variety*, April 9, 1958: 112.

Page 168   **"the new film-based companies . . ."**: Howard Cook, "Pic-Based Diskeries Step Up Impact on Best Seller Charts," *Billboard*, April 27, 1959: 1.

Page 169   **"Teenage Crush," "based on . . ."**: "Kraft 'Idol' Sells to Fox for Movie," *Billboard*, February 9, 1957: 3.

Page 169   **The estimate was conservative:** "Storm over Sands," *Life*, June 3, 1957: 92.

Page 170   **"As uncomplicated as . . ."**: "Teen-Age Crush," *Time*, May 13, 1957: 46.

Page 170   **like AIP monsters, "white teen idols . . ."**: Dick Clark and Richard Robinson, *Rock, Roll, and Remember* (New York: Thomas Y. Crowell, 1976): 155.

Page 172 **"in these days when . . .":** Alex Harrison, "An Open Letter to Exhibitors from Twentieth about Tommy Sands," *Variety,* January 1, 1958: 12.

Page 172 **Sands undertook a personal-appearance tour:** "Tommy Sands Draws Screaming Teens," *Variety,* February 5, 1958: 2.

Page 172 **"The young and recording-tested . . .":** *"Sing, Boy, Sing!" Motion Picture Herald,* January 18, 1958: 681.

Page 172 **"It was a good personal appearance":** "'Sing, Boy, Sing!' Is Yanked in Houston, Tommy Sands' Habitat," *Variety,* February 12, 1958: 4.

Page 173 **Byrnes's teen idol status:** Bob Johnson, "Accent on Youth," *TV Guide,* May 9–15, 1959: 17–19.

Page 173 **"I was offended . . .":** John S. Wilson, "How No-Talent Singers Get 'Talent,'" *New York Times Magazine,* June 21, 1959: 16.

Page 173 **the "pic offers employment . . .":** *"Reform School Girl," Variety,* August 28, 1957: 6.

Page 174 **"This personable chap . . .":** *"Reform School Girl," Motion Picture Herald,* August 8, 1959: 364.

Page 174 **"Somehow I sense . . .":** Ren Grevatt, "On the Beat," *Billboard,* November 10, 1958: 6.

Page 174 **"If my voice sounds too weak . . .":** Davidson, "Strange World of Dick Clark": 111. In his congressional testimony, Clark denied the accuracy of Davidson's article.

Page 175 **"It's no secret . . .":** Bob Stahl, "Can They Really Sing?" *TV Guide,* June 25–July 1, 1960: 10–11.

Page 175 **"will be in the tradition . . .":** Alex Harrison, "A Statement from Twentieth about Fabulous Fabian and 'The Hound Dog Man,'" *Motion Picture Herald,* September 5, 1959: 11–13. In *The Psychotronic Encyclopedia of Film* (New York: Ballantine, 1983), Michael Weldon lists the many ways *Hound Dog Man* rips off Elvis Presley's debut vehicle, *Love Me Tender,* including the appropriation of the latter's wardrobe by the former.

Page 176 **"Fabian is really . . .":** "Twentieth Audit of Its New Faces," *Variety,* December 16, 1959: 18.

Page 176 **"In an effort to discover . . .":** June Bundy, "Movies Reach for Pens as Juve Disk Stars Hit Top Ten," *Billboard,* April 13, 1959: 2.

Page 178 **". . . the nation's theaters would perish":** "Casting to Everyone's Taste," *Variety,* June 1, 1960: 7.

Page 178 **"product of the assumption . . .":** Greg Shaw, "The Teen Idols," in Jim Miller, ed., *The Rolling Stone Illustrated History of Rock 'n' Roll,* rev. and updated (New York: Random House, 1980): 100.

Page 178 **"Pop Music":** Wilson, "How No-Talent Singers Get 'Talent'": 52.

Page 179 ***Billboard* defined "payola":** "Payola Growing Faster than Jack's Beanstalk," *Billboard,* October 6, 1958: 2.

Page 179 **the first exhaustive probe . . .":** Mildred Hall, "Exhaustive Probe for Whole Music Industry on Way," *Billboard,* December 21, 1959: 1; "Sub-committee Hooks Set for Payola Probe," *Billboard,* December 7, 1959: 2.

Page 180 **Freed got royalties:** In his autobiography, Chuck Berry recalls that Freed's cowriting contribution was news to him. "I didn't have any idea that Alan Freed was being compensated for giving special attention to 'Maybellene.' . . .

My first royalty statement made me aware that some person named Russ Fratto and the Alan Freed I had phoned were also part composers of the song." See *Chuck Berry: The Autobiography* (New York: Harmony Books, 1987): 110.

Page 180   **In May 1960, the self-proclaimed:** Jack Roth, "Alan Freed and Seven Others Arrested in Payola Here," *New York Times*, May 20, 1960: 1, 62. See also "Rock 'n' Roll Pied Piper": 62, in the same issue.

Page 181   **by 1957, they claimed 70 percent:** "Indies Hit '57 Tape with 70% of Pop Single Hits," *Billboard*, January 13, 1958: 17.

Page 181   **"Payola really got started . . .":** Ed McKenzie, "A Deejay's Expose—and Views of the Trade," *Life*, November 23, 1959: 46.

Page 183   **personal endorsement to *Gidget*:** "Gimmicks for Gidget," *Motion Picture Herald*, January 31, 1959: 38.

Page 183   **Clark's reputation:** "Tout Dick Clark's Video Fan Mail as Tipping Teens' Theater Tastes," *Variety*, February 11, 1959: 7.

Page 183   **Charges against Clark:** "Dick Clark Cos. Controlled 27% of His TV Spins," *Variety*, April 27, 1960: 1, 58.

Page 184   **" . . .an awful lot of royola":** U.S. Congress, *Hearings of the Subcommittee of the Committee on Interstate and Foreign Commerce: "Payola,"* 86th Congress (Washington, D.C.: U.S. Government Printing Office, 1960): 1204.

Page 185   **" . . .is not payola":** Ibid.: 1304.

Page 185   **Clark's "gross income . . .":** Ibid.: 1305.

Page 186   **"The singer appears . . .":** Ibid.: 1341–42.

Chapter 8: Generation after Generation of Teenpics

Page 187   **"It's hard to tell . . .":** Walter Brooks, "Selling Approaches," *Motion Picture Herald*, September 7, 1957: 35.

Page 187   **"American civilization . . .":** Grace Hechinger and Fred M. Hechinger, *Teen-age Tyranny* (New York: William Morrow and Company, 1963): x.

Page 187   **A front-page headline:** "Film Future: GI Baby Boom," *Variety*, March 5, 1958: 1.

Page 188   **In 1968, Jack Valenti:** "Pix Must 'Broaden Market,'" *Variety*, March 20, 1968: 1, 78.

Page 188   **The Yankelovich survey:** "Pix Must Broaden Market,": 1, 78.

Page 188   **"In the summer of 1960 . . .":** Thelma C. Purtell, *The Intelligent Parents' Guide to Teenagers* (New York: Paul S. Eriksson, Inc., 1961): 157.

Page 189   **After citing statistics:** *Motion Picture Herald*, May 10, 1958: 13–15.

Page 189   **For the $15 million epic:** "Teen Interest Is High in 'Ben Hur,'" *Motion Picture Herald*, June 20, 1959: 10, 15.

Page 191   **Film historian Peter Biskind:** Peter Biskind, *Easy Riders, Raging Bulls: How the Sex-Drugs-and-Rock 'n' Roll Generation Saved Hollywood* (New York: Simon and Schuster, 1998): 14.

Page 191   **As teenagers become "youth":** Seth Cagin and Philip Dray, *Hollywood Films of the Seventies: Sex, Drugs, Violence, Rock 'n' Roll and Politics* (New York: Harper & Row, 1984): 76.

Page 192   **Writing in 1979:** James Monaco, *American Film Now: The People, the Power, the Money, the Movies* (New York: New American Library, 1979): 60. For a more appreciative treatment, see William Paul, *Laughing Screaming: Modern Hollywood Horror and Comedy* (New York: Columbia University Press, 1994).

Page 198   **Traditionally, horror**: For a different view, see Robin Wood, *Hollywood from Vietnam to Reagan* (New York: Oxford University Press, 1986): 70–94.

Page 208   **Regardless of how academic disciplines**: For a provocative discussion of Hollywood's ratings system, see Jon Lewis, *Hollywood v. Hardcore: How the Struggle over Censorship Saved the Modern Film Industry* (New York: New York University Press, 2000).

Page 211   **"In a decade of spiraling . . ."**: Dade Hayes, "Box Office: Reel Fine in '99," *Variety*, January 10, 2000: 9–10.

Page 211   **In 1953, in a famous essay**: Dwight Macdonald, "A Theory of Mass Culture," in Bernard Rosenburg and David Manning White, eds., *Mass Culture: The Popular Arts in America* (New York: Free Press, 1957): 60.

Page 212   **"Teen movies have suddenly . . ."**: Carl DiOrio, "No Pop in Zit Pix," *Variety*, April 2, 2001: 7, 41.

Selected Filmography

Culled mainly from the pages of *Variety*, this is a suggestive, though surely not exhaustive, list of 1950s teenpics. The following designations may serve as a rough guide to film content:

(JD)   Juvenile Delinquent; a film dealing with troubled or aberrant youth

(CT)   Clean Teenpic

(M)   Mainstream; a respectably budgeted film with teen-oriented subject matter and potential crossover appeal for adults

(M-M)   Motor-Mad; a filmed vehicle for hot rods or motorcycles

(R&R)   Rock 'n' Roll; a musical aimed at a teen music "craze"

(V)   Vice; teen-targeted licentiousness

(W)   Weirdie; an offbeat science fiction or horror film, as well as hybrids of any of the above

The Alligator People (1959). Twentieth Century-Fox release of a Jack Leewood production. Directed by Roy Del Ruth. Screenplay by Orville H. Hampton. Featuring Beverly Garland, George Macready, Richard Crane, Lon Chaney. 73 min. B&W. (W)

The Amazing Colossal Man (1957). American International release of a Bert I. Gordon production. Directed by Bert I. Gordon. Screenplay by Mark Hanna and Bert I. Gordon. Featuring Glenn Langan, Cathy Downs, William Hudson, James Seay, Larry Thor. 81 min. B&W. (W)

April Love (1957). Twentieth Century-Fox release of a David Weisbart production. Directed by Henry Levin. Screenplay by Winston Miller from the novel by George Agnew Chamberlain. Featuring Pat Boone, Shirley Jones, Dolores Michaels, Arthur O'Connell, Matt Crowley. 98 min. Color and CinemaScope. (CT)

The Astounding She-Monster (1958). American International release of a Golden State (Samuel Z. Arkoff-Alex Gordon) production. Directed by Edward L. Cahn. Screenplay by Lou Rusoff. Featuring Chester Morris, Marla English, Tom Conway, Cathy Downs. 76 min. B&W. (W)

Attack of the Crab Monsters (1958). Allied Artists release of a Roger Corman production. Directed by Roger Corman. Screenplay by Charles Griffith. Featuring

Richard Garland, Pamela Duncan, Russell Johnson, Leslie Bradley. 62 min. B&W. (W)

Attack of the 50 Ft. Woman (1958). Allied Artists release of a Bernard Woolner production. Directed by Nathan Hertz (Juran). Screenplay by Mark Hanna. Featuring Allison Hayes, William Hudson, Yvette Vickers, Roy Gordon. 65 min. B&W. (W)

Attack of the Puppet People (1958). American International release of a James H. Nicholson–Samuel Z. Arkoff production. Produced and directed by Bert I. Gordon. Featuring John Agar, John Holt, June Kenny, Michael Mark, Marlene Willis. 78 min. B&W. (W)

The Beast with 1,000,000 Eyes (1955). American Releasing Corporation release of a David Kramarsky production. Directed by David Kramarsky. Screenplay by Tom Filer. Featuring Paul Birch, Lorna Theyer, Donald Cole, Dick Sargant. 78 min. B&W. (W)

The Beat Generation (1959). Metro-Goldwyn-Mayer release of an Albert Zugsmith production. Directed by Charles Haas. Screenplay by Richard Matheson and Lewis Meltzer. Featuring Steve Cochran, Mamie Van Doren, Ray Danton, Fay Spain, Maggie Hayes, Jackie Coogan, Louis Armstrong and His All-Stars. 95 min. B&W and CinemaScope. Also known as *This Rebel Age*. (V)

Because They're Young (1960). Columbia release of a Jerry Bresler production. Directed by Paul Wendkos. Screenplay by James Gunn from the novel *Harrison High* by John Farris. Featuring Dick Clark, Michael Callan, James Darren, Doug McClure, Tuesday Weld. 102 min. B&W. (CT)

Bernardine (1956). Twentieth Century-Fox release of a Samuel G. Engel production. Directed by Henry Levin. Screenplay by Theodore Reeves based on the play by Mary Chase. Featuring Pat Boone, Terry Moore, Janet Gaynor, Dean Jagger, Richard Sargent, James Drury, Ronnie Burns. 94 min. Color and CinemaScope. (CT)

The Big Beat (1958). Universal release of a Will Cowan production. Directed by Will Cowan. Screenplay by David P. Harmon. Featuring William Reynolds, Gogi Grant, Andra Martin, Hans Conried, Fats Domino, the Del Vikings, The Diamonds, The Four Aces. 82 min. Color. (R&R)

Blackboard Jungle (1955). Metro-Goldwyn-Mayer release of a Pandro S. Berman production. Directed by Richard Brooks. Screenplay by Richard Brooks from the novel by Evan Hunter. Featuring Glenn Ford, Anne Francis, Vic Morrow, Sidney Poitier, Richard Kiley. 101 min. B&W. (JD)

The Blob (1958). Paramount release of a Jack H. Harris production. Directed by Irvin S. Yeaworth Jr. Screenplay by Theodore Simonson and Kate Philips from an idea by Irvine H. Millgate. Featuring Steve McQueen, Anne Corseaut, Earl Rowe. 86 min. Color. (W)

Blood of Dracula (1957). American International release of a Herman Cohen production. Directed by Herbert L. Strock. Screenplay by Ralph Thornton (Herman Cohen and Aben Kandel). Featuring Sandra Harrison, Louise Lewis, Gail Ganley, Jerry Blaine. 68 min. B&W. (W)

Blue Denim (1959). Twentieth Century-Fox release of a Charles Brackett production. Directed by Philip Dunne. Screenplay by Philip Dunne and Edith Sommer based on the play by James Leo Herlihy and William Noble. Featuring

Carol Lynley, Brandon de Wilde, MacDonald Carey, Marsha Hunt, Warren Berlinger. 89 min. B&W and CinemaScope. (M)

Bop Girl Goes Calypso (1957). United Artists release of a Bel Air production. Produced by Aubrey Schenck. Directed by Howard W. Koch. Screenplay by Arnold Belgard. Featuring Judy Tyler, Bobby Troup, The Mary Kaye Trio, The Goofers, Lord Flea and His Calypsonians, Nino Tempo. 80 min. B&W. (R&R)

The Brain Eaters (1958). American International release of an Edwin Nelson production. Directed by Bruno VeSota. Screenplay by Gordon Urquhart. Featuring Edwin Nelson, Alan Frost, Jack Hill, Joanna Lee, Jody Fair. 60 min. B&W. (W)

The Brain from Planet Arous (1958). Favorite Films release of a Jacques Marquette production, presented by Howco International. Directed by Nathan Hertz (Juran). Screenplay by Ray Buffam. Featuring John Agar, Joyce Meadows, Robert Fuller, Thomas B. Henry, Henry Travis. 70 min. B&W. (W)

A Bucket of Blood (1959). American International release of a James H. Nicholson and Samuel Z. Arkoff production. Produced and directed by Roger Corman. Screenplay by Charles B. Griffith. Featuring Dick Miller, Barbara Morris, Anthony Carbonise, Ed Nelson, Burt Convy. 66 min. B&W. (W)

Calypso Heat Wave (1957). Columbia release of a Sam Katzman production. Directed by Fred F. Sears. Screenplay by David Chandler from a story by Orville H. Hampton. Featuring Johnny Desmond, Merry Anders, The Terriers, The Hi-Lo's, Maya Angelou. 86 min. B&W. (R&R)

Calypso Joe (1957). Allied Artists release of a William P. Broidy production. Directed by Edward Dein. Screenplay by Edward and Mildred Dein. Featuring Herb Jeffries, Angie Dickinson, Edward Kemmer, The Easy Riders, Lord Flea and His Calypsonians. 76 min. B&W. (R&R)

The Careless Years (1957). United Artists release of an Edward Lewis production. Directed by Arthur Hiller. Screenplay by Edward Lewis. Featuring Dean Stockwell, Natalie Trundy, John Larch, Barbara Billingsley. 70 min. B&W. (CT)

Carnival Rock (1957). Howco International release of a Roger Corman production. Directed by Roger Corman. Screenplay by Leo Lieberman. Featuring Susan Cabot, Dick Miller, Brian Hutton, The Platters, The Blockbusters, The Shadows, David Houston, and Bob Luman. 75 min. B&W. (R&R)

City Across the River (1949). Universal release of a Maxwell Shane production. Directed by Maxwell Shane. Screenplay by Maxwell Shane and Dennis Cooper from Irving Shulman's adaptation of his novel *The Amboy Dukes*. Featuring Peter Fernandez, Stephen McNalley, Thelma Ritter, Jeff Corey, and Drew Pearson. 90 min. B&W. (JD)

College Confidential (1960). Universal release of an Albert Zugsmith production. Directed by Albert Zugsmith. Screenplay by Irving Shulman. Featuring Steve Allen, Jayne Meadows, Mamie Van Doren, Conway Twitty. 91 min. B&W. (V)

Compulsion (1959). Twentieth Century-Fox release of a Darryl F. Zanuck Productions presentation. Produced by Richard D. Zanuck. Directed by Richard Fleischer. Screenplay by Richard Murphy from the novel by Meyer Levin. Featuring Orson Welles, Diane Varsi, Dean Stockwell, Bradford Dillman, E. G. Marshall, Martin Milner. 103 min. B&W and CinemaScope. (M)

The Cool and the Crazy (1958). American International release of an E. C. Rhoden Jr. production. Directed by William Whitney. Screenplay by Richard C. Sarafian. Featuring Scott Marlowe, Gigi Perreau, Dick Bakalyan, Dick Jones. 78 min. B&W. (JD)

The Creeping Unknown (1956). United Artists release of an Anthony Hinds production. Directed by Val Guest. Screenplay by Richard Landau. Featuring Brian Donlevy, Margia Dean, Jack Warner, Richard Wordsworth. 78 min. B&W. (W)

Crime in the Streets (1956). Allied Artists release of a Vincent M. Fennelly (Lindbrook) production. Directed by Donald Siegal. Screenplay by Reginald Rose from his teleplay. Featuring John Cassevetes, Sal Mineo, Mark Rydell, James Whitmore. 91 min. B&W. (JD)

The Cry-Baby Killer (1958). Allied Artists release of a David Kramarsky–David March production. Produced by Roger Corman. Directed by Jus Addiss. Screenplay by Leo Gordon and Melvin Levy. Featuring Harry Lauter, Jack Nicholson, Carolyn Mitchell. 62 min. B&W. (JD)

The Curse of Frankenstein (1957). Warner release of a Hammer production (Anthony Hinds). Directed by Terence Fisher. Screenplay by Jimmy Sangster based on the novel by Mary Shelley. Featuring Peter Cushing, Christopher Lee, Hazel Court, Robert Urquhart, Valerie Gaunt. 82 min. Color. (W)

Cyclops (1957). Allied Artists release of an A. B. and H. production. Produced, directed, and written by Bert I. Gordon. Featuring Gloria Talbott, Lon Chaney Jr., Tom Drake. 66 min. B&W. (W)

Daddy-O (1959). American International release of an Elmer C. Rhoden Jr. production. Directed by Lou Price. Screenplay by David Messinger. Featuring Dick Contino, Bruno Ve Sota, Sandra Giles. 74 min. B&W. (M-M)

Dangerous Youth (1958). Warner Bros. release of an Anna Neagle production. Directed by Herbert Wilcox. Screenplay by Jack Trevor Story. Featuring Frankie Vaughn, Carole Lesley, George Baker. 98 min. B&W. (JD)

Date Bait (1960). Filmgroup release of an O'Dale Ireland production. Directed by George Reppas. Screenplay by Robert Slaven and Ethelmae Page. Featuring Gary Clark, Marlo Ryan, and Richard Gering. 71 min. B&W. (V)

Daughter of Docter Jekyll (1957). Allied Artists release of a Jack Pollexfen production. Directed by Edgar G. Ulmer. Screenplay by Jack Pollexfen. Featuring John Agar, Gloria Talbott, Arthur Shields, John Dierkes, Mollie McCart. 67 min. B&W. (W)

The Day the World Ended (1956). American Releasing Corporation release of a Golden State (Roger Corman) production. Directed by Roger Corman. Screenplay by Lou Rusoff. Featuring Richard Denning, Lori Nelson, Adele Jergens, Touch Connors. 78 min. B&W. (W)

The Delicate Delinquent (1957). Paramount release of a Jerry Lewis production. Directed and written by Don McGuire. Featuring Jerry Lewis, Darren McGavin, Martha Hyer, Richard Bakalyan. 100 min. B&W. (M)

The Delinquents (1957). United Artists release of a Robert Altman production. Directed and written by Robert Altman. Featuring Tom Laughlin, Peter Miller, and Richard Bakalyan. 72 min. B&W. (JD)

Diary of a High School Bride (1959). American International release of a Burt Topper production. Directed by Burt Topper. Screenplay by Burt Topper, Mark Lowell, and Jan Lowell. Featuring Anita Sands, Ronald Foster, Chris Robinson, Wendy Wilder. 72 min. B&W. (JD)

Dino (1957). Allied Artists release of a Bernice Block production. Directed by Thomas Carr. Screenplay by Reginald Rose from his teleplay. Featuring Sal Mineo, Brian Keith, Frank Faylen, Susan Kohner. 93 min. B&W. (JD)

Don't Knock the Rock (1956). Columbia release of a Sam Katzman production. Directed by Fred F. Sears. Screenplay by Robert E. Kent and James B. Gordon. Featuring Bill Haley and the Comets, Alan Dale, Alan Freed, Little Richard, The Treniers. 84 min. B&W. (R&R)

Dragstrip Girl (1957). American International release of an Alex Gordon production. Directed by Edward L. Cahn. Screenplay by Lou Rusoff. Featuring Fay Spain, Steve Terrell, John Ashley, and Frank Gorshin. 69 min. B&W. (M-M)

Dragstrip Riot (1958). American International release of an O'Dale Ireland production. Directed by David Bradley. Screenplay by George Hodgins. Featuring Yvonne Lime, Gary Clarkes, Fay Wray, Bob Turnbull, Connie Stevens. 68 min. B&W. (M-M)

Eighteen and Anxious (1957). Republic release of an AB-PT production. Produced by Edmond Chevie. Directed by Joe Parker. Screenplay by Dale and Katherine Eunson. Featuring Mary Webster, William Campbell, Martha Scott, Jackie Loughery, Jim Backus. 93 min. B&W. (JD)

Fear Strikes Out (1957). Paramount release of an Alan Pakula production. Directed by Robert Mulligan. Screenplay by Ted Berkman and Raphael Blau based on the story by James A. Piersall and Albert S. Hirschberg. Featuring Anthony Perkins, Karl Malden, Norma Moore, Perry Wilson, Adam Williams. 101 min. B&W. (M)

The Fiend Who Walked the West (1958). Twentieth Century-Fox release of a Herbert B. Swope Jr. production. Directed by Gordon Douglas. Screenplay by Harry Brown and Philip Yordon from the screenplay for *Kiss of Death* by Ben Hecht and Charles Lederar. Featuring Hugh O'Brien, Robert Evans, Dolores Michaels, Linda Christal. 101 min. B&W and CinemaScope. (W)

The Fly (1958). Twentieth Century-Fox release of its own production. Produced and directed by Kurt Neumann. Screenplay by James Clavell from the story by George Langelaan. Featuring Al Hedison, Patricia Owens, Vincent Price, Herbert Marshall. 94 min. Color and CinemaScope. (M)

Frankenstein—1970 (1958). Allied Artists release of an Aubrey Schenck production. Directed by Howard W. Koch. Screenplay by Richard Landau and George Worthing Yates from a story by Aubrey Schenk and Charles A. Moses. Featuring Boris Karloff, Tom Duggan, Jana Lund, Donald Barry. 83 min. B&W and CinemaScope. (W)

Ghost of Dragstrip Hollow (1959). American International release of a Lou Rusoff production. Directed by William Hole Jr. Screenplay by Lou Rusoff. Featuring Jody Fair, Martin Braddock, Russ Bender, Leon Taylor. 65 min. B&W. (W)

Gidget (1959). Columbia release of a Lewis J. Rachmil production. Directed by Paul Wendkos. Screenplay by Gabrielle Upton based on the novel by Frederick Kohner. Featuring Sandra Dee, Cliff Robertson, James Darren, Arthur O'-Connell, The Four Preps. 95 min. Color and CinemaScope. (CT)

The Girl Can't Help It (1956). Twentieth Century-Fox release of a Frank Tashlin production. Directed by Frank Tashlin. Screenplay by Frank Tashlin and Herbert Baker from a story by Garson Kanin. Featuring Tom Ewell, Jayne Mansfield, Edmond O'Brien, Fats Domino, Gene Vincent and the Blue Caps, The Platters, Little Richard, Eddie Fontaine, The Chuckles, Julie London, Nino Tempo, April Stevens, Eddie Cochran. 96 min. Color and CinemaScope. (M/R&R)

Girls Town (1959). Metro-Goldwyn-Mayer release of an Albert Zugsmith production. Directed by Charles Haas. Screenplay by Robert Smith from a story by Robert Hardy Andrews. Featuring Mamie Van Doren, Mel Torme, Paul Anka, Ray Anthony, and the Platters. 92 min. B&W. Also known as *The Innocent and the Damned*. (V)

Going Steady (1958). Columbia release of a Clover production (Sam Katzman). Directed by Fred F. Sears. Screenplay by Budd Grossman from a story by Budd Grossman and Sumner A. Long. Featuring Molly Bee, Alan Reed Jr., Bill Goodwin, Irene Hervy. 82 min. B&W. (CT)

Go, Johnny, Go! (1959). Hal Roach Studios/Valient release of an Alan Freed production. Directed by Paul Landres. Featuring Alan Freed, Jimmy Clanton, Chuck Berry, "the late" Ritchie Valens, Jackie Wilson, Eddie Cochran, Harvey Fuqua, Jo Ann Campbell, The Cadillacs, The Flamingos. 75 min. B&W. (R&R)

High School Big Shot (1958). Filmgroup release of a Stan Bichman production. Directed and written by Joel Rapp. Featuring Tom Pittman, Virginia Aldridge, Howard Veit, and Malcolm Atterbury. 70 min. B&W. (JD)

High School Caesar (1960). Filmgroup release of an O'Dale Ireland production. Directed by O'Dale Ireland. Screenplay by Ethel Mae Page and Robert Slaven. Featuring John Ashley, Gary Vinson, Lowell Brown, and Steve Stevens. 63 min. B&W. (JD)

High School Confidential (1958). A Metro-Goldwyn-Mayer release of an Albert Zugsmith production. Directed by Jack Arnold. Screenplay by Lewis Meltzer and Robert Blees. Featuring Russ Tamblyn, Mamie Van Doren, Jan Sterling, Jackie Coogan, John Drew Barrymore, Jerry Lee Lewis. 85 min. B&W. (V)

High School Hellcats (1958). American International release of a Charles "Buddy" Rogers production. Directed by Edward Bernds. Screenplay by Mark and Jan Lowel. Featuring Yvonne Lime, Bret Halsey, Jana Lund, Suzanne Sidney, Heather Ames. 68 min. B&W. (V)

Horror of Dracula (1958). Universal release of a Hammer production. Directed by Terrence Fisher. Screenplay by Jimmy Sangster from the novel by Bram Stoker. Featuring Peter Cushing, Michael Gough, Melissa Stribling, Christopher Lee, Carol Marsh. 82 min. Color. (W)

Horrors of the Black Museum (1959). American International release of a Herman Cohen production. Directed by Arthur Crabtree. Screenplay by Aben Kandel and Herman Cohen. Featuring Michael Gough, June Cunningham, Graham Curnow, Shirley Ann Field. 94 min. Color, CinemaScope, and "Hypnovision." (W)

Hot Car Girl (1958). Allied Artists release of a Gene Corman production. Directed by Bernard L. Kowalski. Screenplay by Leo Gordon. Featuring Richard Bakalyan, June Kenny, John Brinkley, Jana Lund, Robert Knapp. 71 min. B&W. (M-M)

Hot Rod Gang (1958). American International release of a Lou Rusoff production. Directed by Lew Landers. Screenplay by Lou Rusoff. Featuring John Ashley, Jody Fair, Steve Drexel, Gene Vincent, Harry McCann. 71 min. B&W. (M-M)

Hot Rod Girl (1956). American International release of a Norman T. Herman (Nacirema) production. Directed by Leslie Martinson. Screenplay by John Mc-Greevey. Featuring Lori Nelson, John Smith, Chuck Conners, Frank J. Gorshin. 75 min. B&W. (M-M)

Hot Rod Rumble (1957). Allied Artists release of a Norman T. Herman production. Directed by Leslie H. Martinson. Screenplay by Meyer Doblinsky. Featuring Leigh Snowden, Richard Hartunian, Joey Forman, Wright King, Brett Halsey. 79 min. B&W. (M-M)

Hound Dog Man (1959). Twentieth Century-Fox release of a Jerry Wald production. Directed by Don Siegel. Produced by Jerry Wald. Screenplay by Fred Gipson and Winston Miller from the novel by Fred Gipson. Featuring Fabian, Stuart Whitman, Carol Lynley, Arthur O'Connell. 87 min. Color and Cinema-Scope. (CT)

House on Haunted Hill (1958). Allied Artists release of a William Castle–Robb White production. Directed by William Castle. Screenplay by Robb White. Featuring Vincent Price, Carol Ohmart, Richard Long, Alan Marshall, Carolyn Craig. 75 min. B&W and Emergo. (W)

How to Make a Monster (1958). American International release of a James H. Nicholson–Samuel Z. Arkoff production, produced by Herman Cohen. Directed by Herbert L. Strock. Screenplay by Kenneth Langtry and Herman Cohen. Featuring Robert H. Harris, Paul Brinegar, Gary Conway, Gary Clarke. 75 min. B&W and Superama. (W)

I Married a Monster from Outer Space (1958). Paramount release of a Gene Fowler Jr. production. Directed by Gene Fowler Jr. Screenplay by Louis Vittes. Featuring Tom Tyron, Gloria Talbott, Peter Baldwin, Robert Ivers, Jean Carson. 78 min. B&W. (W)

It Conquered the World (1956). American International release of a Sunset (James H. Nicholson–Roger Corman) production. Produced and directed by Roger Corman. Screenplay by Lou Rusoff. Featuring Peter Graves, Beverly Garland, Lee Van Cleef, Sally Fraser. 68 min. B&W. (W)

It! The Terror from Beyond Space (1958). United Artists release of a Vogue Picture production. Produced by Robert E. Kent. Directed by Edward L. Cahn. Screenplay by Jerome Bixby. Featuring Marshall Thompson, Shawn Smith, Kim Spalding, Ann Doran, Dabbs Greer. 68 min. B&W. (W)

I Was a Teenage Frankenstein (1957). American International release of a Herman Cohen production. Directed by Herbert L. Strock. Screenplay by Kenneth Langtry. Featuring Whit Bissell, Phyllis Coates, Robert Burton, Gary Conway. 72 min. B&W with color sequence. (W)

I Was a Teenage Werewolf (1957). American International release of a Herman Cohen production. Directed by Gene Fowler Jr. Written by Ralph Thornton

(Herman Cohen and Aben Kandel). Featuring Michael Landon, Whit Bissell, Yvonne Lime, Tony Marshall, Don Richard, Guy Williams. 76 min. B&W. (W)

Jailhouse Rock (1957). Metro-Goldwyn-Mayer release of a Pandro S. Berman production. Directed by Richard Thorpe. Screenplay by Guy Trosper based on a story by Ned Young. Featuring Elvis Presley, Judy Tyler, Mickey Shaughnessy, Dean Jones, Vaugh Taylor. 96 min. B&W and CinemaScope. (R&R)

Jamboree (1957). Warner Bros. release of a Max J. Rosenberg and Milton Subotsky production. Directed by Roy Lockwood. Screenplay by Leonard Kantor. Featuring Kay Medford, Paul Carr, Freda Holloway, Bob Patene, Jerry Lee Lewis, Fats Domino, Carl Perkins, Frankie Avalon, Lewis Lymon and the Teenchords, Slim Whitman. 87 min. B&W. (R&R)

Joy Ride (1958). Allied Artists release of a Ben Schwald production. Directed by Edward Bernds. Screenplay by Christopher Knopf from a story by C. B. Gilford. Featuring Rad Fulton, Ann Doran, Regis Toomey, Nicholas King, Jim Bridges, Robert Levin. 65 min. B&W. (M-M)

Juke Box Rhythm (1959). Columbia release of a Sam Katzman production. Directed by Arthur Dreifuss. Screenplay by Mary C. McCall Jr. and Early Baldwin from a story by Lou Morheim. Featuring Jo Morrow, Jack Jones, Brian Donlevy, George Jessel, The Earl Grant Trio, The Nitwits, Johnny Otis, The Treniers. 82 min. B&W. (R&R)

Juvenile Jungle (1958). Republic release of a Coronado production. Produced by Sidney Picker. Directed by William Witney. Screenplay by Arthur T. Horman. Featuring Richard Bakalyan, Corey Allen, Anne Whitfield, Rebecca Welles, Joe Di Recta. 69 min. B&W. (JD)

King Creole (1958). Paramount release of a Hal B. Wallis production. Directed by Michael Curtiz. Screenplay by Michael V. Gazzo and Herbert Baker based on the novel *A Stone for Danny Fisher*, by Harold Robbins. Featuring Elvis Presley, Carolyn Jones, Walter Matthau, Dolores Hart, Dean Jagger, Vic Morrow, 116 min. B&W and VistaVision. (R&R/JD)

Let's Rock (1958). Columbia release of a Harry Foster production. Directed by Harry Foster. Screenplay by Hal Hackady. Featuring Julius La Rosa, Phyllis Newman, Conrad Janis, Paul Anka, Danny and the Juniors, The Royal Teens, Roy Hamilton, Wink Martindale, The Tyrones. 78 min. B&W. Also known as *Keep It Cool.* (R&R)

Life Begins at 17 (1958). Columbia release of a Sam Katzman production. Directed by Arthur Dreifuss. Screenplay by Richard Baer. Featuring Mark Damon, Dorothy Johnson, Ed Byrnes, Ann Doran, Hugh Sanders, Luana Anders. 74 min. B&W. (CT)

Live Fast, Die Young (1958). Universal release of a Harry Rybnick and Richard Kay production. Directed by Paul Henreid. Screenplay by Allen Rivkin and Ib Melchoir based on a story by Ib Melchior and Edwin B. Watson. Featuring Mary Murphy, Norma Eberhardt, Sheridan Comerate, Michael Conners, Jay Jostyn, Troy Donohue. 82 min. B&W. (JD)

Love Me Tender (1956). Twentieth Century-Fox release of a David Weisbart production. Directed by Robert Webb. Screenplay by Robert Buckner from a story by Maurice Geraghty. Featuring Richard Egan, Elvis Presley, Debra Paget, William Campbell, Neville Brand. 94 min. B&W. (M/R&R)

Loving You (1957). Paramount release of a Hal B. Wallis production. Directed by Hal Kanter. Screenplay by Herbert Baker and Hal Kanter from a story by Mary Agnes Thompson. Featuring Elvis Presley, Lizabeth Scott, Wendell Corey, Dolores Hart. 101 min. Technicolor and VistaVision. (R&R)

Macabre (1958). Allied Artists release of a William Castle production. Directed by William Castle. Screenplay by Robb White (pseudonym for thirteen people). Featuring William Prince, Jim Backus, Christine White, Jacqueline Scott. 73 min. B&W. (W)

Mister Rock and Roll (1957). Paramount release of a Ralph B. Serpe and Howard B. Kreitsak production. Directed by Charles Dubin. Screenplay by James Blumgarten. Featuring Alan Freed, Rocky Graziano, Teddy Randazzo, Lois O'Brien, Fisher and Marks, Lionel Hampton and His Band, Chuck Berry, Little Richard, The Moonglows, Clyde McPhatter, Frankie Lymon and the Teenagers, LaVern Baker, Brook Benton, Ferlin Husky. 86 min. B&W. (R&R)

Monster on the Campus (1958). Universal release of a Joseph Gershenson production. Directed by Jack Arnold. Screenplay by David Duncan. Featuring Arthur Franz, Joanna Moore, Judson Pratt, Nancy Walters, Troy Donahue. 77 min. B&W. (W)

Motorcycle Gang (1957). American International release of a Golden State production (Alex Gordon). Directed by Edward L. Cahn. Screenplay by Lou Rusoff. Featuring Anne Neyland, Steve Terrell, John Ashley, Carl Switzer. 78 min. B&W. (M-M)

The Mummy (1959). Universal release of a Michael Carreras production. Directed by Terence Fisher. Screenplay by Jimmer Sangster. Featuring Peter Cushing, Christopher Lee, Yvonne Furneaux, Eddie Byrne. 86 min. Color. (W)

My Teenage Daughter (1956). British Lion release of a Herbert Wilcox production. Directed by Herbert Wilcox. Screenplay by Felicity Douglas. Featuring Anna Neagle, Sylvia Syms, Normand Wolland, Wilfred Hyde White. 100 min. B&W. (M)

No Time to Be Young (1957). Columbia release of a Columbia Pictures production. Produced by Wallace McDonald. Directed by David Rich. Screenplay by John McPartland and Raphael Hayes from a story by John McPartland. Featuring Robert Vaughn, Roger Smith, Tom Pittman, Dorothy Green, Merry Anders. 81 min. B&W. (JD)

The Party Crashers (1958). Paramount release of a William Alland production. Directed by Bernard Girard. Screenplay by Bernard Girard. Featuring Mark Damon, Bobby Driscoll, Connie Stevens, and Frances Farmer. 78 min. B&W. (JD)

The Phantom from 10,000 Leagues (1956). American Releasing Corporation release of a Jack and Dan Milner production. Directed by Dan Milner. Screenplay by Lou Rusoff from a story by Dorys Lukather. Featuring Kent Taylor, Cathy Downs, Michael Whalen, Helen Stanton. 80 min. B&W. (W)

Platinum High School (1960). Metro-Goldwyn-Mayer release of a Red Doff production. Directed by Charles Hass. Screenplay by Robert Smith based on a screenplay by Howard Breslin. Featuring Mickey Rooney, Terry Moore, Dan

Duryea, Yvette Mimieux, Warren Berlinger, Conway Twitty, Richard Jaeckel, Elisha Cook, Jr. 93 min. B&W. Also known as *Trouble at 16*. (JD)

The Plunderers (1960). Allied Artists release of a Joseph Pevney production. Directed by Joseph Pevney. Screenplay by Bob Barbash. Featuring Jeff Chandler, John Saxon, Dolores Hart, Marsha Hunt, Jay C. Flippen. 94 min. B&W. (JD)

The Rebel Set (1959). Allied Artists release of an Earl Lyons production. Directed by Gene Fowler Jr. Screenplay by Louis Vittes and Bernard Girard. Featuring Gregg Palmer, Kathleen Crowley, Edward Platt, Ned Glass, Don Sullivan. 72 min. B&W. (JD)

Rebel Without a Cause (1955). Warner Bros. release of a David Weisbart production. Directed by Nicholas Ray. Screenplay by Stewart Stern, adapted by Irving Shulman. Featuring James Dean, Natalie Wood, Sal Mineo, Jim Backus, Corey Allen, Edward Platt, and William Hopper. 111 min. Color and CinemaScope. (M)

Reform School Girl (1957). American International release of a Carmel Production, produced by Robert J. Gurney Jr. and Samuel Z. Arkoff. Directed and written by Edward Bernds. Featuring Gloria Castillo, Ross Ford, Edward Byrnes, Ralph Reed, and Luana Anders. 71 min. B&W. (JD)

The Restless Years (1958). Universal release of a Ross Hunter production. Directed by Helmet Kautner. Screenplay by Edward Anhalt from the play *Teach Me How to Cry*, by Patricia Joudry. Featuring John Saxon, Sandra Dee, Margaret Lindsey, Teresa Wright, Luana Patten, James Whitmore. 86 min. B&W and CinemaScope. (CT)

The Return of the Fly (1959). Twentieth Century-Fox release of a Bernard Glasser production. Directed and written by Edward L. Bernds. Featuring Vincent Price, Brett Halsey, David Frankham, John Sutton. 78 min. B&W and CinemaScope. (W)

The Revenge of Frankenstein (1958). Columbia release of an Anthony Hinds production. Directed by Terrence Fisher. Screenplay by Jimmy Sangster with additional dialogue by Hurford James. Featuring Peter Cushing, Francis Matthews, Eunice Gayson, Michael Gwynn. 89 min. Color. (W)

Riot in Juvenile Prison (1959). United Artists release of a Vogue Pictures production. Produced by Robert E. Kent. Directed by Edward L. Cahn. Screenplay by Orville H. Hampton. Featuring Jerome Thor, Marcia Henderson, Scott Marlowe, John Hoyt, Dick Tyler, Virginia Aldridge, Dorothy Provine. 71 min. B&W. (JD)

Rock All Night (1957). American International release of a Sunset production (Roger Corman). Directed by Roger Corman. Screenplay by Clarles B. Griffith from a story by David P. Harmon. Featuring Dick Miller, Abby Dalton, The Platters, The Blockbusters. 62 min. B&W. (R&R)

Rock Around the Clock (1956). Columbia release of a Sam Katzman production. Directed by Fred F. Sears. Screenplay by Robert E. Kent and James B. Gordon. Featuring Johnny Johnston, Alix Talton, Lisa Gaye, Alan Freed, Bill Haley and the Comets, The Platters, Freddie Bell and the Bellboys. 77 min. B&W (R&R)

Rock Around the World (1957). American International release of an Anglo-Amalgamated Film. Produced by Herbert Smith. Directed by Gerard Bryant. Screenplay by Norman Hudis. Featuring Tommy Steele, Patrick Westwood, Hilda Fenemore, Charles Lamb. 71 min. B&W. Also know as *The Tommy Steele Story*. (R&R)

Rock, Baby, Rock It (1957). Freebar release of a J. G. Tiger production. Directed by Murray Douglas Sporup. Featuring Johnny Carrol, Kay Wheeler, The Cell Block Seven, The Five Stars, Rosco Gordon, Preacher Smith and the Deacons, Don Coats, The Bon Airs, The Belew Twins. 77 min. B&W. (R&R)

Rock, Pretty Baby (1956). Universal release of an Edmond Chevie production. Directed by Richard Bartlett. Screenplay by Herbert Margolis and William Raynor. Featuring John Saxon, Sal Mineo, Luana Patten, Edward C. Platt, Fay Wray, Rod McKuen. 89 min. B&W. (R&R)

Rock, Rock, Rock! (1956). Distributors Corporation of America release of a Vanguard Production (Max J. Rosenberg and Milton Subotsky). Directed by Will Price. Screenplay by Milton Subotsky. Featuring Tuesday Weld, Fran Manfred, Alan Freed, Teddy Randazzo, the voice of Connie Francis, Jimmy Cavallo and the House Rockers, The Moonglows, The Flamingos, Chuck Berry, Johnny Burnette, La Vern Baker, Frankie Lymon and the Teenagers. 85 min. B&W. (R&R)

Rockabilly Baby (1957). Twentieth Century-Fox release of a William F. Claxton production. Directed by William F. Claxton. Screenplay by Will George and William Driscoll. Featuring Virginia Field, Douglas Kennedy, Les Brown, Irene Ryan. 81 min. B&W. (R&R)

Rockin' the Blues (1956). Austin Productions release of a Fritz Pollard Associates production. Directed by Arthur Rosenblum. Featuring Flournoy Miller and Mantan Mooreland, The Harptones, The Wanderers, The Hurricanes, Honey Carroll, The Miller Sisters, Pearl Woods. 70 min. B&W. (R&R)

Rumble on the Docks (1956). Columbia release of a Sam Katzman production. Directed by Fred F. Sears. Screenplay by Lou Morheim and Jack DeWitt from the novel by Frank Paley. Featuring James Darren, Laurie Carroll, Michael Granger, Jerry Janger, Robert Blake, Edgar Barrier. 84 min. B&W. (JD)

Runaway Daughters (1956). American International release of an Alex Gordon production. Directed by Edward L. Cahn. Screenplay by Lou Rusoff. Featuring Marla English, Anna Sten, John Litel, Lance Fuller, Adele Jergens, Mary Ellen Kaye, Steve Terrell. 90 min. B&W. (JD)

Running Wild (1955). Universal release of a Howard Pine production. Directed by Abner Biberman. Screenplay by Leo Townsend from the novel by Ben Benson. Featuring William Campbell, Mamie Van Doren, Keenan Wynn, Kathleen Chase, Jan Merlin, John Saxon. 81 min. B&W. (JD)

Satellite in the Sky (1956). Warner Bros. release of an Edward J. and Harry Lee Danziger production. Directed by Paul Dickson. Screenplay by John Mather, J. T. McIntosh, and Edith Dell. Featuring Kieron Moore, Lois Maxwell, Donald Wolf, Bryan Forbes. 84 min. Color and CinemaScope. (W)

Shake, Rattle, and Rock! (1956). American International release of a James H. Nicholson production. Directed by Edward L. Cahn. Screenplay by Lou Rusoff. Featuring Fats Domino, Joe Turner, Touch Conners, Lisa Gaye, Sterling Holloway, Raymond Hatton, Margaret Dumount, Choker Campbell and His Band. 74 min. B&W. (R&R)

Sing, Boy, Sing! (1958). Twentieth Century-Fox release of a Henry Ephron production. Directed by Henry Ephron. Screenplay by Claude Binyon from *The Singing Idol*, a teleplay by Paul Monash. Featuring Tommy Sands, Edmund O'Brien, Nick Adams, Lili Gentle, John McIntire, Diane Jergens. 90 min. B&W and CinemaScope. (CT)

Sorority Girl (1957). American International release of a Roger Corman production. Directed by Roger Corman. Screenplay by Ed Walters and Leo Lieberman. Featuring Dick Miller, Susan Cabot, Barboura O'Neill, June Kenny, Barbara Crane, Fay Baker. 60 min. B&W. (JD)

Speed Crazy (1959). Allied Artists release of a Viscount Production. Produced by Richard Bernstein. Directed by William Hole Jr. Screenplay by Richard Bernstein and George Walter. Featuring Brett Halsey, Yvonne Lime, Charles Wilcox, Slick Slaven. 75 min. B&W. (M-M)

The Spider (1958). American International release of a James H. Nicholson–Samuel Z. Arkoff production. Produced and directed by Bert I.Gordon. Screenplay by Laszlo Gorog and George Worthing Yayes from a story by Bert I. Gordon. Featuring Ed Kemmer, June Kenny, Gene Persson, Gene Ruth. 72 min. B&W. (W)

Summer Love (1958). Universal release of a William Grady Jr. production. Directed by Charles Haas. Screenplay by William Raynor and Herbert Margolis. Featuring John Saxon, Molly Bee, Rod McKuen, Judy Meredith, Jill St. John, John Wilder, Shelley Fabares, Troy Donahue. 85 min. B&W. (CT)

Tammy and the Bachelor (1957). Universal release of a Ross Hunter production. Directed by Joseph Pevney. Screenplay by Oscar Brodney from the novel by Cid Ricketts Sumner. Featuring Debbie Reynolds, Leslie Nielsen, Walter Brennan, Mala Powers, Mildred Natwick. 87 min. Color and CinemaScope. (CT/M)

T-Bird Gang (1959). Filmgroup release of a Stan Bickman production. Directed by Richard Horberger. Screenplay by John Brinkley and Tony Miller. Featuring John Brinkley, Ed Nelson, Pat George, Beach Dickerson, Tony Miller. 75 min. B&W. (JD)

Teenage Bad Girl (1957). Distributors Corporation of America release of a Herbert Wilcox production. Directed by Herbert Wilcox. Screenplay by Felicity Douglas. Featuring Sylvia Sims, Anna Neagle, Norman Wooland. 100 min. B&W. Also known as *Bad Girl*. (JD)

Teenage Caveman (1958). American International release of a James H. Nicholson-Samuel Z. Arkoff production. Produced and directed by Roger Corman. Screenplay by R. Wright Campbell. Featuring Robert Vaughn, Sarah Marshall, Leslie Bradley, Frank De Kova. 65 min. B&W/Superama. Also known as *Prehistoric World*. (W)

Teenage Crime Wave (1955). Columbia release of a Sam Katzman production. Directed by Fred F. Sears. Screenplay by Harry Essex and Ray Buffum. Featuring Tommy Cook, Mollie McCart, Sue England, Frank Griffin, James Bell. 77 min. B&W. (JD)

Teenage Doll (1957). Allied Artists release of a Woolner Brothers production. Produced and directed by Roger Corman. Directed by Roger Corman. Screenplay by Charles B. Griffith. Featuring June Kenny, Fay Spain, John Brinkley, Collette Jackson. 67 min. B&W. (JD)

Teenage Monster (1958). Favorite Films release of a Jacques Marquette production. Produced by Howco International. Directed by Jacques Marquette. Screenplay by Ray Buffum. Featuring Anne Gwynne, Gloria Castillo, Stuart Wade, Gilbert Perkins. 65 min. B&W. (W)

Teenage Rebel (1956). Twentieth Century-Fox release. Produced by Charles Brackett. Directed by Edmund Goulding. Screenplay by Walter Reisch and Charles Brackett from the play *A Roomful of Roses*. Featuring Ginger Rogers, Michael Rennie, Mildred Natwick, Rusty Swoop, Lili Gentle, Louis Beavers, Warren Berringer. 94 min. B&W and CinemaScope. (M)

Teenagers From Outer Space (1959). Warner Bros. release of a Tom Graeff production. Directed and written by Tom Graeff. Featuring David Love, Dawn Anderson, Harvey B. Dunn, Bryan Grant. 85 min. B&W. (W)

Teenage Thunder (1957). Howco release of a Jacques Marquette production. Directed by Paul Hemlick. Screenplay by Rudy MaKoul. Featuring Charles Courtney, Melinda Byron, Robert Fuller, Tyler McVey. 78 min. B&W. (M-M)

Teenage Wolfpack (1956). Distributors Corporation of America release of Wenzel Luedecke production (Germany). Directed by Georg Tressler. Screenplay by Will Tremper. Featuring Henry Bookholt, Karen Baal, Christian Derner. 89 min. B&W. (JD)

Teenage Zombies (1957). Governor release of a Jerry Warren production. Directed by Jerry Warren. Screenplay by Jacques Le Cotier. Featuring Don Sullivan, Steven Conte, Katherine Victor. 73 min. B&W. (W)

Terror from the Year 5,000 (1958). American International release of a Robert J. Gurney Jr. production. Directed and written by Robert J. Gurney Jr. Featuring Ward Costello, Joyce Holden, John Stratton, Frederic Downs. 66 min. B&W. (W)

The Tingler (1959). Columbia release of a William Castle production. Directed by William Castle. Screenplay by Robb White. Featuring Vincent Price, Judith Evelyn, Darryl Hickman, Patricia Cutts. 80 min. B&W, Red, and Percepto. (W)

Too Soon to Love (1960). Universal release of a Richard Rush production. Directed by Richard Rush. Screenplay by Laszlo Gorog and Richard Rush. Featuring Jennifer West, Richard Evans, Warren Parker, Ralph Manza, Jack Nicholson. 85 min. B&W. (JD)

The Unguarded Moment (1956). Universal release of a Gordon Kay production. Directed by Harry Keller. Screenplay by Herb Meadows and Larry Marcus from a story by Rosalind Russell and Larry Marcus. Featuring Esther Williams, George Nader, John Saxon, Edward Andrews, Les Tremayne, Jack Albertson. 95 min. Color. (M)

Untamed Youth (1957). Warner Bros. release of an Aubrey Schenck production. Directed by Howard W. Koch. Screenplay by John C. Higgins. Featuring Mamie Van Doren, Lori Nelson, John Russell, Don Burnett, Eddie Cochran, Lurene Tuttle, Yvonne Lime, Michael Emmett. 80 min. B&W. (JD)

War of the Colossal Beast (1958). American International release of a James H. Nicholson–Samuel Z. Arkoff production. Produced and directed by Bert I. Gordon. Screenplay by George Worthing Yates from a story by Bert I. Gordon.

Featuring Sally Fraser, Dean Parkin, Roger Pace, Russ Bender. 68 min. B&W. (W)

War of the Satellites (1958). Allied Artists release of a Roger Corman production. Directed by Roger Corman. Screenplay by Lawrence Louis Goldman from a story by Irving Block. Featuring Dick Miller, Susan Cabot, Richard Devon, Eric Sinclair. 66 min. B&W. (W)

The Wild One (1953). Columbia release of a Stanley Kramer production. Directed by Laslo Benedek. Screenplay by John Paxton from "The Cyclists' Raid," a *Life* magazine story by Frank Rooney. Featuring Marion Brando, Mary Murphy, Robert Keith, Lee Marvin, Jay C. Flippin, Peggy Maley. 79 min. B&W. (M-M/JD)

The Wild Ride (1960). Filmgroup release of a Harvey Berman production. Directed by Harvey Berman. Screenplay by Ann Porter and Marion Rothman. Featuring Jack Nicholson, Georgianna Carter, and Robert Dean. 86 min. B&W. (M-M)

Young and Dangerous (1957). Twentieth Century-Fox release of a William F. Claxton production. Directed by William F. Claxton. Screenplay by James Landis. Featuring Mark Damon, Lili Gentle, Eddie Burns, Francis Mercer, Dabbs Greer. 77 min. B&W/Regalscope. (JD)

Young and Wild (1958). Republic release of an Esla production. Directed by William Witney. Screenplay by Arthur T. Horman. Featuring Gene Evans, Scott Marlowe, Carolyn Kearney, Robert Arthur. 69 min. B&W. (JD)

The Young Captives (1959). Paramount release of an Andrew J. Fenady production. Directed by Irvin Kershner. Screenplay by Andrew J. Fenady from a story by Gordon Hunt and Al Burton. Featuring Steve Marlo, Luana Patten, Tom Selden, James Chandler, Ed Nelson. 66 min. B&W. (JD)

The Young Don't Cry (1957). Columbia release of a Philip A. Waxman production. Directed by Alfred L. Werker. Screenplay by Richard Jessup from his novel. Featuring Sal Mineo, James Whitmore, J. Carrol Naish, Gene Lyons. 89 min. B&W. (JD)

The Young Stranger (1957). RKO-Universal release of a Stuart Millar production. Directed by John Frankenheimer. Screenplay by Robert Dozier. Featuring James MacArthur, Kim Hunter, James Daly, James Gregory, Whit Bissell. 83 min. B&W. (JD)

Index to Film Titles

251

General Index